Author
Lucy Bullivant

Subject
UK architecture's
rising generation

british built

Princeton Architectural Press
New York

ABOUT THE AUTHOR

Lucy Bullivant is an architectural critic, author, and curator of exhibitions and conferences. Born in London, she studied art history at Leeds University and cultural history at the Royal College of Art, London, and worked as an art curator for many years before becoming Heinz Curator of Architectural Programmes at the Royal Academy of Arts (1993–94). Her exhibitions include "Leading Edge" (AXIS, Tokyo,1989–90), "The near and the far, fixed and in flux" (Milan Triennale,1996), "Kid size: the material world of childhood within and beyond the Western world" (Vitra Design Museum,1997–2005), and "Space Invaders: new UK architecture" with Pedro Gadanho (the British Council, 2001–3). Her conferences include "4dspace," "Spaced Out III/Smart Practices in a Complex World," (ICA, London, 2003; 1997), and "Home Front" (AA, 2003). She writes for *Domus* (Italy), *AD* (UK), *Harvard Design Magazine* (US), *The Plan* (Italy), and *Indesign* (Australia). Her books include: *4dspace: interactive architecture* (AD/Wiley, 2005), and *Kinaesthetic: responsive environments*, (V&A, 2006).

ACKNOWLEDGMENTS

British Built would simply not exist without the advanced wisdom, generosity and goodwill of the featured architectural practices and their staff, to whom I am hugely grateful. Innumerable professional peers in the UK and internationally freely gave me their shrewd insights and facilitated meetings and visits of benefit to the project. Lucas Dietrich, my stalwart and good-humoured commissioning editor, gave me consistent support and encouragement throughout. Graphic designer and trapeze artiste Melanie Mues confidently shook up architectural book design orthodoxies with her conceptual agility and grasp of visual pacing, without losing sight of the rigour that must accompany it. Thanks are also due to all at Thames & Hudson. For supporting my research and writing through a grant, I am most grateful to the Trustees of the Oppenheim-John Downes Memorial Trust, as I am to JAL Airlines and the Great Britain Sasakawa Foundation for enthusiastically sponsoring my Japanese research trips. The clear friendship of Dan Knight, Christine Styrnau, Shona Kitchen, Fiona Dunlop, Tobias Kommerell, Danielle Tinero, Nico Macdonald and Torsten Neeland made the crossing seem far more navigable, and, for their solidarity and presence, a resonant thanks to my father Dargan and mother Pat – their Architectural Association-trained architectural genes seem to be wearing well – and my sibling posse Helena, Alexander and Victoria.

Princeton Architectural Press
37 East Seventh Street
New York, New York 10003

For a free catalog of books, call 1.800.722.6657
Visit our web site at www.papress.com

Published by arrangement with Thames & Hudson Ltd, London
© 2005 Thames & Hudson Ltd, London
Text © 2005 Lucy Bullivant
Photographs © the individual photographers
08 07 06 05 4 3 2 1 First edition

Library of Congress Cataloguing-in-Publication Data
Bullivant, Lucy.
 British Built : UK architecture's rising generation / Lucy Bullivant. —1st ed.
   p.   cm.
 ISBN 1-56898-553-3 (alk. paper)
 1. Architecture—Great Britain—21st century. I. Title.
NA968.6.B85 2005
720'.941'090511—dc22

Printed and bound in China by Everbest Printing Co.

PICTURE CREDITS

[B=bottom; L=left; R=right; M=middle; T=top]
>4 © Hélène Binet >5 © MUST >6, 7L © London 2012 >7R © London Development Agency >8–9 © Sarah Wigglesworth Architects >10, 11L © Nick Hufton/VIEW >11R © CABE/ McDowell + Benedetti >12–13 © Hélène Binet >14 © Kilian O'Sullivan >15 © Softroom >16 © Peter Gunzel >17 © Holger Kehne/Plasma Studio >18–21 © Lyndon Douglas >21R. 22T, 23 © Adjaye Associates >22B, 24–25T © Lyndon Douglas >25B © Adjaye Associates >26–27T © Tim Soar >26–27B, 28B © Adjaye Associates >28T, 28R, 29T © Tim Soar >29B © Lyndon Douglas >31, 32T, 32BR © Adjaye Associates >32BL © Lyndon Douglas >35, 36 © Adjaye Associates >38–39, 40T © Dennis Gilbert/ VIEW >40B © Alison Brooks Architects >41 © Chris Gascoigne/VIEW >43T, 43BL © Alison Brooks Architects >43R © Dennis Gilbert/VIEW >43BR © Alison Brooks Architects >44, 45B © Christoph Kicherer >45T, 46–51 © Alison Brooks Architects >52–53 © Tim Soar >54L © AHMM >54R, 55 © Tim Soar >56TL © AHMM >56–57, 58 © Tim Soar >59B © AHMM >60–61, 62T © Tim Soar >62BL © AHMM >62BR, 62–63 © Matt Chisnall >64L © Wyn Davis >64–65 © Smoothe >65 © Wyn Davis >66–70 © Hélène Binet >70–71T © Caruso St John >72, 73T © Hélène Binet >73B, 74, 75, 76T, 77 © Caruso St John >76B, 78 © David Grandorge >79 © Caruso St John >80–82, 83T © Alex de Rijke >83B © dRMM >84T © Alex de Rijke >84B © dRMM >84–85 © Alaistair Nicholson >86, 87T © Michael Mack >87B © Alex de Rijke >88, 88–89B © dRMM; >88–89T © Alex de Rijke >90–91L © Sue Barr/ Architectural Association >91T © dRMM/AA students >91B, 92–93T © Alex de Rijke >92–3B © Janek Schaefer/Philip Marsh >95T, 95BL © Michael Mack >95BR © Sue Barr/Architectural Association >96–97 © Michael Mack >98–99, 100–1 © Hélène Binet >102 © DSDHA >103 © Carley Wright >104–5, 106, 107T © Martine Hamilton-Knight >107BR, 108–11 © DSDHA >112–13 © FAT >114 © Morley von Sternberg >115 © FAT >116–17T © Oscar Paisley >116–7B © Morley von Sternberg >118 © FAT >119 © Andy Keate >120, 121L © Reinout van den Bergh >121R © FAT >122BL, 123B © Josh Pulman >122T, 122BM, 122BR, 124–27 © FAT >128–29 © Katsuhisa Kida >130 © Ushida Findlay >131, 132T, 133 © Katsuhisa Kida >132B © Ushida Findlay >134, 135 © Katsuhisa Kida >136–37 © David Churchill >138–39, 140T © Ushida Findlay >140B, 141T © Hélène Binet >141B, 142–43 © Ushida Findlay >144–50 © Satoru Mishima >151 © FOA >153T © Satoru Mishima >153MT, 153MB, 153B © FOA >154T © FOA >154B, 155 © Kristian Daem >156, 157 © Christian Richters >158–63 © FOA >164–67 © Tim Soar >168L © Gollifer Langston >168R © Tim Soar >170–71, 172L, 172TR © James Brittain >172BR © Tim Soar >174L © Gollifer Langston >174R © James Brittain >175 © James Morris >176TL © Gollifer Langston >176BL, 176–77 © Morley von Sternberg >178–79 © Kozo Takayama >180–82 © Katsuhisa Kida >183L © Kozo Takayama >183R, 184 © KDa >185 © Kozo Takayama >186, 187 © Katsuhisa Kida >188–89 © Jun Takagi >189 © Kozo Takayama >190T © KDa >190B, 191 © Kozo Takayama >192, 193B © KDa >193T © Kozo Takayama >194–97 © Jason Lowe >198 © muf >199 © Jason Lowe >200, 201 © Etienne Clément >202BL, 202BR © Jason Lowe >202T, 203 © muf >204TL © Oliver Claridge >204TR © muf 204B, 205 © Jason Lowe >206–7 © muf >208–11 © Hélène Binet >211R, 212T, 213T © Sergison Bates >212B, 213B, 214, 216, 217B © Hélène Binet >217T © Sergison Bates >218, 219B © Hélène Binet >219T © Sergison Bates >220, 221BL © Hélène Binet >221TL, 221TR © Sergison Bates >222–27 © Jan Bitter >227R, 228, 229B © S333 >229T © Patrick Reynolds >230–31, 232–33B, 233 © Luuk Kramer >232L © S333 >234–41 © S333 >242 © Paul Smoothy >243 © Sarah Wigglesworth Architects >244L © Tonkin Liu Architects >244M, 244R © Mike Tonkin, Tonkin Liu Architects >245L © East >245M © Nils Norman/General Public Agency >245R © ZM Architects >246L, 246M © Gross.Max >246R © East >247L, 247M © Nicholas Kane/ARCAID >247R © Julian Cornish-Trestrail >248, 249L © Piercy Conner >249R © Paul Smoothy

ON THE COVER

Klein Dytham architecture, Leaf Chapel, Kobuchizawa, Japan, 2004. Photographer: Kozo Takayama

The emerging ethos

> Fluid: <u>Derwent Gateway Centre cricket hall and grandstand</u>, Derby, 2004; multi-purpose hall with café and gym

Architecture is not what it was. Instead of carrying the heavy utopian baggage of the 20th century, younger architectural practices, and not just in the UK but globally, are progressively reinventing the identity of the profession, reinvigorating it with new processes. It is traditionally the prerogative of the young, driven by a passion to test the limits and not prepared to perpetuate tired old ways of doing things, to find unconventional solutions to challenges. Lateral thinking is architecture's lifeblood, and architecture and urban design, building and masterplanning, for too long perceived as independent fields of activity, are evolving through new approaches by young architects into mutually enhancing layers of action.

As this book seeks to demonstrate, architecture is also about fostering a public engagement that continues after the project has been completed. The themes presented in *British Built* are necessarily selective about architectural practices in the UK and their activities nationally and internationally. The choices are guided by their professional connections with the country rather than by nationality alone. What makes the contemporary milieu so fertile is that the sensibilities uniting the featured practices transcend nationality: their traces extend across the globe. In the European Union, transport and information networks are bringing physical and virtual connectivity to such an extent that national borders are waning in importance.[1] At home, the UK's contemporary multicultural identity – both in terms of makers and the process of making buildings, spaces and facilities – means that architecture has become a synergistic art. It fosters improvisation rather than colonization, and cross-fertilization of places, systems and users instead of their segregation. The practices who received their first sparks of media recognition in the last fifteen years are multi-scalar, multi-context and multi-tasking. They are omni-practices in an era of omni-need. Their multivalent practice counters the onward rush of global urbanization and its logic of homogeneity – creating a present without a past, a world without cultural nuances or climatic, topological and ecological sensitivities – with a variety of strategies. We know that the gritty realities permeating urban life transcend architectural problem-solving, but a willingness to ask new questions about recurring and contemporary issues that get beyond formulaic approaches to either urban healing or utopian visions is prevalent. The engagement of the architects featured in *British Built* with their projects is site-specific and as responsive to the needs of local communities as it is to those of public and private sector clients. Their work raises a mirror to the embedded layers of history and culture in the UK, as well as to its urban neglect. It articulates positions that override – even as they may play with – brand culture. It is an ethos that naturally makes a virtue of ephemerality or limited budgets; in practice it is about an informality of context and the transcendence of outworn boundaries and social codes. This generation works from the bottom-up not top-down, extending architecture further than ever before, and not through decades of experience but through lateral approaches.

Cutting their teeth on small, and occasionally large-scale competition wins and highly varied commissions, the younger firms profiled in this book can be seen as pioneers who did not let the recession of the early 1990s weaken their courage to go it alone. Today, the role of the architect involves more controversy and risk than it used to: architects have to broker deals with a far wider range of

> <u>Unicity</u>, research project by Dutch architects and urbanists MUST, analyzing the cross-national urban field resulting from north-west Europe's High Speed Train network, 2003-4

stakeholders, invariably including both public and private funding. Patrons of young architects in the UK come in a variety of guises, with a myriad of types of briefs. A close reading of the fluid social and cultural conditions, processes, materials and resources enables architects to combine building with deft microplanning (i.e. at small scales) in difficult urban situations. The challenge remains to upgrade the fabric of the UK's eroded public realm and overcome the dearth of first-rate public buildings, a hangover from the 1980s and 1990s when little was commissioned or built of quality.

The coincidence of increased government concern for urban and environmental conditions and a more socially engaged generation of young architects is serendipitous and could not have been anticipated at the beginning of the 1990s, when many architects chose to avoid the traditional career route of continuing to work for bigger practices and instead set up their own offices, some in their own front rooms, in the style of Microsoft or *Dazed and Confused* magazine. Of the wave of practices featured in this book, most were established during the 1990s' recession by architects dissatisfied at sitting in the passenger seats of mainstream practices when inexorable changes were affecting cities and regions. The incentive for young architects to set up on their own was fostered as early as the mid-1960s when the RIBA started its important initiatives to educate the profession, giving proactive guidance on management; while the knowledge structures of the specialist architectural media, such as *The Architects' Journal* and *Building Design*, have provided invaluable advice and information on real life issues.

Architecture as a profession has always revered maturity, but the command by the youthful of its technological processes is realigning that traditional equilibrium. Lords Foster and Rogers have moved to a situation within their practices where more of their responsibilities are steered by young architects. The middle generation of timeless figures like Zaha Hadid and David Chipperfield hold enormous sway internationally. They have emerged, and, as their skills base deepens, the stakes go on getting higher; but they continue to incubate new processes and strategies of lasting worth. Certain figures have been influential. The distinctive trajectory of Rem Koolhaas – trained at the Architectural Association, London, and, with his practice, OMA, recently selected to masterplan <u>White City</u> in west London – as both cultural critic and A-list architect and his focus on programme has drawn interest and envy across generations of UK architects. The growing openness to contemporary architecture and urbanism, and its cultural role that his activities have helped to foster, requires the support

of younger operators to sustain it. Yet, in spite of all the new freedoms that have opened up for younger architects, this generation inevitably continues to find itself in direct competition with longer established, invariably more corporate practices with bigger budgets to spend on presentations to impress competition judges. In the UK, the world of architecture is small and often claustrophobic. In such a scenario, a proposition works on its own terms: its value stems from the fact that it conceptualizes but also makes architecture out of its engagement with the complex spirit of the age, finding a response to the cultural and political forces of globalization, that adjusts the impact of forces hitting a downtown area of a city or the inequalities of public-private sector relationships that can be felt in every field of public life one cares to imagine. Through their processes of making, their ethos, and their redefinition of the public-private topography, the work of these practices reflects how far the definitions of the fabric and the functional categories of society have changed.

Transforming the generic into the specific, taking the hermetic into a state of wider relationships, their activities work with what is there rather than a tabula rasa. Everything is negotiable. Every win counts as some kind of improvement. The pragmatism that exists places emphasis on the prototypical, the topographical, the local, and the incremental, rather than on the typological, the singular, the abstract or the visionary. Earlier architectural tactics of creating collages of arbitrary elements do not work in the face of globalization; a more decisive positioning is necessary, creating inclusive systems that nonetheless allow many things to happen simultaneously. This emerging sensibility reflects multicultural realities, with a respect for difference that has strong repercussions for the already pronounced internationalism of architectural practice. Operating with an unprecedented diversity of players in terms of gender and cultural background, younger architects are dealing with the final stages of the shift within the UK

from a welfare state to a market-led society. Their territory is global capitalism's impact on local communities. Whatever the scheme, it is invariably a case of using architecture as a tool to stake out fresh terms for urban renewal that can sustain itself in that system but also maintain an independent ethos of community.

With so many stakeholders, adding value is the binding nexus of younger architects in private practice. Although most of an entire younger generation has never benefited from the largesse of, for example, capital funding of building schemes through the National Lottery, the need to re-think the way architecture is marketed is a widespread legacy of its establishment. Unlike a few earlier Lottery-funded projects, the recent award of £5 million for Rivington Place, the new arts centre in Shoreditch for IVA and Autograph ASP[2], by Adjaye Associates, through the Arts Council of England's Capital Lottery Programme 2, was made in response to a highly credible plan based on the enrichment of communities.

While there are many traces of 1960s' experimentalism in the work discussed here, the collaged reinterpretations of public space associated with Archigram have been replaced by a synthesis of processes: visualizations are rarely collaged (with the exception of FAT's work); research is extensive and inclusive; techniques and technologies have become far more versatile; and technocratic solutions have been replaced by many more accessible and ingenious construction technologies, and isolated structures by sensuous or convivial buildings that engage in a dialogue with the landscape[3]. What remains, perhaps, is the English tradition of modernism, which tries to reconcile a sentimental view of a bucolic past with the industrial city, city and country, nature and culture. What is new is the sheer myriad of ways in which initiatives in architecture and urbanism are focused on resistance to neglect, preservation of the status quo and cultural homogeneity. UK architecture is renowned for its pragmatism, and high-tech has been its most successful architectural export since the 1960s, but the hybrid activities and approach of the latest generation demonstrates that the country's long-standing idiosyncratic counterculture of experimentation is being calibrated by these practices.

Young architects' interest in and commitment to society began to develop after the era of deregulation, privatization and reduction in spending on public services during Margaret Thatcher's term of office, famously justified by her statement, 'there is no such thing as society: there are individual men and women, and there are families.' Under her aegis, London Docklands was built without planning controls. Now planning mechanisms, adjusted through successive government legislation, are best seen as part of a continuous process, and, like procurement processes, are there to be part of a debate.

> The London 2012 Olympic Village: (left) visualizations of the Olympic park site, 2004; (right) part of the Lower Lea Valley Olympic regeneration masterplan by EDAW, Allies and Morrison, Foreign Office Architects, HOK Sport and Fluid, 2003-4

If the advent of the welfare state in the late 1940s meant social research was in the hands of government, now diversified public-private client alliances and, above all, inexorable shifts in social patterns and the fast-changing nature of technological resources has meant that a brief offered to an architect frequently involves re-evaluating and designing the programme – not just regenerating a school, or a block of housing, but expanding and making its identity viable. Analytical skills used not to be a major part of an architect's education, but architecture has become a far more knowledge-based profession.

The current focus on research-led architecture by younger architects is a huge asset at a time when the discipline is having to compete with commercial forces and processes in a construction world that largely ignores the value of design. This contrasts with the pattern of much of the post-Second World War period, when from the 1940s to the 1970s the architectural profession in the UK had no tradition of conducting research into human requirements, technical innovation and standards. Architects were still working in the same tradition as Sir Edwin Lutyens (1869–1944), but without the craftsmen to support them; and were only very rarely engaged with the social brief. This was because research was in the hands of central and local government, with local authorities, not private practices, operating as employers – of up to 200 architects – and clients. Although before the Second World War architects were almost entirely private practitioners offering a generalist set of skills, their post-war equivalents, designing facilities with very limited resources, were not empowered to research or design briefs. When post-war private practices first began to receive work from government sources, they were given very detailed briefs that constrained solutions.

Two exceptions offer a striking example of architects engaged to develop the brief: the Barbican Centre by Chamberlin, Powell and Bon, and Centrepoint, one of the first office blocks in London, designed by Richard Seifert. The latter, at 385 metres high the second tallest building in London, was extremely audacious for its time (1963–67), and was regarded by younger architects as beyond the pale because during post-war reconstruction years, materials and planning permission were tightly controlled by government. Centrepoint was a sizeable asset for the developer, but it remained empty for years. Apart from the fact that in the 1950s architects' roles were largely limited to designing social facilities, in many sectors there was little recognition of the need for research: the housing market was originally seen as not requiring much research, just space standards, which were handed down by government. Now, younger architects are keen to break down the embedded design

norms of housing into diversified patterns, and to address the integration of social housing in cities, a situation slowly being matched by the best developers' aspirations (for example, Urban Splash; Countryside, Alison Brooks Architects' developer for the Brooklands Avenue scheme in Cambridge; and, in the field of social housing, the Peabody Trust) as the market becomes more vocal about its needs, and sensitivity to those of lower-income citizens is heightened.

The new generation of architects is in a far stronger position than its socially concerned precedessors in the 1950s: it can give multi-dimensional, multi-skilled attention to society. Responses to the changes brought about by global capitalism and the struggle between public and private interests over urban space have made microplanning an art in British architecture. Sloughing off the social codes that prescribed earlier generations of built form, especially in education and housing, is a continuous process, which engages political and social forces through the testing of prototypes.

Recent political conditions favour these tactics: although the centralized functioning of government has changed drastically since the commitment by the Labour government in the late 1940s and 1950s (led by Prime Minister Clement Attlee) to social building, the public urban realm is now the subject of countless new central and local government policy initiatives. Although no one can be sure how long these might last, many have stemmed from the 105 recommendations by the government's Urban Task Force, chaired by Richard Rogers, in June 1999, for improvements to British cities and towns, which were included in the Urban White Paper, 'Our towns and cities: the future' (2000), a government policy document looking at the delivery of urban renaissance throughout the country. Although in 2001, following devolution, Scotland committed to a national policy, as yet there is no national architectural policy in England. Some of the White Paper's recommendations encouraged

higher density building, the bringing back into use of brownfield sites, mixed tenure, and an integrated approach to design-led regeneration of different types of urban environments. Developers are encouraged to step-change their cultural ambitions and play a larger role in funding what were once welfare state-supported facilities as well as locations undergoing change. Taken as a whole, there are sophisticated mechanisms in place to promote urban regeneration, but they need design-led intelligence to make real headway. The green shoots of activity by younger practices navigating these structures demonstrate that the concerns of the Urban Task Force are being tested out on the ground in urban communities in a range of ways, and that a dialogue with and about government initiatives, and what more needs to be done, is continuing.

Government-funded schemes include the New Deal for Communities[4], a community-based regeneration programme for which £1.9 billion has been allocated for up to thirty-eight bids over the next ten years from local agencies to improve deprived areas via grants that focus on the economy, environment, IT, crime, health, education, community and neighbourhood management. The £22 billion Sustainable Communities plan, launched in 2003, and the new Urban Regeneration Companies[5] work with a range of public and private sector partners in localities around the UK, as well as in conjunction with other social schemes aimed at improving educational and nursery school facilities. There is also the Millennium Communities programme to nurture sustainable communities, the first example of which was the Greenwich Millennium Village[6], adhering to mixed tenure, higher density and the reversal of the customary dominance of the pedestrian by the car.

Another opening for lateral thinking has been the badly needed reinvention of educational facilities, which has been backed by initiatives such as the Department for Education and Skills' (DfES) Building Schools for the Future and Exemplar Designs. This has resulted in dRMM's Kingsdale School in Dulwich, south London (see p. 92), as well as the Big Rug School[8], by Sarah Wigglesworth Architects, whose designs, together with those by Sergison Bates, were selected as pilot projects for the DfES's Classrooms of the Future scheme. The need for exemplars, prompted by changes and developments in education, ICT, wider community use of schools, diversity in pupils and their needs, and the desire for sustainability, has given projects like Kingsdale and Big Rug the challenge of becoming benchmarks: they fulfil local needs but must also be seen as inspirational talking points about future provision rather than prescriptive templates.

The Urban Task Force's[9] recommendations represented a pivotal moment and gave new impetus to urban development in the UK. Not only have the subsequent government-funded schemes provided work for the rising generation of architects, but they have also given them the opportunity to speculate on the preconditions needed for increased common ground between interdependent bodies – local government, commercial clients, development agencies and firms – and to read and respond to specific cultural needs. The London bid for the 2012 Olympics entails the regeneration of the Lower Lea Valley based on a masterplan by a multi-disciplinary team, including Foreign Office Architects (FOA) and Fluid, alongside EDAW[10], Allies & Morrison and HOK Sport, with an opportunity to create fresh ways of approaching urban renewal. The mantra of urban renaissance has had a pervasive impact, which can be seen in cities like Manchester and Birmingham, as well as in town and regional initiatives. Urban conurbations have advanced, and even a previously war-torn city like Belfast has discovered a new youthful optimism, if not yet progressive urban plans. However, there are centres, such as Edinburgh, that are subject to restrictive planning regulations, or have not begun to foster a younger architectural scene, except

within academia. In Wales, the award of the expansion of the Oriel Mostyn Gallery to Dominic Williams of Ellis Williams, architects of the BALTIC visual arts centre in Gateshead, is a confident decision. In south-west England, Jamie Fobert[11], who set up his practice in London in 1996, was selected in 2005, beating fifty practices, to design a new building for the Tate St Ives, intended to nurture the town's future. Through their work, younger architects are promoting an informed awareness of the factors in urban change, and a research-led, site-specific interpretation of issues: how desirable urban intensity can be achieved; how to grow new, flexible facilities; how to develop propositions that counter the arbitrary, banal anonymity of the 'non-place'[12] prevalent in urban environments. The Urban Task Force can now be seen to be an important point of no return with its requirements for higher density, better urban design, use of brownfield sites, and mixed use. But what kinds of architecture will provide the necessary corrective to the transformation of city centres into vast shopping malls, or the development of retail temples to soothe the modern soul on tracts of rural land, such as Bluewater, which was built in a Kent chalk pit? There is at the same time a continual thread of creative activity – video projects, photography, writing, art, graphic design and websites[13] – as exemplified by some of the work of Sergison Bates or the now New York-based architects David Turnbull and Jane Harrison (practising as atopia[14]), taking the anthropological pulse of the UK's changing urban, suburban and rural environments in which the old concept of place as a site-based notion is at risk of being shrinkwrapped into obscurity.

Transparency in architecture's social role and hence in the process of making architecture is common in the Netherlands but far less pervasive in the UK, with its erratic record of urban policy management and labyrinthine planning legislation. Unyielding bureaucratic protocols make it hard for younger practices to break through and demonstrate the value and legitimacy of their ideas. In what can often seem like a closed shop, personal contacts still add leverage in the increasing numbers of sectors of society (not just primary and secondary but further education) re-evaluating their physical environments. Although advanced architectural thinking coexists in the UK, with examples of huge client bravery, a failure of political will on the part of too many clients prevails when it comes to adding architectural value to large-scale projects. High-quality buildings are still few and far between. Zaha Hadid's competition-winning design for the Cardiff Bay Opera House was vetoed by the client, in spite of its virtuoso quality. Only in 2004 did her hundred-strong practice win a major commission on home ground, the £50 million Transport Museum in Glasgow, part of a major

redevelopment by the City Council to regenerate the banks of the River Clyde; and in 2005 she won the Architecture Foundation's international competition for its new headquarters in Southwark, London, and one for the city's £40 million Olympic Aquatic Centre that is to be built for public use. Yet internationally she has well over eighty buildings under construction or completed, mostly in the public sector[15]. There is also David Chipperfield, whose body of built works internationally far outnumbers those commissioned at home. The slowness of local patrons to come forward to forge working relationships with some of the UK's most outstanding architects even prompts the biblical aphorism that 'a prophet is not without honour, save in his own country.'

The misconception that if architecture is too high up the agenda in a development it will lead to a more expensive building needs to be quashed, again and again, by promoting examples where this has not been the case. What was once an old boys' network is now much more of a meritocracy in which it is necessary to gamble in order to get jobs. It is undeniably true that beyond the publicity mechanisms that promote emerging practices, there are few bridges to support architects in the transitional stages of their careers. Competitions represent one route to commissions, but they are insufficient in number and sometimes not adequately managed. The system for enabling public projects through the RIBA Clients' Advisory Service is effective yet limited in scale, with just twenty-six clients successfully enabled in 2004. Several institutions, including The Architecture Foundation and architectural centres like The Lighthouse in

Glasgow, promote contemporary architecture, competitions and public debate to ensure that new ideas are given a chance. The champions of architectural competitions argue that it is a better method of decision-making than judgements made via more traditional networks. Policies which offer opportunities to younger architectural practices as well as international ones need to be put in place in a way that sustains the continued evolution of this method of selecting designs. The criteria for choosing a team need careful scrutiny. The panel of judges should consistently match the aspirations of clients and the public, and include a higher percentage of architects. In France, for instance, every public project with an architectural fees budget above €90,000 is put to competition and is subsidized by the state. There is a commitment there to include one younger practice and one international practice on each shortlist. An open competition win can define the future course of a practice, as happened, for example, when S333, the multidisciplinary studio of architects and urbanists, won the Europan 3, the European housing competition for young architects. Winning the international competition for the £150 million Yokohama Port Terminal in 1994 gave Foreign Office Architects an immediate media profile, which their £22 million BBC Music Centre competition success in 2003 further invigorated.

The legacy of Margaret Thatcher's government has arguably made for nervous styles of architectural procurement in certain sectors and meant that clients had fewer opportunities to learn how to get the best from their relationships with architects. It created a schism in thinking about culture and economics that has continued with the current Labour government (for example, PFI [Private Finance Initiative] and policies for the design of hospitals), and has held the UK back. Architects' fortunes are highly sensitive to shifts in the cultural, political and economic climate, but the legitimacy of their designs and the roles they decide to play should stem from an independence of thinking. Rather than selling out, younger practices have been lucky to find like-minded, cosmopolitan patrons, such as the department store Selfridges, or Laforet in Japan, with precise ideas about what they want in terms of cost and quality. Being based in a city that is an international gateway helps London architects. The Greater London Assembly's Architecture and Urbanism Unit, to which Richard Rogers and Richard Burdett[16] are architectural advisors, champions good design through comprehensive strategies and projects for public space and compact housing, for instance.

In the private sector, the pugilistic procurement of architecture by select international corporate brands is led by the needs of sectors like art museums and galleries, and retailing, to differentiate themselves and thereby stay in the public eye. Here, architectural patrons favour young talent, but competition processes are often protracted, with uncertain outcomes. In engaging Caruso St John to design his latest gallery in King's Cross, London, at the frontline of the regeneration of this area, Larry Gagosian, the world's most successful art businessman, has acquired something fashionably local to complement his global outlook. Design-led urban gentrification of former industrial districts or pockets of cities in the UK has brought huge benefits. The work of proactive, enlightened developers such as Simon Silver of Derwent Valley, Roger Zogolovitch of Solid Space – who is an architect[17] – and Tom Bloxham, founder of Urban Splash, whose initiatives in Manchester and Liverpool, in particular, converting industrial buildings into housing (for instance, The Collegiate in Liverpool, a former school transformed by ShedKM) and mixed-use schemes, as well as the firm's new-build projects and housing, has contributed a new momentum to their city centres. Other cities – not just London and Birmingham – keen to breed cosmopolitan values, are welcoming schemes by larger, highly design-literate developers like Hammerson and Land Securities that will help them stand out as distinct civic communities.

Younger architects are attuned to the art of such individualist statements. As well as fitting themselves into the frame of rules, limits, standards and stereotypes operating within society and to which their clients may well be subject, they are motivated to find ways of outstepping them. Certain sectors, such as education, which are governed by protocols, are showing signs of opening up; others need initiatives, such as the Commission for Architecture and the Built Environment's[18] (CABE) Healthy

McDowell + Benedetti: (right) proposal for garden, CABE's Healthy Hospitals initiative, 2003

Hospitals scheme, to prise open the door to new ways of thinking about holistic, humane solutions. However, few young practices would bother with restrictive PFI-funded commissions, as this procurement method for billion pound jobs that minimize risk is one in which design is not a high priority in itself. Design expertise in such a context is usually regarded by clients solely as a tool to secure planning permission.

Shifting ground in cultural identity

The reality of the architects featured is that of a profound and delicately layered multicultural ethos born of diverse origins, history, experiences, circumstances and freedoms, the impact of which cannot be ignored even by anyone imagining that architecture is the preserve of middle-class white males. The demographic make-up of teams working at each of the practices (for example, David Adjaye's office of forty includes at least six black members of staff and others who are of Chinese, South American, Indian or Asian origin) can be identified as a highly geographically mobile generation in the sense that, like the cultural make-up of the UK's architectural student population, they possess a richness of diverse personal histories derived from a myriad of locations. As a name, Foreign Office Architects, now an office of eighteen architectural staff, evokes the external perspective and creative agency of the foreigner. The UK continues to be porous to the infiltration of other cultures, a fact well chronicled by observers of other art forms, such as photography and typography. The signs are that the country is attracting architects – not just as students which the leading schools continue to encourage – who are happy to be based here as practitioners, and to teach and work internationally as well as locally. Both Plasma Studio in London, co-founded by Eva Castro, who is Argentinian, and Holger Kehne, who is German, and Meta Infrastructural Domain (MID), the practice set up by Sebastian Khourian and Ciro Najle, also Argentinians, have in recent years been highly placed in The Young Architect of the Year Award run by *Building Design*.

Being schooled in complexity theory, perceiving urban culture through the lenses of many disciplines, from the visual arts and anthropology to genetics, has evolved a particular kind of nomadic architectural identity that is tied up with changes in how place is seen. Intervening in many cultures, basing themselves internationally, either permanently or temporarily as opportunities arise, is a way of being in the world that loosens ties with place of origin and heightens exposure to and exchange with 'the other'. Global references are essential and the shifting set of relationships

between global and local cultures become part of a practice's rationale for design and creation of new spaces that are themselves often hybrid. In the case of KDa, based in Tokyo since 1988, their scavenging of indigenous influences and materials was shrewd. With the prospect of fresh markets generated by the enlargement of the European Union, cross-border collaborations are more likely to succeed where there is a commitment to open-mindedness and risk-taking. Moving bases or spreading bases – as David Adjaye is doing by setting up a second office in New York – increases the depth of involvement with projects. A Japanese base during the executive design and construction of Foreign Office Architects' Yokohama International Port Terminal meant the practice could work alongside the contractors.

When S333 won Europan, in 1994, it moved its base to Amsterdam, and is now regarded as a Dutch practice, although two of its members are English, another is Canadian and the fourth a New Zealander. However, today S333 is

> Fluid: <u>Derwent Gateway Centre</u>, Derby, 2004; (left) cricket hall; (right) multi-purpose hall adjoining the cricket hall

increasingly involved in the country that it left a decade ago, bringing to bear specific advanced urban design skills that the UK needs. The public-sector bodies behind Thames Gateway, the major urban regeneration project in the south-east, have given Dutch architects and planners Maxwan and West 8 key masterplanning and development roles. S333's refocus on the UK, taking advantage of this fluidity in intellectual trading based around the regeneration of place, can be seen as a tactically productive strategy, facilitating political and cultural exchange across national boundaries.

Research-driven activities, adhering to flat models of management structures, advanced interdisciplinary collaborations and a proactivity in programmatic responsibilities: all these factors are changing the style of architectural practice. So far this generation has had relatively few commissions that provide an opportunity to work collectively on solving problems. The UK currently lacks clients who favour the multi-team approach; but the practices featured in this book could easily apply their high-level participative skills in this way, modelling themselves on the 'swarm' loved by emergence theorists[19]. They just need the right opportunities and clients who are able to take a risk.

Identifying what you do is now part of identifying who you are. Once architectural practices were invariably named after their founders. Following the introduction of more loosely based groups – Archigram in the 1960s being an early example – it became popular to identify the values of the team with a noun. Nouns can express purpose and denote strategies, philosophies and desired impacts. For every conventionally titled firm (Witherford Watson Mann, a two-year-old practice that has converted factory buildings into Amnesty International's headquarters), two or more trust to acronyms (such as the multidisciplinary AOC, nascent

Agents of Change), almost as if their meaning confers magical powers. Nouns convey a sense of the architect being engaged in global cultural espionage, which of course they are. Parallels with this research-led, network-driven activity can be detected in the work of practices based outside the UK; for example, Field Operations in New York (run by James Corner, who was born in Manchester in the UK); Crimson in Rotterdam, who are collaborating with FAT; Stefano Boeri's Multiplicity in Milan; PLOT in Denmark; BAR (Base for Architecture and Research) in Berlin; or EZCT, the French/Dutch practice.

Bespoke holism

Architecture is one of the few generalist professions with a broad view of the world. The times demand customized applications tailored to context; they require both this broad view and specialist skills. The days of placing emphasis on standardized design solutions rather than on modular systems are over. Instead there is a range of strategies to cover process, programme, technique and so on. That is why the issue of 'non-style' is so important to many of the featured architects and their peers: a style implies repetition, not a fresh, bespoke response to a situation or cultural context. In formal terms, these architects reject universal recipes in favour of ingenious custom-designed solutions that are not bombastic or self-referential. For them, a building needs to work holistically as an urban space, contributing to the construction of the city and its sense of civitas, by offering a generosity of character. By exploiting construction techniques, younger architects use the means of production to reinvent the programme. Their approach to form is not about CAD concepts scaffolded into three-dimensional reality: rather than being purely a means to an aesthetic end, choices about how a building is constructed carry a polemical objective. The intention of many of AHMM's designs, for example, is to 'make the vernacular more explicit', as Simon Allford puts it, and 'the making of it is the finish, not build and skin'. Their architecture is not a system finessed by the language of the skin: maximizing use of space is favoured over the ability to upgrade finishes.

The Pompidou Centre in Paris, designed by Richard Rogers and Renzo Piano, both in their early thirties when it was completed in 1978, challenged every architectural orthodoxy. Foreign Office Architects' Yokohama Port Terminal, completed in 2002, also does this. Its material continuum removes the distinction between the load-bearing structure and the building envelope. A vectorial rather than a Cartesian grid without coded, segmented elements, its unconventional construction followed a morphogenetic

process of complex material organization generated through the integration of various 'orders', from circulation flows to flexion resistance and climate via the medium of the diagram. These processes are expressed in an accumulation of millefeuille layers of steel. Foreign Office Architects prioritize the process of 'growing buildings', combining ambitions concerning surface and topography as well as the desire for their buildings to blend into their environment.

The interleaving of building and context has many distinctive contemporary qualities. David Adjaye's designs aim to 'corrupt' pure modernist forms with experiential spatial tactics. Alison Brooks favours the weightlessness of origami-type structures; in common with Foreign Office Architects and DSDHA, she uses form to dissolve boundaries. dRMM is preoccupied by form's reconfigurability and transparency. When the surface is a preoccupation, it can be surprisingly upfront, as with FAT's attachment to façades, promoting a polemic in favour of liberating taste from its association with lifestyles deemed to be fashionable by the media. Structural engineering now actively serves architects' creativity in what has become a strong convergence between the disciplines[20]. This shared chemistry, optimally involving conversations very early on in a design process, is noticeable on projects for which architects engage their favourite young innovative engineering firms. Adams Kara Taylor has worked with numerous practices, including Zaha Hadid, and is currently involved with Foreign Office Architects' BBC Music Centre; Michael Hadi was responsible for the inflated ETFE roof of Kingsdale School designed by dRMM; and architect-trained Charles Walker, under the mentorship of Cecil Balmond at Ove Arup & Partners, founded the Advanced Geometry Unit (AGU) in 2001.

Spatial interventions by other young practices organize

environments around patterns of movement and a variety of uses with subtlety and ingenuity. Plasma Studio's conversion of an industrial building in Hackney, east London (2002–3), into a mixed-use space creates zones of varying degrees of openness and enclosure, with pods defined by vectors filled by sliding translucent doors slicing space into 'a jig of relationships', as they

put it. For a silversmith's live/work space (2000–1), also in Hackney, the architects maximize workspace by introducing platforms of steel grating. Like the silver forms the owner makes, their relationship echoes the evolution of metallic form from two to three dimensions. They transmit as well as deflect light and produce a continuous, interlinked succession of small gallery spaces through which visitors move towards the skylight at the top. Surface, which is interested in 'topological surfaces, distorted to suit all conditions, rather than discreet or "strong" building elements such as walls and roofs', designed The Ambiguous Object (2004) at the Medical School Library, Queen Mary College, University of London. It is set in a deconsecrated church and includes a concealed lift platform which provides disabled access to the crypt of the Grade II listed building. With its upper portion free to oscillate as a pendulum, the photo-etched aluminium structure plays on ambiguities of material, weight and scale while fulfilling its functional brief. The sensibilities of younger architects lead them to transcend either/or categories of 'iconic' and context to emerge into an interwoven territory of investigation. Fluid's commission for the Derwent Gateway Centre building in Derby (completed in 2004), a facility intended to signal local regeneration, came as a result of masterplanning work that the practice was doing in the area. As a structure it reconciles its various functions as a cricket club, grandstand and community centre. A sense of ownership of each facility is achieved by contrasting form and materials: polycarbonate and playfully coloured curved walls distance the community spaces from institutional trappings. At the same time the boundaries between each are dissolved.

Discerning how far singular strategies are the preserve of a younger generation is not easy. But their calibration of experiments in relation to contemporary realities is a constant process. Architecture has become as fluid as the social patterns it is entrusted to accommodate, with its meanings easily appropriated or debased to make a fashion or marketing statement. To ask younger British architects or interior designers, engaged as they frequently are by consumer brands, to define the sense of place in their work is a loaded request now that so many projects have a short lifecycle. It may not affront architecture's contemporary social role to emphasize experience, or a sense of 'occasion', instead of 'place'. Reflecting social change without being socially determinist, and allowing the process of production to transform the initial idea for the project; these are some of the design parameters that distinguish the finest work of this rising generation from that of any generation that asks too much or too little from architecture. The predetermined, self-referential sculptural presence of building is no longer the

> Surface: The Ambiguous Object, Queen Mary Medical School Library, Whitechapel, east London, 2004; north and west elevations

primary means by which architecture is made to communicate; that approach has been transcended by the marriage of process, socio-spatial concerns and adaptation to new information and uses. The vulnerable nature of architecture as a profession, a result of its loss of its master-mason status, is counteracted by an intensely multivalent strategy of engagement in the world. After all, with our pliable sense of time and place, why should abstraction still be of much value?

It is far too soon to predict the shape or depth of the potential legacy by the most successful of the UK's younger architects, but polite modernism, stemming from an over-association with the kind of social status Margaret Thatcher made fashionable (a description of the Achilles' heel occasionally heard on the UK architectural circuit which, apparently, characterizes too many of them), will, as this book makes clear, scarcely feature on the list. A culturally profound platform has been created in the last five years, established on a socially driven ethos that embraces cultural and corporate responsibilities. Architects have always been highly skilled at balancing conflicting forces; indeed, they are trained to do so. Architectural entrepreneurialism has its own particular chameleon-like identity, and perhaps that is what brings out the cynics long recognized at the table of UK culture. But architecture is synthetic; practices are corporate: how else does a practice function with credibility and legitimacy in financial relationships with clients? Like the best entrepreneurs, architects take massive risks in making the

corporate cultural on every conceivable level by self-funding countless competition entries. To make this work, they design structures that allow the directors and staff maternity and paternity leave and family time, practising in a meritocratic long-hours profession, in a country with a long-hours culture, in a way that is as flexible as possible. Signs that an entrepreneurial spirit may be waning among UK-based late-twenty-somethings may have something to do with the overall buoyancy of ever brand-conscious international practice sustaining careers, rather than cold feet in the face of what continues to be a tough procurement environment characterized by too many closed shops and a box-ticking, risk-averse climate lacking a progressive competition structure.

Just as it would be unrealistic and naive to hang the future fortunes of younger architects solely on current government initiatives, it is also too much to expect that the market will provide the full range of opportunities they need to make their mark. The ideal situation is one in which both play their part, take risks and make architecture a central part of their ongoing capital programme.

A bridge needs to be created that allows more of the lateral thinking, high level research and new proposals in UK architecture to be applied to society's myriad needs. Architecture's capacity for proposing sustainable projects for urban communities is not yet sufficiently understood or valued in the UK. It does not help that the Prince of Wales derides ecologically advanced schemes like Bill Dunster's award-winning zero energy BedZED affordable housing in Beddington, Sutton, built in 1999–2001 for the Peabody Trust[21] (the project's making as a bottom-up scheme is documented in Dunster's *From A to ZED*[22]), nor that funding bodies to higher education have until recently been prone to judge architecture in an unfairly narrow way – leaving the School of Architecture at the University of Cambridge vulnerable to closure for a time – although now this myopia towards the value of design-led research is being overcome through revised criteria for judgement.

The instability and fluidity of the times demand not just that architectural experimentation gets more airtime but that it is properly invested in. Banishing architecture's traditional attachment to hierarchies and orders and self-image as a profession responsible for drawing board utopias is an ongoing and necessary process. On the other hand, 'make do and mend' was a slogan from the Second World War that in the 21st century we do not need to continue to haunt our ambitions for architecture as a social art. This globally transferable generation has shown itself to be capable of constructing advanced counterintuitive relationships between theory and practice. In their heyday its now

oftroom: design for <u>The Wireworks</u>, a new-build development of apartments and commercial units, Southwark, south London, 2003-

internationally known predecessors relied far more on the weight of theory alone. Now it is time that the accumulated riches of ideas and strategies resulting from the cultural metamorphosis of the entire younger generation of UK architects are better understood internationally and employed at home more often. It is time for higher levels of subsidies for research, from industries that stand to gain from improved urban and environmental conditions, to allow the whole architectural culture of the UK to undergo further change in support, which it is long overdue. It is time to raise the game still further. If not now, when?

Notes

1. Unicity, a research project by the Dutch architects and urbanists MUST (established in Amsterdam in 1998), not yet exhibited in the UK, commissioned by a group of Dutch and British urban bodies including the Thames Gateway, South East England and the Cross River partnership, analyzes the potential of the cross-national urban field that has come about as a result of the impact of north-west Europe's High Speed Train network (2003–4).
2. InIVA is the Institute of International Visual Arts; Autograph is a photographic arts agency.
3. Sam Jacob of FAT, in his essay 'Archigram's Pastoral Futurism', published on his website www.StrangeHarvest.com, argues that young architects are still seduced by technology.
4. Office of the Deputy Prime Minister (ODPM), created as a central department in its own right in 2002, and responsible for policy on housing, planning, devolution, regional and local government, the fire service, the Social Exclusion Unit, the Neighbourhood Renewal Unit and the Government Offices for the Regions.
5. For instance, Liverpool Vision, New East Manchester and Sheffield One.
6. Launched in 1997.
7. Building Schools for the Future (BSF), launched by the Department for Education and Skills in 2003, is the single biggest UK government investment in improving school buildings for over fifty years, aiming to rebuild or renew every secondary school in England over a ten to fifteen-year period.
8. A primary school.
9. 1997–99.
10. EDAW was incorporated in 1967 in the USA as Eckbo, Dean, Austin, Williams, a land-based planning and design firm, and now has a European office based in London.
11. Forty-two-year-old, Toronto-born, London-based architect.
12. As the French anthropologist Marc Augé defined it.
13. For example, architect Ian Abley's www.audacity.org.
14. Established in London in 1995.
15. For example, the Phaeno Science Centre in Wolfsburg, Germany (2000-5).
16. Founding Director of the Architecture Foundation, Richard Burdett is also currently Centennial Professor of Architecture and Urbanism at the London School of Economics, London.
17. The 'Z' in CZWG, established in London in 1975.
18. A non-departmental public body set up by the Government in 1999 to encourage the development of well-designed homes, streets, parks, offices, schools, hospitals and other public buildings.
19. Self-organizing systems that are complex, adaptive and bottom up, which start producing emergent behaviour, i.e. that lies one scale above them, for instance, local agents creating new urban districts.
20. Architectural critic David Taylor has termed this convergence 'engitecture' (2004, in conversation with engineer Hanif Kara).
21. Stands for Beddington Zero Energy Development.
22. *From A to ZED* by Bill Dunster, Bill Dunster Architects/ZED Factory Ltd, 2003.

> Plasma Studio: <u>loft refurbishment for mixed use</u>, east London, 2002-3; (left) office and living area with sliding door; (right) corridor formed as an interstice between inserted volumes

asma Studio: <u>silversmith's workshop</u>, east London, 2000-1; platforms of steel grating form a spiral staircase

Adjaye
Associates

> <u>Dirty House</u>, Shoreditch, east London, 2002

projects kıck the structural components of modernism as a truth, and knock you out of customary perceptions.'

> <u>Dirty House</u>, Shoreditch, east London, 2002; (left) top floor studio; (centre) building with its cantilevered roof

> (far right) ground, first and second floor plans

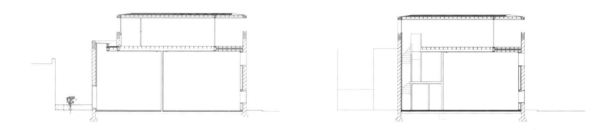

> <u>Dirty House</u>, Shoreditch, east London, 2002; (top, from left to right) sections through studio one/two, studio one/living room, studio two/office/bedroom/living room; <u>Elektra House</u>, Whitechapel, east London, 1998-2000; (bottom left) the house from the rear

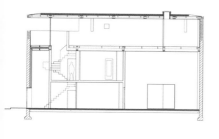

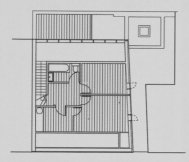

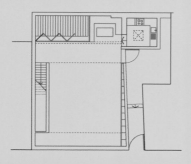

Inspired by his belief that 'architecture has an incredible psychological presence', David Adjaye's experiments with its substance emerge from the tension created by his interest in the abstracting power of modernism and a sensual reading of spatial experience. His desire to integrate within his work an 'imprecise geometry and certain imperfections' is critical to his commitment to initiate new hybrid programmes for architecture in urban contexts. It will be fascinating to see how he applies his art-driven language to functional challenges as the focus of his practice shifts from small scale private commissions to larger projects in the public realm. Now the first wave of public schemes by Adjaye's forty-strong practice is under way, building on a sequence of private houses, it is clear that he differentiates space through an innovative agenda that is more concerned with experiential distinctions than with establishing functional boundaries. As a conceptual architect wedded to a lateral view of culture, his approach cuts across notions of architecture as a purely pragmatic, technically driven practice, or as a visual language based on certain conceits; instead he prefers to investigate the possibilities of more fluid spatial solutions, reinventing the changing programmatic identities and relationships of cultural buildings and living environments. Adjaye has always been very vocal on the relationship between architecture, culture and urban context. At a time of change in social and working patterns, he sees houses and institutions 'collapsing and compressing into each other which has immense implications for how materials and spaces are read'.

Adjaye was born in Dar es Salaam, Tanzania, of Ghanaian parents. His father was a peripatetic diplomat, and Adjaye spent his childhood in East Africa, Egypt and the Lebanon before moving to London in 1975, when he was nine, completing his education at a city comprehensive. This background influenced his ability to negotiate layers of different cultures from a very young age. Adjaye studied art and sculpture before working for David Chipperfield Architects in London, returning to train in architecture to postgraduate level at the Royal College of Art (RCA). He spent time in Kyoto, Japan, on a scholarship, as well as in Oporto, Portugal, working for Eduardo Souto de Moura Architects, before establishing a practice in 1994, a year after leaving the RCA, with fellow RCA architecture graduate William Russell, which lasted until 2000 when Adjaye set up Adjaye Associates, with eight employees and Karen Wong as managing director.

The team rapidly became known for its designs for private apartments, in some cases incorporating studio space, for artists Chris Ofili and Jake Chapman, actor Ewan McGregor, and photographer Jürgen Teller. Adjaye relished the freedom offered by art, and collaborations with friends like Ofili, another RCA graduate. By deft means, the architects played up the

(bottom right) ground floor; (far right from top) first floor plan, second floor plan

sensuous qualities of basic materials like lacquered chipboard or honeycomb aluminium panelling in London projects like Lunch, a café on Exmouth Market in Clerkenwell, the Social bar in NoHo (north of Oxford Street) and Browns Focus boutique in Mayfair. The budgets for their projects varied widely, ranging from a reported £80,000 for Elektra House, for an artist couple and their children in Whitechapel, east London, to £3 million for a penthouse in Kensington Park Gardens.

A fluid way of thinking about public and private spaces permeates Adjaye's work, but now he is actively exploring his relationship to the parallel discussion between modernism and tropical architecture. In the West, we tend to have a single view of modernity, but Adjaye proposes that there are many modernities, one of which comes from the diaspora of West Africa. His projects show signs of his desire 'to write a second story', one in which he combines his knowledge of the history of Western architecture with his early experiences of architecture and design in Africa. They represent attempts to 'flip the way a project is perceived' by welding these disparate approaches towards function and representation together into a singular system so that they are indivisible.

This is the duality that he makes frequent reference to. The strong patterns that can be identified in the architecture of Nigeria, Ghana and West Africa provide its means of representation and are a response to a need to limit exposure to the sun and keep things cool; they have a natural identity that can be seen repeated as icons or symbols in textiles, jewellery and other artefacts. Adjaye's fascination with pattern systems informs his 'making a freeze moment from a surface, a geometric' where, for example, windows which are not straight become powerful details guiding the viewer's responses, or façades assert a new identity through the way the composition of their 'skins' is treated; and he will often combine contrasting materials. Through such stimulating devices Adjaye is able to 'kick the structural components of modernism as a truth'. His grasp of modernism, Swiss in particular, is solid and deeply informed by art practices, and the work of artists like sculptor Walter de Maria or David Hammons, the American conceptual artist, as well as musical composition.

This conceptual starting position means Adjaye favours achieving a degree of genericism in his design, but one that can incorporate 'bespoke moments beyond the system'. He also believes that 'too much knowledge about architecture stops people from really doing it', and that many of the inherited tools of the discipline are becoming inadequate to deal with the scale of cultural changes taking place. When faced with the 'pluralistic mess' of the urban context, his tactic is not to try to mend the

> Kensington Park Gardens apartment, London, 1999-2001; (centre) corridor/living room; (top right) hallway

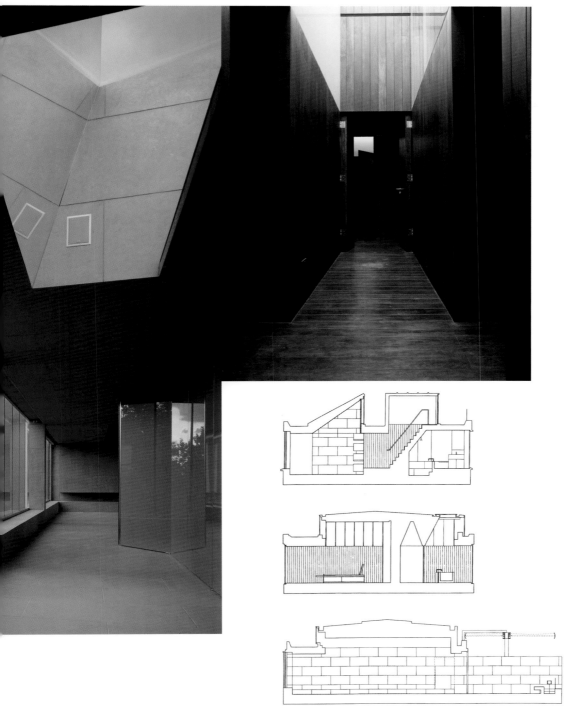

> (bottom right, from top) sections through library and guest bedroom, master bedroom/bathroom, main living space and terrace

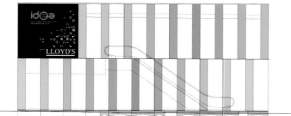

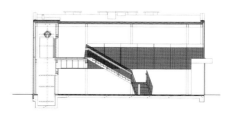

> <u>Idea Store</u>, Poplar, east London, 2001-4; (top left) east-facing windows of library; (top right) the building over an existing arcade of shops; (bottom left) south/front elevation; (bottom centre) cross-section

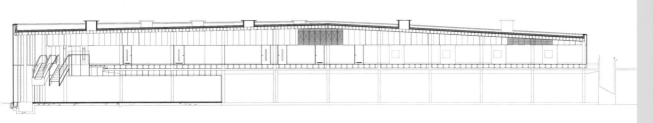

> (bottom right) longitudinal section

> <u>Idea Store</u>, Poplar, east London, 2001-4; (top left) curved furniture in the library; (bottom left) podium level plan;
(middle) the building seen from the main road; (top right) coloured glass window; (bottom right) staircase to the podium library level

urban environment, but to forge a credible response that impacts on what is already there, something Adjaye likes to call 'condition impact'. There is no secret formula, and it is something that he is continually experimenting with, relating to the idea that architecture can be a 'corrupting system (based on human rather than system intelligence) of what the culture is'.

One of Adjaye's tactics is to apply pattern to a building as a way of generating form that avoids hierarchy. In his collaborations with the artist Chris Ofili, architecture and art have been allowed to transform each other's characteristics. The Folkestone Library foyer (2002) with a translucent glass screen was certainly about blurring the lines between the two. Adjaye points out that this was a neo-classical trick, so that the art work becomes a function and a device that becomes a corridor. Flanked by Ofili's doodles screenprinted behind clear glass or sandwiched between clear and coloured glass, the design draws on the materiality of the space. At the Venice Biennale in 2003, Adjaye worked with the iconography in Ofili's paintings and created a starburst ceiling that hovered, hanging from a space-frame structure constructed inside the room but separate from the walls. While in the past, axis might have ruled architecture, colour – including dark tones – is the verb in Adjaye's work, helping, he maintains, to create an overall scalelessness. 'The articulation of colour breaks down mass and allows you to understand the whole; but it also allows you to play,' he says. The vernacular modernism of Egyptian architect Hassan Fathy is one of his biggest influences, and it could be said that Adjaye strives for a multicultural contemporary vernacular. Shada, a storytelling pavilion for families, a collaboration with artist Henna Nadeem (1999–2000), located within the playground space of a new housing development at Limehouse Fields Estate in London, again shows how architectural structure and art work can become the same thing. Above a 6 metre piece of Corten steel, a steel disc canopy perforated by laser cutting projects a shadow image of leaves on a tree that acts like a huge timepiece in the playground.

His winning design for the 2002 competition for the Nobel Peace Center in Oslo demonstrates how he can articulate a complex theme. The conversion of a former railway station into an area for exhibitions and presentations begins with a new Corten steel gateway canopy, leading to a lobby where pixellated circles create illuminated apertures like an alternative map of a borderless world based on capital and secondary cities rather than land and water, boundary and territory. From the top-floor windows, the view leads down to the gateway structure with another 'map' of the world, with land masses and sea cut out of the steel, solid yet punctuated by tiny holes.

Adjaye has also designed and built a substantial number of private houses, most of them in London. He calls them 'prototype houses' as many are studio-houses for clients with lifestyles that demand a high degree of flexibility and, therefore, innovative solutions. The 130 square-metre Elektra House (1998–2000), for an artist couple, which came soon after his split from Russell, is geared to the couple's needs for closely involved living and working/display spaces. Elektra has a blank street façade, which is a wall of dark, phenolic resin coated plywood cladding, totally windowless and enigmatic. The building's unconventional proportions and hermetic character are set in play with a third factor, the relationship between 'artificial versus natural light'. This theme can be traced through much of his work: large skylights contrasting with windowless rooms full of unusually placed lighting. 'The project had to find a new expression beyond the cellular layout of a standard house,' Adjaye explains. He avoids repetitive elements and makes the compact space appear larger by suspending the upper floor of bedrooms and bathroom facing the all-glass rear wall behind the front façade, leaving room for double-height spaces.

Adjaye grapples, he says, with how he can make architecture express a sculptural quality. His desire is for 'a very present silhouette', applying geometry 'designed to make the maximum dissolve, and the diagonals shift'. While the design of Elektra House centred around spatial perception and scale, that of Dirty House (2001–2), in Chance Street, Shoreditch, for artists Tim Noble and Sue Webster, tackles relationships in scale between living and working space, immateriality in form and language while achieving clarity in organization. Adjaye converted a dilapidated warehouse into a three floor 5,000 square-metre space for living, with a double-height studio and entrance lobby. He adapts the building by giving it textural mass, covering the exterior in dark chocolate-coloured anti-graffiti paint that still allows the years of successive brickwork treatments to be read. This intensification of the surface of a volume has been described by some commentators as primitivist. The transformation operates like a wrap, with the exterior merely a skin, and the windows – tinted on the ground floor, with deep-set ones above – unrelated to the floor levels inside.

While the ground floor is a very 'lofty, thinking space', the top floor, with its extreme horizontality, is a glazed courted pavilion that frames a panoramic view of the surrounding urban environment. Standard timber decking positioned on its reverse side unites the floor of the interior and two-sided terrace. In a reversal of expectations, you descend from this domestic floor – completely hidden from the street – into the high ceilinged spaces below, experiencing the differentiation Adjaye creates between levels.

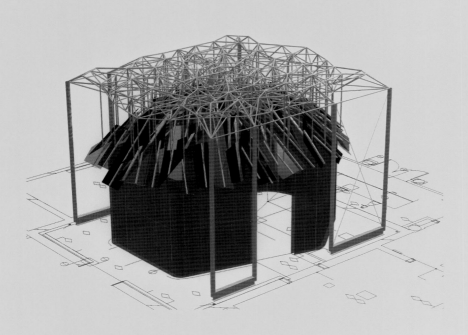

> With artist Henna Nadeem, <u>Shada storytelling pavilion</u>, Limehouse, east London, 1999-2000 (top); <u>British</u> <u>Pavilion for artist Chris Ofili</u>, Venice Biennale, 2003; (bottom) 3D model of starburst ceiling supported by space-frame structure

> <u>Nobel Peace Center</u>, Oslo, Norway, 2002-; (top) visualization of the gateway canopy in front of former railway station building; <u>Folkestone Library</u>, Kent, 2002; (bottom left) corridor with screenprint by Chris Ofili between screen of clear and coloured glass

The cantilevered roof, held above the glass wall of the building by steel rods – a slab with a white glow of light set in the parapet wall beneath it and reflected off the floor onto the roof lining above – seems to float. This impression is heightened at night, when the base becomes a dark mass, in stark contrast to the white roof of the building, highlighting the sense of an outer structure – in this case a pre-existing one, historically part of its location – protecting something independent and 'other' inside but emerging above it: a striking example of the duality that Adjaye seeks. Kensington Park Gardens (1999–2001) is a 1,664 square-metre penthouse at the top of a late 1960s apartment building by Richard Seifert. It was converted by Adjaye for a computer industrialist. Portuguese limestone in 300 millimetre panels was used to line the walls and ceiling of the public areas of the apartment. This contrasts with the dark smoked oak and West African macassar timber that is applied to the private living quarters. The bedrooms are lined with sycamore. The design demonstrates the power of materials to create a sense of luxury. It brings to mind Adolf Loos's Müller House in Prague, which also focused on the structural nature of materials, rather than their traditional value. At the centre of the penthouse, stone and timber collide and reveal their differences. On the street side of the apartment, there is a 60 metre wall of Privalite glass which can be switched electronically from opaque to transparent. A skylit corridor evokes Craig Ellwood's treatment of rooflights, opening up space to the sky.

By spring 2003, Adjaye was working on twenty houses and his list of public commissions had also grown, giving him the chance to experiment on a larger scale and to challenge the identity of 'civic' building. In his public architecture, the key issue for Adjaye has been how you read an urban context. His Idea Stores, two new-build libraries for the London Borough of Tower Hamlets, reinvent the typology, along with a number of other new examples in the UK. They are among a number of initiatives aimed at providing information and continuous education to a multicultural citizenship in inner city areas where ownership of computers at home is low. The concept began in France with the mediathèque, and this new kind of civic space aims to be more like a living room than a traditional library. Adjaye Associates won the Idea Store competition in June 2001, and completed the first building, on Chrisp Street in Poplar in the East End, in July 2004. (The five times as big, five-storey £7 million flagship on Whitechapel Road is due for completion in autumn 2005.) Sited on the main road, next door to a supermarket on the edge of the 1951 Lansbury Estate, it incorporates a library, adult education facilities, free computer and Internet facilities, a café and a crèche. As Adjaye explains, the idea was 'to make a building that doesn't cut out the richness of life, and the light', one that is 'a new

> Bernie Grant Centre for the Performing Arts, Tottenham, east London, 2001-; (bottom right) visualization of the site with theatre, studios, enterprise units and landscaping

public intellectual playground for people of all ages, where people can make their own journeys and discoveries'.

As a result of Adjaye's attempt to 'try and find a form generated from context and a reading of the site', the east side of the building, above a row of small pre-existing ground floor shops, is flat and reflective, incorporating a double-height entrance, and almost 'disappearing' into the stacked structure of the estate, while the other is bent and higher, a stepping up that allows the library its place on the main road and creates variety within the local context. Adjaye's interpretation of the site lets what would otherwise be a pure form become corrupted. It looks at first like an orthogonal prismatic box, but it is not. The façade is a double skin of full-height coloured glass (four different blues and greens) and aluminium insulating panels in vertical strips positioned randomly around the building which, from the calm seclusion of the interior, frame the views outside. The design is a reworking of the curtain wall which establishes an efficient system for maximum transparency. Adjaye hijacks that more conventional language which is about economy of materials, creating a design that is inherently driven by pattern.

The large hall of the main library space, which runs obliquely on plan at the front, its coloured verticals seeming to dissolve in front of the streetscape, tapers towards the rear. It offers a view of timber illuminated by skylights which cast dappled shadows amidst the green hue from the windows. Such effects are a common feature of Adjaye's spatial choreography. The custom-designed hanging lights, angled like the building crank, add visual dynamism. The furniture and fittings using recycled timber are also entirely custom-designed, with shelving that deliberately avoids a cellular fitout. Historically, a public building would not present itself in a commercial way; nor would a library traditionally be constructed of glass. Idea Store is a chameleon in its retail context, a jewel of a social project that promotes proximity and interaction with its neighbours and neighbourhood. Adjaye's agenda is to reassess traditional boundaries of exclusivity, confronting the user with contradictions in the way space has customarily been treated, thereby deinstitutionalizing public buildings, and making them less formal.

Soon after the Idea Store competition was awarded, Adjaye scooped a £10 million commission to design the Bernie Grant Centre in Tottenham, north-east London, a cultural/educational centre dedicated to the memory of the MP and civil rights leader. It is due for completion in 2006. In plan it is like a campus, a relatively unusual solution for an urban art quarter. The site will include a 300-seat theatre space and studios, enterprise units and a new civic square, which will regenerate the area. The landscape is laid out like a carpet that draws people into the site,

> <u>Rivington Place arts centre</u> for inIVA and Autograph, Shoreditch, east London, 2003-; visualization

> <u>Museum of Contemporary Art</u>, Denver, Colorado, 2004-; visualization

with the cultural centre presented as three separate structures faced with wood, Corten steel and ceramic. The theatre is clad in a rain screen of purply pink Caribbean timber, its softly crumpled form like an insect at pupa stage, representing the acoustic nature of the structure. The rooms are lined with woven slatted timber weave, an acoustic material, with tessellated batik patterns. As with Adjaye's houses, their character is not indicated by the façade, which is dissolved through a process of scarification. Its surface marks, like scars on a human body, create a sense of scale and break down the volume. There will be 'no single orthogonal line', he says; the cross-section shows the auditorium, rehearsal room and foyer as three chambers of equal size, deliberately avoiding compartmentalization and hierarchy.

The brief for <u>Rivington Place</u>, a new £5 million Shoreditch-based arts centre, home of the cultural institutions inIVA (Institute of International Visual Arts) and Autograph ABP, was for a non-hierarchical space. Adjaye Associates, appointed in 2003, designed a triple-height meeting space as a threshold between the white box of the gallery and the black box of the auditorium, which acts as a condenser of people. 'It will have an urban scale when you enter the building,' says Adjaye, who likes to place his entrances on the side rather than the front. The façade is perforated, broken down into a series of units pegged together with stainless steel dowels, a diagonal surface that envelops the building. The intention is for the building to be understood not as a formal or generic box but as a 'volume of experience' with 'a sense of being able to be discovered'.

The commission that Adjaye won in 2004 for the <u>Museum of Contemporary Art</u>, in the downtown area of Denver, Colorado, now being regenerated, contains elements of the atelier-like ambience of the studio he designed for Ofili. It is three discrete buildings with triple- and double-height spaces like chambers, with a T-shaped atrium dividing them, wrapped by a long walkway entry around the periphery ('the slowest entry ever', says Adjaye), rising up initially as a tunnel. Creating an autonomy – like a mini-city – was important at Denver. So was the sensuousness of the design: the façade is a clear glass skin and woven fibre polypropylene sandwich that reflects people's shadows. Off-white, it will take on the colour of the sky. Adjaye likes to focus on the materiality of his designs, 'achieving a little hallucinogenic moment when the visitor is deceived into thinking a building is not an institution'. His is mysterious, yet highly engaging and emotive architecture: a building 'has to interpret its remit so well that it is astonishing, but also a mystery'. With interiors that belie external appearances and create hybrid worlds, his projects are exercises in how to achieve an elusive balance of public and private, architecture and art.

Alison Brooks Architects

(ABA)

> <u>VXO House</u>, Hampstead, north London, 2001-4; (top left) view from dining area to entrance; (bottom left) site plan; (right) staircase in front of house

Alison Brooks loves the complexity in architecture that can emerge from a simple approach: 'the baroque effect you can get through relatively few gestures'. For her, this is 'better than working with something complicated and trying to make it simple'. Brooks's emerging body of work strongly demonstrates her interest in transforming architecture out of its customary context and into landscape, giving it new character beyond the boundaries of tectonic convention.

Working and living in Toronto until 1989, when she moved to London, she craved 'the intensity and density' of London as a place where 'eccentricity is nurtured'. She became a founding partner of Ron Arad Associates in 1991, and their combined architectural energies produced One Off Studios on Chalk Farm Road (1991), the Tel Aviv Opera House foyer (1994), Belgo Noord (1995), a stone's throw from One Off, and the 300-seat Belgo Centraal in Covent Garden. In 1996 she left Arad's practice and set up Alison Brooks Architects. 'I was determined to get out of interiors and into urbanism. I hated the idea that housing was a ghetto. Housing is city building: it should be a site for experimentation.'

Even her reinvention of a hotel brand demonstrates that everything she does is intensely site-specific, and cross-fertilized with other disciplines as well as singular materials and processes. She says that 'this approach is necessary to 'unframe' the design problem, and allow the social to engage with the technological, creating an open cultural context in which the project can evolve.' Her design for Atoll, a new-build spa hotel on the German island of Helgoland (1997–98), was based on the concept of 'a sensory adventure, where every expectation is overturned'. Its interior is a liquid, tranquil space defined by its organic visual connections, employing sensuous materials inspired by the 'atoll', a circular steel vessel originally used as a deep sea diving platform. The foyer floor is pierced to reveal views of the pool, while over the edges of a carved-out mezzanine, in the centre of the teardrop-shaped bistro facing the main island pier, a table top splayed like a starfish can be spied below.

At VXO House in Hampstead (2001–4) bold forms intervene in the secluded garden location of a 1960s' family house. Brooks's conversion opens the building up to the landscape, creating a dialogue with all the different areas of the garden surrounding it. The clients wanted the entrance to become transparent, so Brooks extended the brick building with a 100 square-metre timber-clad cube supported by a structural 'V' and fronted by floor-to-ceiling glazing. This brought movement into the façade, making it 'a canvas for things to happen'. The open, light-filled foyer is a frame rather than a plane. With its slate flags, it 'masquerades as a covered outdoor terrace. I am trying to dissolve the boundary. You

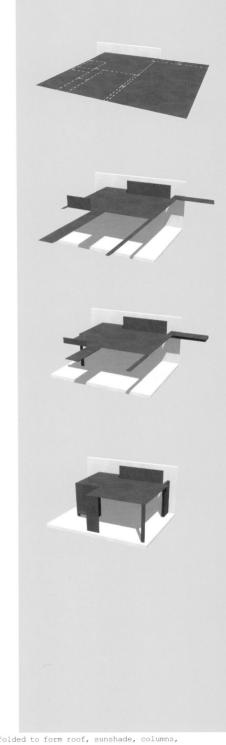

> Fold House, Wandsworth, south London, 2001-4; (left) single planar surface cut and folded to form roof, sunshade, columns, walls and bench

> (top) exterior; (bottom left) exterior at night; (bottom right) floor plan

> <u>Atoll hotel</u>, Helgoland, Germany, 1997-98; (top) swimming pool; (bottom) mezzanine above starfish-shaped table in bistro

are always puncturing your space. That horizontal boundary (the floor and roof) is waiting to be broken,' says Brooks.

Suspended and hovering, a new translucent steel staircase hung upside down from the first floor to the floor below, comes into view, an eye-catching sculptural object. The idea was to create 'a staircase that didn't look like any other. I used a walkway grating to suspend the stair. It creates a kind of veil, which changes as you walk around it, becoming alternately opaque and transparent'. To the right, *Ohm Sweet Ohm*, a trompe l'oeil of a blue screen wall made by artist Simon Patterson, reworks a 1960s amplifier wiring diagram: 'The electrical codes are replaced by a lexicon of musical performers from the 18th century to the present.' This veiling and layering makes the entrance area feel like a Moorish arcade with a secret courtyard.

Throughout the house, internal spaces are opened up to create new circulation routes, flowing living spaces and a double-height glass-roofed gallery over the dining area. 'We took the darkest part of the house, and made it the lightest,' Brooks says. Sliding glass walls with bar code etching designed by ABA offer another variation on the theme of language. A chain mail 'curtain' hangs over the fireplace, and the skirtings are of zinc. A year after the extension was built, Brooks was commissioned to design an independent gym and guest house, and a car port, each linked to the main house via Ipe timber decks across the redesigned garden.

The car port is a simple timber deck raised up and supported on an 'O'-shaped column. It has the feel of a garden folly. The grass-roofed guest house is formed by two 'folded', superimposed pavilions. One, a rear concrete plate, faces the house and is clad in black pebbles like a garden wall; the other timber-clad plate screens the space from zinc-clad storage and bathroom spaces and faces the garden. The grass roof is lifted above the walls by two X-shaped columns, leaving a continuous clerestory strip of frameless glazing. Each element tells a different story. Brooks makes her structural elements – the V, X and O – function as expressive events: 'In trying to communicate ideas that are readable it is sometimes good to make things slightly tongue-in-cheek. People laugh when they see that the structure is formed of letters.'

In the eight years since ABA was founded, the practice has maintained its commitment to experimental work in urban design, housing, interiors and landscape. Her designs for competition schemes during this period included urbanDNA (Diverse Neutral Accommodation) for Britannia Basin (1999), a prototype exploiting fast-track production systems, economies of scale and the urban character of a brownfield site.

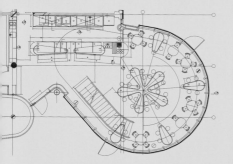

> (top) bistro plan; (bottom) solarium in spa

Touching on her desire to transform was Ful House ('future urban life'; 1999), 'a critique and metamorphosis of the Victorian-Edwardian terraced house,' with 7.5 metre-wide living zones, spatial variations and a strong sense of flow.

ABA is building three housing types in an emerging scheme that has already won an RIBA Housing Design Award (2003) and is increasingly recognized as an exemplar in relation to the PPG3[1] (Planning Policy Guidance on Housing) guidelines issued by the UK Government in 2000 and its sustainability agenda for new buildings. Brooklands Avenue (started in 2002) in Cambridge, for Countryside Properties, will be the largest modern housing development in the city since 1965. Countryside wanted to achieve a high eco-homes rating, with courtyard houses built at high density in a context of car-free streets. Brooks describes her involvement as 'participating in a process of city building rather than house-building per se'. Forty units within three different building types, each with a distinct character, are part of a 400-unit masterplan designed by Feilden Clegg.

In the tradition of Cambridge University's academic morphology, the apartment buildings are composed like campus buildings in a landscape, with a central boulevard spine. However, what is certainly not normative is ABA's cladding in copper on fractured façades. The units are excellent test cases for the exploration of individuality within communal building forms and offer new spatial models for the single family house. 'We take a completely site-specific approach,' she adds, aiming to create 'architecture that has the potential for non-specific occupation'. The first of the three building types is a loft structure, with 'spaces interlocking like rubic cubes'. Brooks not only orientates individual spaces to the sun but expresses each apartment as a piece in the overall structure. On the ground floor are four apartments; all the other floors repeat over two levels five different types of maisonette (in a total of four storeys), containing one to three bedrooms. Each one has a void 'to provide a visual link between the different levels and accentuate the open-plan layout'; and the L-shaped 'sky patios' on the north side of the south-facing balconies, with sun-catching screens in a shape developed out of the structural element of the concrete wall/slab, provide a continuation of interior to exterior. As Brooks says, 'I gave the building something that transforms as you go around it.'

'The house building industry here is really ripe for new models and experimentation. Housing design is city building and should be given the most attention as it's the pivot of urban life.'

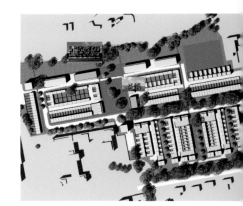

> <u>Brooklands Avenue</u>, Cambridge, 2002–; (left) site plan, with the three buildings in green; (top) perspective of north elevation of twenty-six-apartment building; (bottom) perspective of angled façades of ten-apartment building

The second type is a semi-detached house, three and a half storeys high, with a flexible open-plan layout that has spaces of varied heights and spatial continuity achieved with a split-level staircase and a central void. A curved copper roof wraps over the top of the house and down the rear façade, enclosing a huge top-storey, split-level family room. Windows are arranged as a kind of 'dance' across the front façade, often placed at floor or ceiling level to remove the sense of 'top and bottom' in the room interiors. Although the front of the house is a tight orthogonal box clad in Cambridge yellow stock brick, in compliance with planning restrictions, the rear of the house consists entirely of glass, steel porticoes and curved copper: 'the house melts as it faces the south and opens up to its garden,' says Brooks. Interestingly, Brooklands Avenue is a 'design and build' project, but the process has honoured custom-designed architecture, bucking the trend towards a dilution of design concept.

The third type is a six-storey apartment building clad in faceted brass on the central green of the 400-unit masterplan. 'People call it the giant copper crisp packet,' says Brooks, who wanted to angle the façade so that each apartment has oblique views across the landscape, and long views of the space surrounding the building.' The 'woven' effect of the façade comes from the alternating façades pushing in and out, as though the building were breathing. The external amenity spaces are not separate elements but part of the overall geometry governing the design, notably the cantilevering floor slabs of the levels below which create the external spaces for the balconies above. Brooks did not want to make 'an apparition between the greenery', but to 'try to dissolve the overall form into the canopy of trees. Sometimes the building will be light and transparent – at night the building will dematerialize into little cubes of light, scattered around. I think of the whole thing in movement. I like the idea that baroque devices of illusion and movement can be used in 21st-century housing.'

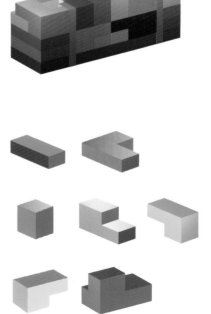

Fold House in Wandsworth, south London (2001–4) clearly shows Brooks's interest in dematerialization. A 390 square-metre conversion and extension of a huge Victorian terraced family house in a conservation area, it has a singular living/dining space generated by a repeatedly folded sheet of patinated bronze. This elemental form 'folds away from a glass box', creating a variety of outdoor spaces, including a courtyard located between the existing house and the new extension and a covered outdoor portico, with folded plates acting as light reflectors and benches. The glazing is retractable, allowing two of the façades to be fully opened to the garden. Ever conscious to avoid a static statement, Brooks's three millimetre sheets of patinated bronze will gradually change colour through exposure to sunlight and shifts in temperature and humidity. 'If the architecture can be made into

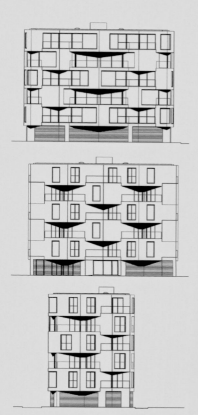

something as simple as cut and folded sheets, it becomes extremely two dimensional, even when it is three dimensional, a bit like working with origami,' she says. 'It's about expressing weightlessness.'

It is rare to see new indigenous architecture created in a maritime context, but <u>Salt House</u> (2002–5), on the coast at St Lawrence Bay in Essex, is a new 300 square-metre hip-roofed atrium house clad in black slates. It sits at the end of a row of rare white clapboard timber 'oyster' cottages. Fitted out with bay windows, these cottages were formerly oyster fishermen's homes. A glazed lantern at the apex of Salt House provides its central focus, while silhouetted timber louvres offer shade and privacy to the large glazed areas around the open-plan ground floor which has wooden decking. The decking opens onto the south and north frontages in stepped terraces.

Like all the houses in the row to which Salt House acts as 'a kind of book end', it has an 'outrigger' to the south, a one-storey extension for guest accommodation. 'Deflecting the façade became the controlling geometry for the whole house,' Brooks says of the faceted first floor perimeter, which is drawn from the language of neighbouring bay windows. This fold in the exterior provides generously shaped bays and brings a sense of flow to the space, breaking down 'the flat, tight skin that separates the exterior from the interior, and being more plastic with it'. Brooks enjoys 'working with planes, bending, folding and lifting',

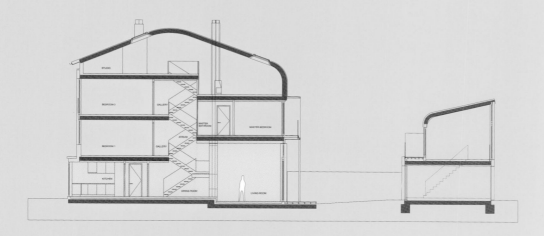

> (top) ten-apartment building: south elevation with maximum glazing, north elevation with minimum glazing, east and west 'transitional' elevations; (bottom, left to right) semi-detached apartment building: section showing open-plan ground floor and top-floor studio

taking her different studies of the upper space through the collapsing geometry so that the compressed effect of the walls 'creates an amazing upward movement'. She tries to explore something new with each project but similar things tend to re-emerge. At the risk of giving Salt House the over-precise faceted quality of an architectural model, her process is about letting a crystalline form emerge, just like a salt crystal.

Brooks is intent on producing a radical new vision for housing and urban design in the UK. The way she sees it, people in the UK 'have already bought into the idea of modern flexible spaces – the loft was part of that shift – and are more open-minded and ready for something different; but there's a time lag in terms of the built environment'. She thinks the house building industry is 'really ripe for new models and experimentation', citing the willingness in mainland Europe to see housing as a territory for exciting ideas. 'There are pockets of enlightened developments here in the UK. The challenge is whether the agenda of the masterplan filters through to the buildings. We should be addressing a different concept of domestic environment as it can improve people's lives on a daily basis: it has a huge social impact.'

She sees the paradigm shift that has come about in the last twenty years in the use of digital technology, computer modelling, software and structural analysis as key in any debate on housing or design. 'We produce three-dimensional models at a very early stage…you can test everything you do, the ideas against the virtual model, the model against the complexities in fabrication and construction, then the virtual model itself tests the concept. It becomes an integrated design process. As people become more demanding with that way of looking at things it will help architecture.'

Brooks wants to extend architecture's boundaries. The way she sees that happening is 'if you can play certain games but also look quite seriously at how you can create an architecture that is unexpected'. She is not moved by formal acrobatics for their own sake. 'It's about creating experiences, enabling people to experience their physical and social environment in more intense and specific ways. I'm trying to connect to the senses, to emotions, to our senses of being human, those things that often get sidelined by the purely architectonic.'

1 Planning Policy Guidance Note 3 (Housing) published by the Department of Transport, Local Government and the Regions, 2000

> <u>Salt House</u>, St Lawrence Bay, Essex, 2002-5; (from top) 3D study of ground-floor layered decks from which the enclosure emerges as a series of continuous folding/unfolding vertical and horizontal planes

(top) view of house from sea, with hip-roof forming giant bay window; (bottom left) south view of house with outrigger framing entrance court; (bottom right) section through house showing folded stair and atrium

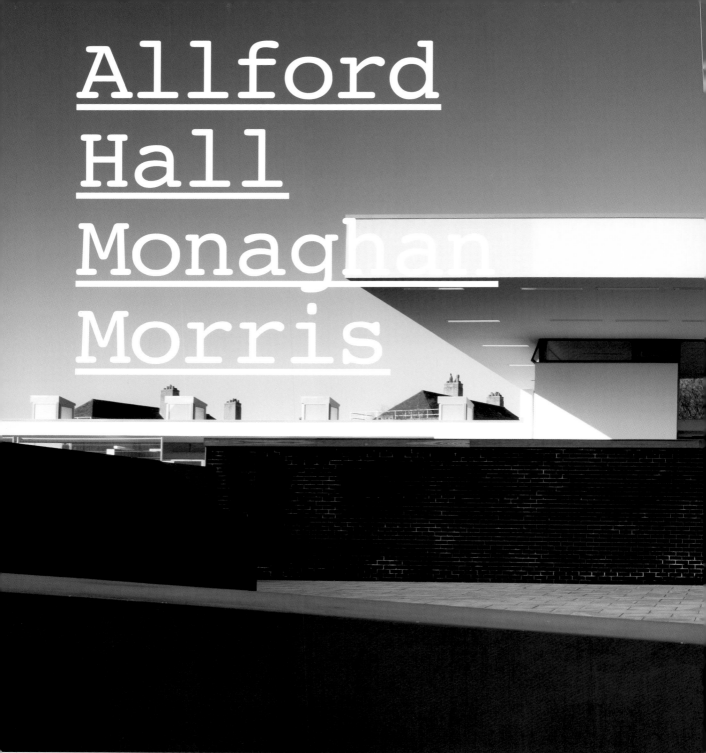

Allford
Hall
Monaghan
Morris

> <u>Jubilee School</u>, Tulse Hill, south London, 1999-2002; cantilevered roof of school hall

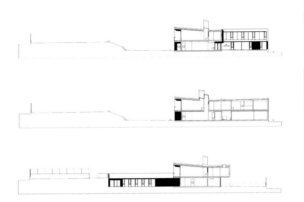

AHMM's stated aim is simple and explicit: 'to set up the architecture where architecture can occur', as partner Simon Allford puts it. The practice has completed over ninety buildings in the UK since it was founded in 1989 by its four partners, Allford, Jonathan Hall, Paul Monaghan and Peter Morris, who were all students at the Bartlett School of Architecture. They launched their practice on graduation, after submitting 'The Fifth Man', a collaborative final project, unusual at a time when solo creativity dominated architecture. AHMM were in their early thirties when they won the competition for one of their most well-known buildings, the bus station in Walsall in the West Midlands (1995–2000).

'Architecture is the management of a delightful mass of contradictions,' says Allford. 'The Fifth Man' framed an approach that they have drawn on ever since, that new architecture should develop from 'understanding issues of site, space, finance, technology, architectural typology and the whole mechanism of the city'. This approach reflects the collaborative ethos of the practice and the added value that mutuality brings to dealing with gritty contexts rather than a clean slate. Whether designing educational buildings on tight budgets, new working spaces, or masterplanning, they maintain a commitment to making more of urban public space, and for them that is largely a matter of pragmatism aiding the creation of a convincing contemporary vernacular architecture. Discussing urban regeneration projects, Allford feels that 'if you design the development equation, you can redesign the architecture'.

'We are trapped in old models of measuring things, for instance, habitable rooms per hectare when something smaller with a better use of space might well be better. We like throwing away the measuring scales.'

> Jubilee School, Tulse Hill, south London, 1999-2002; (left) sections; (right) nursery playground

> <u>Jubilee School</u>, Tulse Hill, south London, 1999-2002; coloured cheek walls and glazed bricks

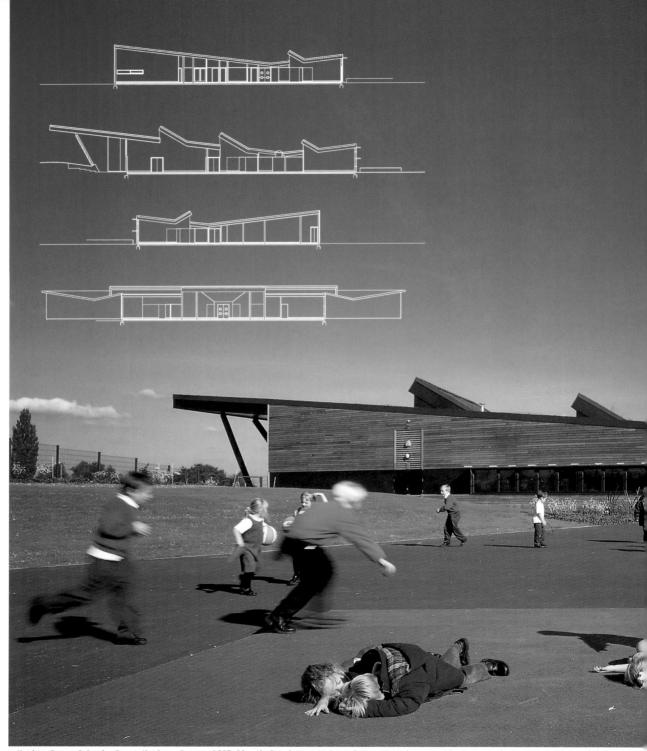

> <u>Notley Green School</u>, Great Notley, Essex, 1997-99; (left) four sections from top to bottom: kitchen to classroom; hall to classroom; classroom and plant; library and internal court; (main picture) view of school from the west

> <u>Notley Green School</u>, Great Notley, Essex, 1997-99; (main picture) south elevation; (bottom centre) the 'prow' of the triangular building; (bottom right) ground floor plan; <u>Walsall bus station</u>, West Midlands, 1995-2000 (bottom left)

The AHMM method found a good solution for Notley Green School, which opened in 1999. It began as a competition held by the Design Council and Essex County Council, which asked for 'a new prototype model sustainable school' on a greenfield site to a standard DfES budget. Rethinking this weighty brief, as well as providing feedback on its principles of sustainability and method of construction to the architectural profession, education and government, was important, so too was designing a building that could be used by the community out of hours.

Notley's triangular form has a commanding presence on site and good floor to wall ratio. Its effectiveness as a design centres around the way AHMM made best use of the budget. By exploiting the building form and maximizing the use of circulation areas for teaching space with just one dedicated corridor, their scheme added two more spaces – a central court and a play area – than required by the brief. This reduced the overall area of the building by 10 per cent, which meant that more could be invested per square metre in its fabric, including numerous recycled, low-energy and environmentally preferred products.

'We are trapped in old models of measuring things when something smaller with a better use of space might well be better. We like throwing away the measuring scales,' Allford observes. He sees what went on in the process of planning Notley Green as a 'microcosm of what we would do with a masterplanning commission'. While masterplanning is often 'a series of classical Beaux Arts observations and plans that result in elegant and less elegant moves', he stresses that the most important part is to understand the possibilities of the context. Their scheme to give Barking town centre a new heart is the first phase of a masterplan arising from a competition that AHMM won in 2002 to improve the environment and encourage more people to live there. Barking is located within the Thames Gateway, an 80,000 hectare area, stretching from Tower Bridge in London to Essex and north Kent, with a high concentration of brownfield land and deprived areas, which the government has committed to regenerating. At Barking, AHMM propose creating a new pattern of linked public spaces – a gateway, library arcade and town hall square – and revitalizing the town centre with new buildings that have an individual identity, including a lifelong learning centre. The architects also plan to add housing on top of the existing library, which will gain its distinctness through a central garden forming the main circulation courtyard for residents, and via cantilevering balconies, each one individually coloured, from olive to yellow, creating a spectral rainbow. Taking a balanced yet decisive approach in line with AHMM's approach to space generally, the architects aim 'not to overprescribe what happens'.

When faced with the challenge of very tight budgets, Allford explains that AHMM 'use devices and tactics to be generous'. They are not obsessed with detailing for status or aesthetics at the expense of the overall quality of the architecture. Their affordable housing for the Joseph Rowntree Foundation in the inner city industrial quarter of Birmingham, one of two CASPAR (City-centre Apartments for Single People at Affordable Rents) social housing developments for single people, was realized in 2000 at a cost of under £52,000 per unit in a scheme of forty-four in two blocks. The strength of the design derives from the clever angled flying bridges linking the two five-storey blocks, rather than shared decks common to older forms of social housing, which support the social life of the scheme and provide space for private entrances to the apartments and front gardens. Made of basic materials, including steel frame, red brick and hardwood, the design of the bridges demonstrates how assuredly AHMM respond to a brief to create a fresh social context at high density. The solutions that they find for their 'principled pragmatism', as CABE Acting Chairman Paul Finch described their approach, often creates an exemplar of its type, whether it be housing, a school building or another form of public amenity.

'You can upgrade finishes but not a space,' says Allford, and a similar ethos pervades the practice's affordable housing schemes at <u>Dalston Lane</u> in Hackney (1998–99), and <u>Raines Court</u> in Stoke Newington (1998–2004), in east London. Both are tough-looking buildings, expressive of the economy in their making. The design for Dalston Lane's eighteen residential units above 750 square metres of retail space, incorporates a double-height entrance space and light-diffusing, insulating Okalux window panels; it shouts its robustness via the big checkerboard pattern on its façade which also reduces the building's sense of scale within the street.

Raines Court is a six-storey scheme of fifty-one apartments and ten live/work units for the Peabody Trust, with a ground floor area of 400 square metres, that introduces diversity within standardization. The Trust's first modular housing scheme of predominantly off-site volumetric construction, its relatively wide (3.8 metre) steel-framed modules generate new layouts and plan types, minimizing circulation and maximizing usable area. Typically, a two-bedroom apartment is made from two steel modules, one for living/dining and kitchen areas, the other for bedrooms and bathroom. Arranged in three separate blocks linked by a central circulation core, the scheme has a street-facing 'civic' side which is clad with zinc shiplapped panels and modulated by deep recessed balconies. There is a softer, inner side facing south, with private courts off the walkway which are incorporated into the modules. To customize the standard nature of the scheme right through to the

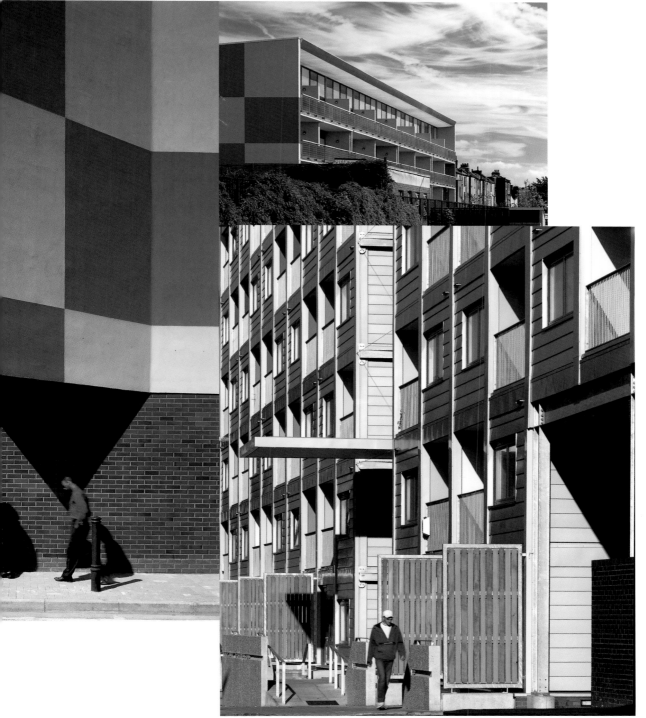

> <u>Dalston Lane housing and retail building</u>, east London, 1998-99; (left) checkerboard façade; (top right) exterior;
<u>Raines Court housing and live/work units</u>, Stoke Newington, east London, 1998-2004; (bottom right) exterior

> <u>Raines Court housing and live/work units</u>, Stoke Newington, east London, 1998-2004; (top) exterior; (bottom far left) ground floor plan with individual flat plans

details, each recessed balcony has been decorated in a different colour within a palette created by the colourist Charlotte Ingle. Inside, the standardized shells allow a variety of fit-outs. AHMM, working with Peabody, have gone on to exploit their experience of prefabricated construction by developing their design for MoMo ('mobile modular') apartments, a system of quick-fit relocatable housing for short-term needs based on container technology.

AHMM are interested in how you can incorporate elements of made to measure while working with standardization and strict cost limitations. Part of that interest involves – through the use of materials and organization of space and structure – making an overall sense of vernacular space more explicit. The idea of a precast concrete that can be manipulated is appealing, because, as Allford explains, 'the making of it is the finish, it is definitely not about "build and skin"'. 'Build and skin' is not AHMM's style; they do not promote this kind of additive architecture on any level. Instead their strategy in constructing a vernacular is pretty comprehensive as their reinvention of the brief for Great Notley exemplifies. As Monaghan says, this approach has entailed 'using a set of rules and language quite consciously' and evolving them steadily over time. The award-winning Jubilee School (1999–2003) in Tulse Hill, south London, is an accomplished example of AHMM's rigorous thinking about what can be done on a standard budget to create generous architecture. The scheme combined a 420-place primary school, nursery, facility for hearing-impaired pupils and a crèche.

The layout was designed to allow the maximum flexibility of use. Although the building, with its east-facing cantilevered roof to the school hall, is at first glance quite plain and functional looking, it demonstrates how well AHMM play compositional games while making a great virtue out of cost-effective solutions, such as glazed ceramic bricks in vivid colours for the outer walls on the ground floors. The layout of the main spaces includes adjacent break-out areas: a range of spatial experiences is permitted by manipulating the plan of the building. AHMM brought in collaborative 'agents' to help achieve their rigorous layering of objectives, including consultants Studio Myerscough who developed the school's brand identity, Andrew Stafford who designed the custom-designed furniture, and artist Martin Richman who was responsible for the coloured wall and lighting installations.

Legibility and definition are priorities for AHMM's largest on-going project to date: Rumford Place in Liverpool (2003–), a mixed-use two-tower building with 15,000 square metres of offices, 161 residential units and ground floor retail space. Unity Building, a tower for residential use, steps up the corner of the street to create an urban marker as

> private house, St John's Wood, north London, 2001-4; (bottom left) light feature by Martin Richman; (centre) split pitch roof and clerestory window

intentionally strong as its neighbour, but taller and slimmer. The walls and floors are to be made in-situ in cast concrete; and this choice of material 'shapes the whole building, becoming a pure skin', says Allford. An 'exploration of interlocking form, colour and relief', the effect modulates the façade and breaks down the mass of the building. 'Patterns can be used to convey different scales in the city so the building can be read', he adds, referring not just to Rumford Place, but also to Dalston Lane and Raines Court. He quotes Lubetkin's idea of architecture being a carpet made of interlocking geometries that express a wholeness so that people can both read the scheme and appreciate the individuality created by the pattern making.

Instead of heavily prescribing functions, AHMM try to find innovative ways to define spaces. Their project for Tooley Street in Southwark, south London, a mixed-use development of housing and offices, which will be submitted for planning approval in 2005, layers the uses, breaking away from the tradition of London as 'a party wall city'. Allford cites this scheme, as well as another for Union Street nearby, which they are working on with developer and architect Roger Zogolovitch, as urban buildings taking control of their site so that the resulting design is not 'derivative of an arid system, while at the same time clients can see the material benefits'.

In keeping with their thorough approach, hammering out a new spatial coherence rather than just a superficial facelift is an important feature of AHMM's long-term programme of improvement for the many spaces of the Barbican Arts Centre (designed by Chamberlin, Powell Bon and constructed between 1971 and 1982). In the first stage, the art gallery, which reopened in 2004, was reworked and made physically separate from the library. Later phases over the next three years will reinvent the notoriously complex ground-floor foyers with new, integrated elements, including a bridge to transform navigation, signage and redesigned

> Barking town centre masterplan, Essex, 2003; (bottom left) perspective; Rumford Place, Liverpool, 2003–; (centre) mixed-use scheme with buildings for commercial and residential use and a penthouse block; (bottom right) view of Liverpool from across the River Mersey

points of arrival on the roadside and at the lakeside. In contrast, a new-build private house in St John's Wood conservation area in London (2001–5) gave them 'the opportunity to experiment with architecture in a pure way', says Monaghan. Although the building has a traditionally proportioned front façade, there is innovation in the use of materials inside, with some of the full-height and full-width sliding windows at the rear being the largest of their kind in the world, and a light piece by Martin Richman. It has no pretensions to be a universal space but establishes three clear, connected zones – open plan and private areas, and a garden – with views beautifully set up within an effortlessly satisfying composition.

New projects are emerging rapidly from AHMM, which now has nearly fifty staff. 'It is up to us to ensure that the opportunity is grasped,' Allford adds. It is no surprise, given AHMM's commitment to high standards of public design, that they avoid the many PFI (Private Finance Initiative) commissions the industry now offers, which do not have design on the agenda. However, like many of their generation, they are working on buildings that would once have been designed by architects on the public sector payroll. Keen to speculate and strike deals when it comes to innovative solutions for mixed-use space, AHMM know that the concept of a division between the public and private sectors has broken down, and they are happy to be 'forced to think differently' in response.

Caruso St John Architects

> <u>Stortorget</u>, Kalmar, Sweden, 1999-2003; (left) stainless steel masts and rooftops holding red lights; (right) detail showing existing fieldstones, cut stones and new precast paths

Caruso St John are respected for their commitment to an organic realism in architecture, a spatial and contextual approach that engages the everyday, strives for social transparency and brings together all aspects of the site. Partners Adam Caruso and Peter St John established their practice in 1990 after both worked for Florian Beigel and Arup Associates. They became famous for their £21 million Lottery-funded New Art Gallery in Walsall in the West Midlands, which they won in competition in 1995, when they were in their early thirties, and completed in 2000. Five years later, Caruso and St John are aware that the character of their work is now changing, and becoming more elaborate and varied.

Walsall was a landmark building, a model of accessibility, with a strong visual presence. It was proud to be cheek-by-jowl with high street shops such as Woolworth. As a gallery that interspersed art works with art work-sized windows, the design was celebrated for its boldness of gesture and extreme sensitivity to context. However, as a result, the practice became known for making quiet architecture, when in fact they are interested in 'the emotional capacity of building'. The year 2003 appears to have been pivotal, with several varied projects coming their way. Caruso is not worried about Caruso St John becoming 'wildly eclectic', because there is a sensibility that runs consistently through the project. 'When we won Walsall it was a period of concentration on one thing,' adds Peter St John.

> <u>New Art Gallery</u>, Walsall, West Midlands, 1995-2000; (left) view of the gallery from the railway station; (top right) site plan; (bottom right) entrance foyer

Now it seems, there is no risk of the practice becoming typecast. For example, in 2004 the new Gagosian Gallery, which they designed, opened in the King's Cross area of London, a part of the city that is undergoing radical redevelopment. Built on the site of municipal garages, the 1,400 square-metre concrete-floored galleries are simple and robust. The largest gallery is a completely new structure installed at the centre of the site. Drawing out the full potential of the scale of the space, the architects have provided varied gallery conditions within a suite of naturally lit rooms resulting from new and existing structures that will accommodate the work of the fashionable young artists and American masters that Gagosian favours. Their proposed design for a new office building in the southern part of King's Cross shows an interest in variety within an urban scale. Varied, big-scale architecture can be successfully combined with the formation of credible urban streets, say the architects, citing lower midtown Manhattan and South Michigan Avenue in Chicago. Caruso once said that he was into 'tough architecture, not touchy feely architecture', and it would seem that this building aims to give a strongly urban character through a combination of fine vertical grain and surface texture, but also colour. Precast concrete, with natural sands and aggregates – green porphyry and black basalt – are combined with very smooth synthetic formwork to create a smooth, almost ceramic surface.

A constant thread throughout Caruso St John's work has been their interventions to historic buildings. Two competitions with very similar briefs – the first, the renewal of the Cathedral Square at Kalmar in south Sweden; the second, an extension to the Museum in Darmstadt – made strong spatial demands. When it comes to the identity of the museum in the 21st century, the architects relate to the reality that interdisciplinary display is taken very seriously. Their competition scheme for the extension to the Darmstadt Landesmuseum, Germany, 'adds new spatial types on the site', styled by the client as a 'Museum Cluster for the 21st century'. Their new museum extension building 'stands like a glasshouse within the city gardens', its piano nobile galleries arranged like the raised beds of a garden. Large panels of thick cast glass are designed to have a palpable physical presence within the gardens and the adjacent neo-classical structure of the existing museum. The architects adopted a heterogeneous approach to decisions about the degree of restoration needed in order to provide a range of spatial possibilities for extending the way in which the collections can be displayed.

Caruso St John's restoration of the Stortorget in Kalmar, Sweden, completed in 2003, involved another kind of subtle remoulding. Owing to its historical importance, the competition for the project was run by the

'The most radical thing is allowing things to happen, allowing Woolworth and the Art Gallery to be a part of the city.'

> <u>Gagosian Gallery</u>, King's Cross, London, 2003-4; (top left) top-lit main gallery space; (top right) Britannia Street elevation; (bottom) side-lit gallery within existing warehouse; (bottom right) site plan

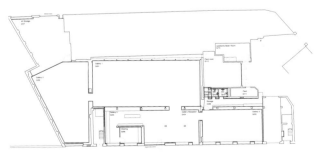

> <u>Bethnal Green Museum of Childhood</u>, east London, 2002-6 (phase 1 and 2); (top) central hall showing new fibreglass furniture

> <u>Bethnal Green Museum of Childhood</u>, east London, 2002–6, phase 2; (top) exterior of new entrance building for the Museum; (bottom left) interior of the new entrance building; (bottom right) site plan

city and the Swedish Public Arts Council with the collaboration of conservationists. For their winning scheme, Caruso St John worked with the artist Eva Löfdahl. The project took four years to construct. The square, with its Baroque cathedral, had a vertical emphasis. Caruso St John reconfigured it as a ceremonial space for today's uses; using contrasting field stones and other large, cut stones they made a seamless flow of new spaces. 'It was about not reinforcing the axes of the cathedral, but trying to redistribute the existing energies on the site,' says Caruso. Smooth paths for wheelchairs are made of huge slabs of precast concrete incorporating a smaller version of the existing granite field stones. 'The design aims to lend dignity to the existing spaces by increasing one's awareness of its physical characteristics,' say the architects. 'Stones come together in an unmediated way – no edgings.' There are masts with handcast jewel-like red lanterns; and the underground fountains which trigger different sounds audible via grilles in the paving surface suggest the infrastructure beneath the city; it is 'like making a celestial layer below the real one'. The space now has an asymmetrical form, much busier on one side than the other; it also has a unified, characterful identity. The project was the most purely public project that Caruso St John have done, with no pressure to introduce retail elements. An RIBA Award winner in 2004, the judges commented that 'the lightest of touches' had led to 'an altogether magical place'.

'No matter how unpromising a situation is, there is no such thing as an uninteresting site: you just add,' believes St John. A good example of this approach is Brick House (2001–5), a private house in west London that the practice is working on. It occupies an extraordinary space that prevents any kind of street frontage but offers the potential to invent a new style of domestic arrangement. Their solution introduces a kind of lung-like building shaped like a horse's head, reached by a ramp leading to a big vaulted interior space not unlike a Baroque chapel, with brick floors and walls. Three courtyards at the corners of the triangular site allow light to enter the interiors and provide intimate gardens for the ground-floor bedrooms. The building can also be read as a cave: with no external openings on the perimeter walls, it is insulated from the city. 'It's like the building's inflated to maximum volume,' says Caruso, while St John sees it as 'an exaggeration of the condition of London, one of many small utopias, but not quite fully formed'.

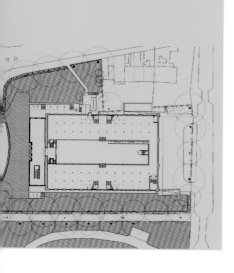

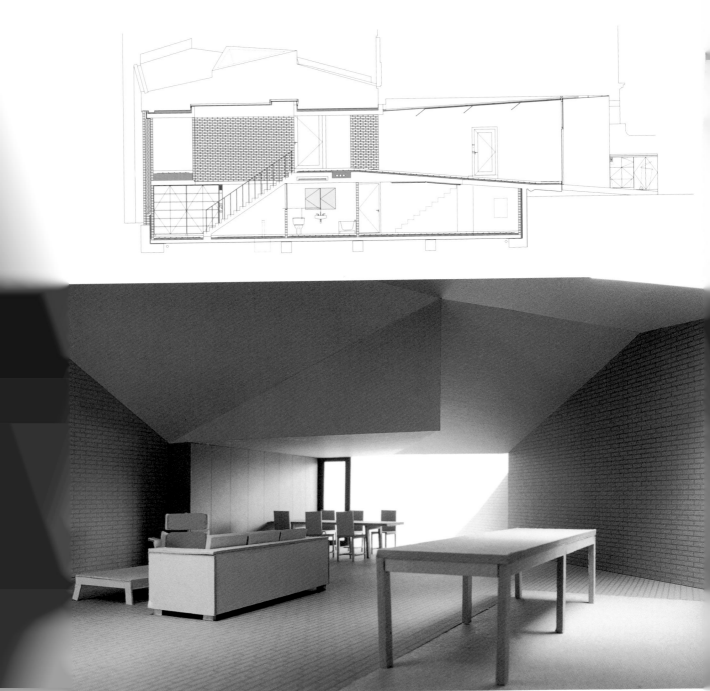

· <u>Brick House</u>, London, 2001-5; (top) section showing entrance ramp; (bottom) view of first floor living room

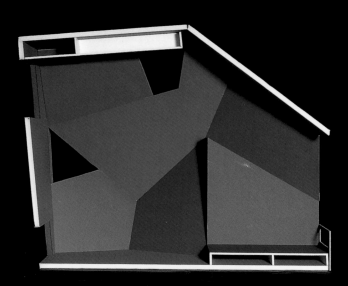

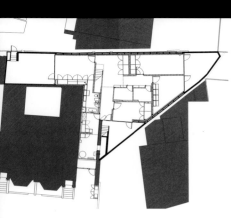

For the recently completed first phase of their refurbishment of the mid-19th-century <u>Bethnal Green Museum of Childhood</u> (2004), the exhibition space, with its vast filigree cast-iron roof structure, was cleaned out and decluttered. Working with the artist Simon Moretti, Caruso St John devised the colour scheme as well as the display systems and new items of furniture, trying to maintain a sense of overall context. Graphic designer Alex Rich created the 'road' signage to differentiate the spaces. When the museum was originally built, it was to have had additional reception buildings along the Cambridge Heath Road frontage, but these were never completed; so for the second building phase, the architects have proposed a new two-storey building with a room stretching the full length of the façade. This will provide circulation space and allow the two gallery levels to be connected in a more generous way and become part of the new centre. In keeping with the original iron structure, it will be a very light building, providing generous views in to its interior life and out to the garden. The scheme features champagne-coloured anodized aluminium, purple, red and grey glass, all referring to the colours of the mosaics on the side of the original building.

> (top) study model of living room ceiling; (bottom) upper floor plan

'We are interested in the emotional capacity of building', Caruso St John have written. 'In our work there is little sense of one material being inherently more valuable than another; instead the choice of a material and the development of its assembly is seen as an opportunity to make connections with the site of each project and to invest interiors with an intense spatial character.' Discussing the public square at Walsall, where they collaborated with Sergison Bates on the design of a new pub (see p. 218), they describe their treatment of the space as characteristically English. 'The most radical thing is allowing things to happen, allowing Woolworth and the Art Gallery to be a part of the city,' says Caruso. This does not mean that their approach is laissez-faire, for elsewhere Caruso and St John have described their techniques as 'knitting, weaving, wrapping and pressing'. Their skill in allowing architecture its place within 'the field of experience'[1] leads to an immensely fine-tuned and powerful way of making space.

1. As Irenée Scalbert describes it in 'On the Edge of the Ordinary', *Archis*, March 1995, pp. 50–61.

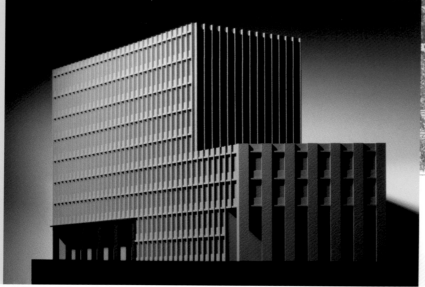

> Office building, King's Cross Central, London, 2003; view from Pancras Square

> <u>Landesmuseum</u>, Darmstadt, Germany, 2003; visualization showing glass additions to the neo-classical building

de Rijke
Marsh
Morgan

> <u>Kingsdale School</u>, Dulwich, south London, 2001-4; big hall and pod

> <u>Kingsdale School</u>, Dulwich, south London, 2001-4; (left) new courtyard

'We've pushed the brief and
the budget as far as it will go,
and we're not just focusing on
buildings but on activities.'

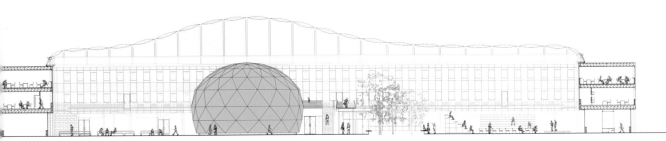

> (top) variable ETFE plastic skin roof; (bottom) section through main building and pod

> <u>Kingsdale School</u>, Dulwich, south London, 2001-4; (top) ITC suite central pod; (bottom left) ground floor plan; <u>Royal College of Art sculpture department's student accommodation,</u> London, 2002; (bottom right) proposal for a plug-in matrix of service pods

de Rijke Marsh Morgan draw on a range of classic modernist principles, creating new hybrids and typologies from UK and European precedents based on an economy of means that suit contemporary living patterns. The practice resists identifying with a particular architectural style or relying on metaphor to define a building, preferring to let function, form and construction be transparent. 'We like to design in a non-architectural way so that people can understand it,' say dRMM.

At home with commissions of all sizes, especially those with a strong social agenda, they apply a highly strategic methodology, inventively adapting various generic and industrial catalogue products and materials in order to create non-standard architectural solutions. In 'Off the Shelf'[1], an exhibition of the architects' work held at the Architectural Association in 2001, emphasizing a new type of 'one-off' or crafted building, a bank of standard archival storage systems with customized cabinets filled the room, serving as a statement about the architects' standpoint.

dRMM, set up in London in 1994 by Alex de Rijke, Sadie Morgan (they were both Royal College of Art graduates) and Philip Marsh, hit the ground running, winning two publicly funded competitions within the first two years. Their Ecostation in London's Docklands (1995), a speculative design for a floating house, and a scheme for the urban planning of Portsmouth city centre offered intelligent thinking about future uses of building and wider urban interventions and helped to put them on the map.

Alex de Rijke was born in London to Dutch parents but went to school in the Netherlands. 'I'm an anglicized Dutchman really,' he says. Marsh studied interior design and architecture and Morgan specialized in interior design. The group chose to base their practice in London rather than the Netherlands because of the challenges the UK presents, with 'extremes that are fascinating, though not always a good thing'.

The studio works as a non-hierarchical, close-knit collaborative team. De Rijke compares their approach to 'total football', the playing method developed by the Dutch football team Ajax in the 1970s, where everyone in the team can play in any position, and, as a result, 'all the players are much better informed and more flexible, and it saves time because you're not waiting for a certain person to make a certain move', explains de Rijke.

dRMM strive for ease of building as well as conceptual clarity. They used stackable blocks reminiscent of LEGO bricks for their 1998 Module Grass House design for brownfield sites. This modular approach addressed

> <u>Centaur Street</u>, Lambeth, south London, 2001-3; a mixed-use apartment building

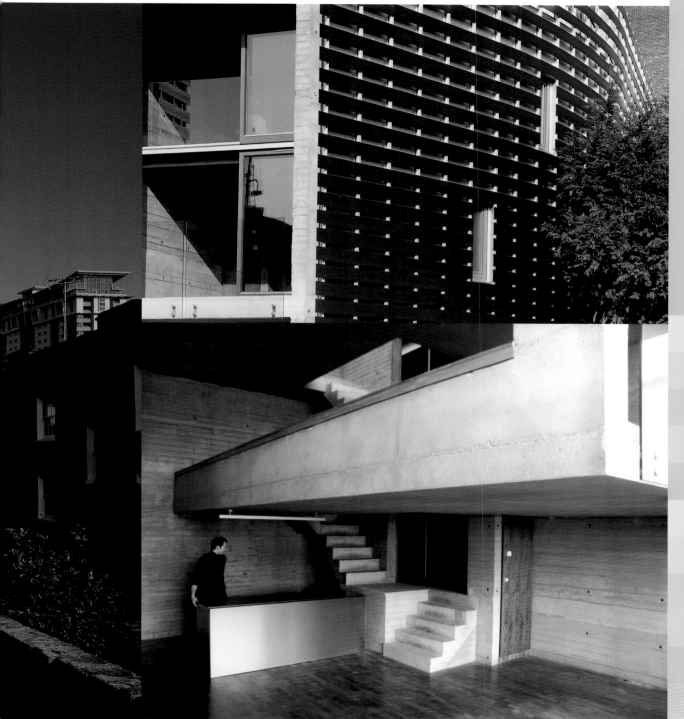

(top) detail of insulated rainscreen exterior; (bottom) the cast-concrete structure creates a Loosianraumplan of open and closed rooms of stepped heights

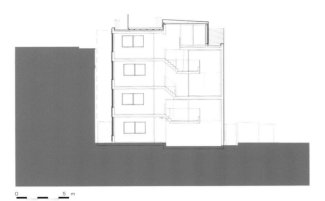

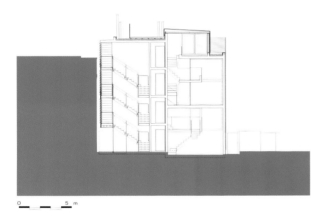

issues of high density and ecology, enabling a quick and reconfigurable assembly, reminiscent of the way Charles and Ray Eames approached housing design by exposing the structural elements. Their use of adaptable forms counters the otherwise predetermining process of building. dRMM's prototypes include a trailer-sized capsule hotel (2001) made up in 1:1 scale clear polycarbonate sheet, a joint project with their students at the Architectural Association. It was conceived as a nomadic communal space, adaptable to different cultural and environmental climates. Their proposed strategy in 2002 for the <u>Royal College of Art's sculpture department</u>, which included student accommodation, featured a plug-in matrix of service pods to optimize the various possibilities for working and living.

Prefabrication is a continuing priority for dRMM. They see it as a means of achieving a transparent architectural language as well as economies in time, cost and ease of construction. <u>HH Huis</u> (2002), a lightweight chalet,

> <u>Centaur Street</u>, Lambeth, south London, 2001–3; (left) sections; (right) first-floor interior and sketch

with open-air rooms, sited on a cliff overlooking the sea in Cornwall, was designed so that it could be constructed by the family that commissioned it. It is made of Steko, a Swiss prefabricated system of big but light recycled wooden blocks that sit on a heavy concrete raft. The house has an optical plan that gathers light into the building. Functions are inverted, with the bedrooms downstairs. A terrace above is treated as an open-air room. 'You could say that it has its roots in modernism in that it's an upside down configuration; but that's perfectly sensible given the site, because you want to get up to see the fantastic view, while the road corresponds with the living room and entry level and each bedroom downstairs has a door straight into the garden,' explains de Rijke.

Achieving greater transparency by removing as many of the internal doors and walls as possible featured strongly in their redesign of the Architects' Registration Board headquarters in central London (2000), banishing the cellular office layout from the traditional nondescript brick and sash-windowed interior, removing as many of the internal doors and walls of this labyrinthine legacy as possible. An 'island' service core and a boardroom made from translucent blue corrugated polycarbonate created a glowing centrepiece for the flexible and palpably more cheerful open-plan working environment.

Moshi Moshi, a Japanese restaurant in Brighton (2001), is also open rather than monumental in design. A simple, light box-shaped pavilion in translucent fibreglass, clear glass and steel, it sits on a raised deck which appears to hover mysteriously. Playfully countering its mundane context – it faces the neo-classical town hall and is bordered by low-quality municipal offices – the pavilion has the exotic presence of a Japanese temple, while the interior, with its casual ambience of an airy beach hut and deck of routed softwood boards, is a constant reminder of the proximity of the sea.

Moshi Moshi introduced the sushi conveyor belt concept to the UK, and dRMM created a correlation between the architecture and the food that is fresh, clean, precise and light by using Kalwall, a translucent composite aluminium/GRP panel. De Rijke explains that it meant 'that diffused light could be combined with privacy, while its low weight meant the façades could be suspended so that the whole thing hangs'. The completely flat façade has a horizontal front door that can slide off completely, opening the restaurant up to the square outside, thereby transforming both the building and its immediate context. 'The frame offers itself as a picture frame in the town square when the façade is closed, and when it is opened and parked in the frame it becomes a screen', explains de Rijke. At night the skirting of clear glass gives the building the effect of floating above its raised deck like a lantern. A skylight appears as a red cross of luminous paint, acting as a connective device, at once part of the outside world as well as the interior. The pavilion is so light that it can also be read as a piece of furniture in a public living room, defying any simple categorization of what is the inside and what is the outside.

The architects' apartment building at Centaur Street in Lambeth, south London, near Waterloo, for developer and architect Roger Zogolovitch, represents a new type of high-density housing, shifting the ground of this archetypal urban model. Completed in 2003, and the winner of the RIBA Building of the Year shortly afterwards, it regenerated a brownfield site, in this case a particularly narrow former scrapyard next to a group of 18th-century cottages, a housing estate and, on the north side, the Eurostar railway viaduct south of Waterloo Station. Here dRMM demonstrate a good command of archetypes, creating a mini-apartment block that is a hybrid of the four-storey European apartment block and the English terraced house. By studying typologies, they have established principles of organization and access which have fed into the design. Each of the four apartments has a spatial structure loosely reminiscent of Adolf Loos's raumplan interiors for social housing, being a combination of open and enclosed rooms of stepped heights. The main spaces are organized as a large, open double-height living area/kitchen, with a mezzanine gallery level, accessed by stairs, which can act as a study, home office, library, den or more secluded living area. One of the upper apartments has a double-height, glass-louvred winter garden. The building's staircase acts as a concrete buffer to the railway.

Centaur Street is a spacious solution that belies its modestly proportioned site. It is a tactile cast concrete structure, where the exposed 'textured' concrete walls are economically overclad externally with insulated rainscreen, horizontal panels of faux wood, a cool, robust and ergonomically sound aesthetic, and what de Rijke calls 'a reversal of the norm'. The graduated sequence of panels, placed at wider and wider intervals, is an effective visual tactic, making the block look solid at the base while appearing to dematerialize at the top. All the components are prefabricated, specified from international sources. dRMM use an unusual Spanish resin plywood, with a quilted diamond pattern, in the passageways between bedroom and bathroom. The block has its own shared planted garden from which the interior can be seen through sliding floor-to-ceiling glazed windows on each set of balconies. The judges of the RIBA's 2003 Domestic Building award admired the fact that the design 'breaks normal rules of decorum and refinement and is all the better for that. It somehow catches the moment'. Centaur Street uses texture rather than colour to command attention, derived from just three materials: cast concrete, wood and glass. In the UK, it is an example of an all too rare prototype of a new breed of high-density housing.

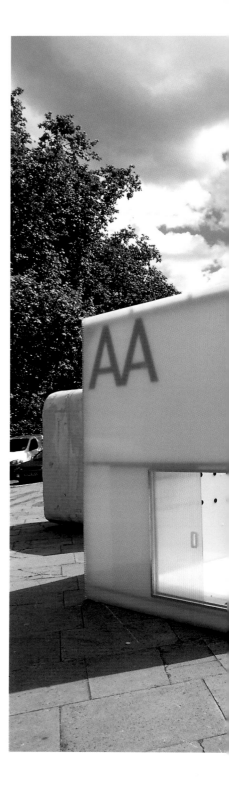

> <u>Capsule Hotel</u>, dRMM/Architectural Association research project with students, 2001; (centre and bottom right) nomadic communal space; (top right) spatial configurations designed with Diploma 4 Unit students at the Architectural Association

> <u>HH Huis</u>, Cornwall, 1999-2002; (top left and right) a timber block house overlooking the sea; <u>Module Grass House</u>, 1998; (bottom left) housing research project proposals for the north of England; (bottom right) proposal for a Dutch polder

Centaur Street was a new-build scheme on a tricky site. When it comes to adapting existing structures, working with givens requires being able to 'twist' them to advantage, says de Rijke. Kingsdale School in Dulwich, south London, completed in 2004, has been dRMM's biggest project to date. School Works, a not-for-profit UK company, commissioned them as part of their mission to develop a new approach to school design, demonstrating the link between architecture and educational standards and the impact that good design can have on the self-esteem of the school community. Kingsdale is School Works' first partner school, a previously troubled comprehensive which was awarded £9 million by the Department for Education and Skills (DfES) to implement new design proposals, including refurbishment of the grounds.

There is no reason why inner-city schools should not be allowed to demonstrate a contemporary identity through investment in infrastructure, but secondary schools have long been stuck in an anachronistic institutional form closer to the 19th-century factory. Some might say that this legacy actively blocks learning. Against this backdrop, Kingsdale is a groundbreaking project setting new standards, including social and programmed education. 'This building has to prove that education can be improved through the architecture,' says de Rijke.

Deciding against demolition, the most common solution since the Second World War for worn out and inadequate school buildings, the architects chose instead to modernize and exploit the potential of the existing late-1950s' building designed by Leslie Martin. It was all glass yet lacking in transparency, 'a very generic school' with an atmosphere of separation and division. Making strategic changes, they replaced the introverted cellular configuration with a cluster model, opening up the ground level and uniting two neglected external courtyards to create an 80 metre x 40 metre space at the heart of the school. They covered this new space with a new roof, a variable skin ETFE, a self-cleaning Teflon-coated plastic that controls solar gain, similar in type to the one used by Nicholas Grimshaw & Partners at their Eden Project in Cornwall.

It was the first time that such a material had been used in a school building, and at 3,200 square metres it is currently the largest of its kind in the world. With a dynamic vector pattern screenprinted on two of the three membrane layers, as a result of the superimposition of scales, when you walk under it the effect is of moiré. It also allows light to be filtered and reduced, from 50 to 5 per cent. Designed by structural engineers Michael Hadi Associates, the structure is light and rests on steel supports rather than the existing framework of the building. The cost of creating such a space may not have been possible to justify to the DfES if the architects had decided on a rebuild.

Everything but the trees was removed from this space, which has been given a highly reflective green resin floor. In this calm area of dappled light, dRMM have placed a huge, distorted geodesic pod in birch-faced plywood. This irregular structure is a 314-seat auditorium for music, cinema and performances. Here, Dutch anarchist artist Joop van Lieshout's line in 'useful art' has provided a cheeky-looking services duct, reminiscent of a cannon, to adjust light, air and sound levels above the steeply raked seating. Each of the school's 'houses' (rather than years) has the use of the auditorium once a week, enabling pupils of different age groups to mix. The treatment of space in the courtyard is fluidly functional to allow for varied activities by the school's population of 1,500 pupils. A library with red walls and carpets fits behind the pod, whose seats have steep raking, between an open dining area (the old school offered a mere 'cattle grid area for standing only'), a garden and an assembly area with bleacher seating for assemblies.

The deft merging of programmes encompassing space age associations rendered what was previously a site full of tension now 'cool enough to chill in'. By blending social with more formal space, dRMM have evolved a new kind of educational facility. High level walkways diagonally connecting east and west stairways and a new 'totem pole-like' lift tower and gallery staircase linking the first and ground floors, 'unlock the circulation', as de Rijke puts it, and create a range of overt connections similar to cloisters around a quadrangle. All the various elements create a social space for the children that 'attacks the orthodoxy of the existing building, unlocking it'. Planned work for the future – a music block and gym, as well as furniture – will ensure that further developments reflect the same new ethos. New pavilion buildings will provide dedicated sport, performing arts and music facilities. 'We've pushed the brief and the budget as far as it will go, and we're not just focusing on buildings but on activities,' explains de Rijke.

Whether it was making sure that every child had his or her own locker, the redesign of the staffroom, remodelling the corridor system, a new network for smart card access, improving sports, library and IT facilities, or making the 'trouble magnet' dining hall more intimate, each aspect of the design was rigorously checked against the clients' and architects' criteria. They undertook a long period of consultation, working closely with the local education authority, the headmaster and the school board, but also with the pupils, who were invited to express views about their desires and dislikes, and not just visually but in terms of space, acoustics and comfort. Together, dRMM and the children co-designed a TV station to broadcast their views on the design. School Works' input resulted in a better understanding of the relationship between the hard and soft elements as seen, for example, in the redesigned timetables.

'The frame offers itself as a picture frame in the town square when the façade is closed, so when it is opened and parked in the frame, it becomes like a screen.'

> <u>Moshi Moshi</u>, Japanese restaurant, Brighton, 2001; (top) exterior; (bottom left) interior;
<u>Off the Shelf</u>, 2001; (bottom right) exhibition of dRMM's work at the Architectural Association

'Life's too short for rhetorical architecture,' says de Rijke. There is a big difference between a cosmetic makeover of a building and the far-reaching programme of changes that dRMM made at Kingsdale, which have had a positive effect both on morale and academic results. By radically re-evaluating the relationship of programme to form and 'being inventive within constraints', the architects have given the school a renewed sense of spatial fluidity, pragmatic provocation and meaning. Influenced by the progress of the Kingsdale scheme, the DfES, already moving ahead with its £2.2 billion Schools for the Future scheme to rebuild or refurbish every secondary school in the country by 2020, commissioned dRMM as one of a number of practices to produce a design for public sector schools. Based on their work at Kingsdale, dRMM have devised a flexible kit of parts for schools to create 'individualized learning environments'. These architects should know what they are doing: Kingsdale serves as a prototype for the future that works from the inside out.

1. 'Off the Shelf', de Rijke Marsh Morgan practice and Unit projects, Architectural Association exhibition catalogue, AA Publications, London, 2001.

> ARB (Architects' Registration Board), central London, 2000; (left) reception; (right) polycarbonate walled boardroom

Deborah Saun
David Hills
Architects

> <u>John Perry Nursery</u>, Dagenham, London, 2002-3; exterior of building with canopy fronted by a landscaped activity zone

(D.SDHA)

> <u>John Perry Nursery</u>, Dagenham, London, 2002-3; (left) soft play area with low-level bench; (right) play area with polycarbonate wall

'We want to make architecture work harder and operate on many levels simultaneously.'

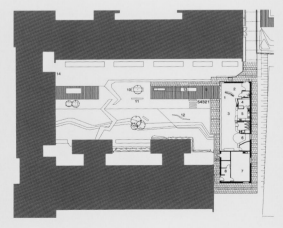

> <u>John Perry Nursery</u>, Dagenham, London, 2002-3 (top) landscape wall the length of the play area; (bottom) ground floor site plan

When asked what really motivates them, Deborah Saunt and David Hills, co-founders of DSDHA, have said that it is 'to span between scales and negotiate between diverse and often contradictory interests in order to find new solutions'. Their progression has not gone unnoticed. In 2004, the architects won two RIBA Awards for Architecture and were shortlisted for the Prime Minister's Better Public Buildings Award. They have also become increasingly known for applying their multidisciplinary design skills widely within the UK to urban framework plans and public consultations.

Their declared driving force was put to the test at an early stage with their infamous <u>Divorced House</u> (2000), designed for a couple in the aftermath of a break-up who wanted to maintain physical proximity in their home, which DSDHA divided into two to fulfil both conditions. They have also designed a multi-faith chapel for a London hospice, 'zones' for teenage children within family homes and adapted a house to accommodate two sets of children from different relationships whose parents now live together. Alongside a desire to invent new housing typologies for sustainable design and a holistic approach, innovative yet sensitive solutions are vital to the pair, 'because new social structures demand new architecture'. Responding directly to hybrid public/private conditions, DSDHA's ambition is 'to make architecture work harder, and operate on many levels simultaneously', says Saunt, and to 'reinstate a sense of civitas', Hills emphasizes.

Established in 1998, DSDHA have kept up a continuous thread of research through their teaching at the University of Cambridge and the Architectural Association, London, where their focus has been on facing the ironies arising from the merger between contemporary public and private space. To achieve this they maintain that it is necessary to 'unstitch the age-old relationship between the city, suburb and countryside in order to reveal the more fluid realities between our collective assumptions'. For the last few years, DSDHA's workload has been dominated by education, with a series of benchmark school projects; but their extensive research work has also given the architects the background to diversify into masterplanning, housing and public buildings, providing them with ample opportunities to test out their cultural rationale.

Their skills in educational projects have been articulated at a public level through design competitions for initiatives for pre-school child care facilities, supported by central government's new lines of funding, allocated in the last couple of years. Both the DfES (Department for

> <u>Stockwell Primary School</u>, south London, 2000-3; curved wall reception, part of new entrance lobby

> <u>Hoyle Early Years Centre</u>, Bury, Lancashire, 2001-3; exterior with illuminated canopy for play and other outdoor activities

Education and Skills) and DWP (Department of Work and Pensions), under the heading of Sure Start, have contributed financially to new DfES and CABE (Commission for Architecture and the Built Environment) initiatives for nurseries.

DSDHA's design for Hoyle Early Years Centre in Bury, Lancashire (2001–3), is an exemplar of its type. It began as a CABE/DfES competition for Neighbourhood Nurseries, focusing on the most socially disadvantaged areas of the country. DSDHA approached their proposal from an urban perspective, and won a commission to refurbish and expand the nursery (for seventy-five children) and propose ways to integrate the requirements of special needs children, without providing a rigid environment. The brief also asked for the relationship and layout between the different functions of the school, including space for parents and children, to be rationalized, and for a new play area. The architects virtually rebuilt the original buildings and made a light and airy environment, 453 square metres in size, with the illusion of space and a sense of calm. The roof was raised to insert a clerestory level, and windows with views outside were positioned at heights appropriate to the users. A new street elevation reinforces the nursery's key role in the local community. A central courtyard garden is accessed by sliding doors that link the main nursery, library, reception area and cloakroom. The

> (top) linear courtyard covered play area; (bottom) room for babies up to two years, with child-height window

nursery rooms, with their cork floors, are flexibly laid out and decorated neutrally to allow the children to provide the colour. The huge (8.5 x 7.5 metres) canopy for sheltered outdoor play is made of translucent cellular polycarbonate.

The site is on a slope, so the building has to work off a ramp. The existing building created a barrier between a residential community and the local park it faced, and part of the brief for the design was to resolve the relationship between the nursery and its context, including preventing it from being a target for vandals. Metal screens and a plinth of dry-stone walling now play a protective role; and, from the inside, the continuous clerestory helps to blur the boundaries and achieve a sense of it as 'a pavilion in a park', taking in constant views of the surrounding landscape. DSDHA have thought carefully about the structure and ambience of the school and the various functions it caters for, reinforcing the sense of a welcoming urban identity rather than making the space an extension of the home.

The scheme's CABE recommendation put DSDHA in a strong position and the practice went on to win a competition led by Barking and Dagenham Borough Council, for John Perry, a nursery school in Dagenham (2002–3). Sited within the government-designated urban regeneration zone of Thames Gateway, phase one has now been completed and provides a new single-storey, twenty-six-place nursery, with phase two, for a fifty-place care facility, on site from 2004. Like Bury, the nursery is situated in a deprived area largely devoid of new architecture, although this lack is being challenged by Irish architect Tom de Paor's landscaping along the A13 and the promise of extensive new regeneration projects along the Thames by West 8 and Maccreanor Lavington. It is in this ambitious climate that DSDHA's design offers a range of contrasting environments: the front wall of the nursery is a skin of polycarbonate punctuated by windows of varying heights. Responding to a need for the children to spend more time outside, an integrated landscaping and outdoor teaching/activity zone complements the indoor classroom spaces which exploit scale and the notion of levels. The dynamic presence of the steel and polycarbonate canopy, cantilevering eight metres over the activity zone, is a vital gesture, blurring the boundary between the courtyard and the nursery, and making the overall space appear much larger.

The combination of different materials and forms, delicate and heavy, in the building reflects the layered nature of the design. Inside, the long, flexed walls of the nursery are designed like a 'landscape', fitted with shelves, and containing toilets, an office, kitchen and a storeroom. 'Children are a very sophisticated audience,' says Saunt, 'a hybrid response

1. reception hall
2. 3-5 years' room
3. library
4. parents' room
5. 2-3 years' room
6. baby room
7. reception
8. head teacher's office
9. staff room
10. covered play area

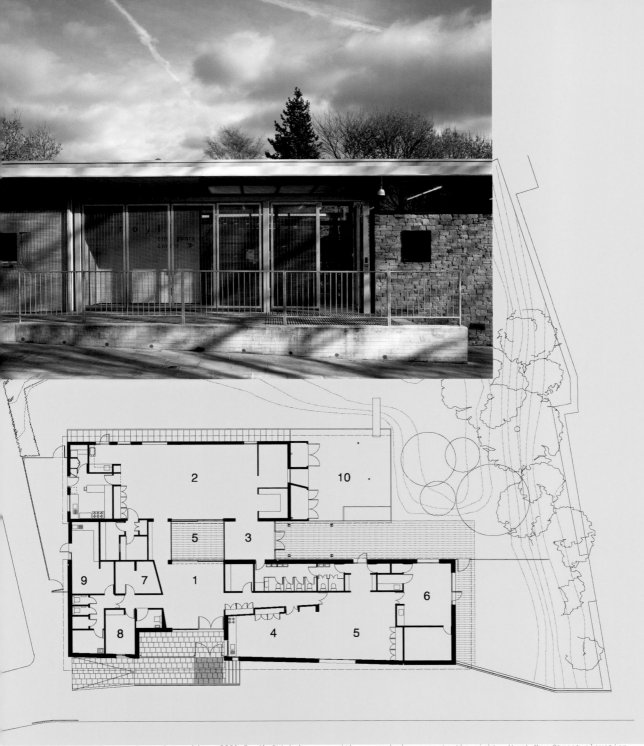

> <u>Hoyle Early Years Centre</u>, Bury, Lancashire, 2001-3; (left) baby room with covered play area to the right; (top) Key Street elevation with galvanized steel security mesh; (bottom) ground floor plan

is very important,' she adds, referring to their first built civic space.
In 2003, DSDHA won the social housing association the Peabody Trust's
Silvertown competition for a block of artists' studios and housing in
London's Docklands, the first mixed-use scheme of its kind. Another
equally novel scheme has been shortlisted by the developer Urban
Catalyst for a project to reconfigure and give status to social housing.
Nicknamed the <u>Bermondsey Twist</u>, DSDHA's design proposal for a tiny
island site is a building with twenty apartments, each with very
generously sized windows and one floor of retail. The design proposal is
for a simple, solid pavilion clad in burnished metal, a rotated form
twisting away from lower, existing housing in order to give the building
maximum site volume over six floors. This means that the size of each
flat changes floor by floor, but that each one maintains a corner view
with a double aspect; some look over Tower Bridge. The apartments sit
above a raised ground floor for retail or restaurant use, embedding the
scheme in the extended public territory of Bermondsey Market. If their
emphasis on public sector work has led DSDHA to run the risk of being
regarded as a safe pair of hands, then projects like this certainly broaden
their identity. 'It's good to stand back and read your own language,'
admits Saunt. With the Twist, 'it is something very legible and unstable
at the same time,' provoking new ideas of social housing that are
pragmatic about costs but also innovative in terms of spatial quality and
landmark status.

One of DSDHA's prevailing concerns has been to consider how suburbia
and the city centre and the American mall and the high street might be
reconciled, as well as to mediate encounters between landscape and
urban environments. But this has not meant a retreat into overly abstract
propositions: 'we do not claim to be poets. We want the city to have a
dynamic future,' Hills says. The partners have a preference for the mixed
nature of cultural influences in architecture; they deeply admire Dutch
architecture. 'We are engaged in an international culture,' says Hills, 'but
at the same time it's absolutely vital for us to understand the realities of
local contextual issues.' Saunt's Australian background may account for
her belief in the power of cities as communities with the confidence to
reinvent themselves. Their winning scheme for the CABE/IPPR (Institute
for Public Policy Research) Designs on Democracy competition (2003) to
reinvent the <u>town hall</u> at Letchworth Garden City, Hertfordshire, is a
strikingly modern design for a building and public square which, with its
panoramic roof terraces and hydroponic vertical garden, pays homage to
garden city ideals. Proposals for a mix of activities appealed to the
judges, as well as the fact that as a new urban space it nonetheless
fuses into the life of the town, creating multiple routes through the site

> <u>Housing and artists' studios</u>, Silvertown, east London, 2003; (top left) street elevation of mixed-use apartment building with
approaches; <u>The Bermondsey Twist</u>, south London, 2004; (bottom) three elevations and night perspective of five-floor housing blc

and to surrounding streets and maintaining vistas through them. Significantly, the design 'interprets interior and exterior as a united landscape', as Hills puts it. One way it does this is by exploring the different levels feasible for public space: a cut into the ground reveals new formal civic meeting rooms beneath the existing town hall. When it comes to describing the way in which the architecture of their town hall manifests itself not just in a civic context but as a civic context in its own right, they, like David Adjaye, call it 'corrupting the box'.

Saunt feels that the UK is in the middle of a real cultural generational shift in architecture: 'An architect like Tony Fretton (who designed the Lisson Gallery in London) has dealt with interior relationships and how they are perceived from outside as well as a dialogue about duality. We don't perceive thresholds between interior and exterior as a dichotomy.' 'Our understanding of landscape is that it extends the opportunity of creating places of social interaction,' adds Hill.

DSDHA's winning design (2004) for <u>Tittle Cott Bridge</u> and underpass, a gateway to the town of Castleford in Yorkshire, bears this out. One of six urban landscape schemes selected for The Castleford Project to help catalyze regeneration, each was developed with the close involvement of the local authority and community. All are bespoke projects with a distinctive narrative of place, weaving the various areas of the town together. The bridge is a gateway that strengthens the connection between new housing and the town centre. Instead of a single arch, it is a design that tackles that neglected sphere of public space, the underpass, reinventing it as an attractive and intimate rather than claustrophobic place, with sheltered seating and a polished mirror wall providing oblique views to reassure users. The bridge is to be made of stacked cedar, a reference to Roman timber towns. Its sedimentary layers of glass, bronze, ceramic and jet fragments will be inscribed with local stories – 'a micro-museum built for and by the community', say the architects. The project bears out DSDHA's commitment to making landscape and intimacy integral components of hybrid urban architecture, spaces with a new relevance that goes beyond simply labelling them public or private.

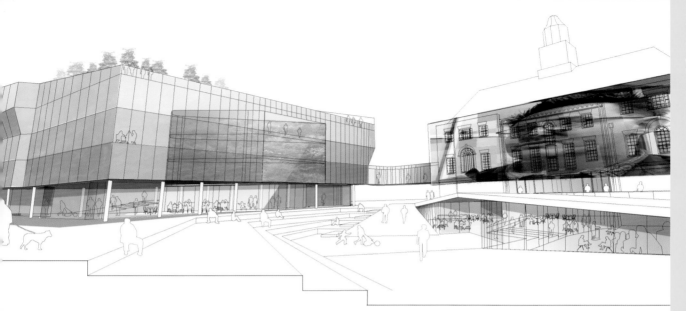

> <u>Town hall and public square</u>, Letchworth Garden City, 2003; (top) perspective view of the new square, civic information hub and council chamber

FAT

> <u>Hoogvliet Heerlijkheid</u>, Rotterdam, the Netherlands, 2002-; illustration of a park-based complex with reception halls, sports facilities, boating lake, workspaces and exhibition space

> <u>Garner Street</u>, Hackney, east London, 1998-2002; street façade of new-build house and office

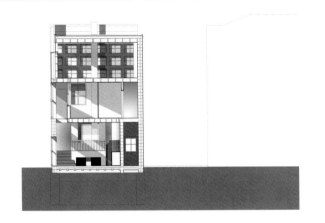

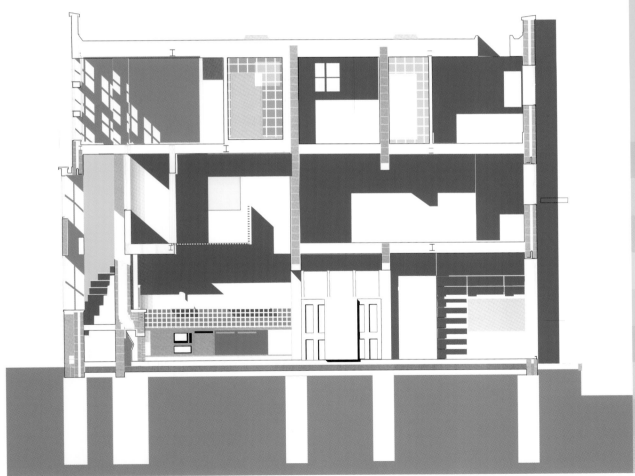

> (top) cross-section through front staircase, kitchen and bedroom; (bottom) longitudinal section

> <u>Garner Street</u>, Hackney, east London, 1998-2002; new-build house and office; (top, left to right) double-height foyer, bedroom, bedroom windows; (bottom left) front and side elevation of house; (bottom right) detail of front wall

'Death to Manifestos…Viva How-tos! How to become a famous architect…a guide which will help you navigate the strange world of design. It will help you achieve what you deserve only if you believe in yourself. Don't fake it.'

One of the most telling essays on the FAT Channel, the group of architects' website, features the motto 'let FAT make the world a better place' and is subsidized by advertising – a Weight Watchers window jumps out at you. It is as if to say, by all means get heavy architecturally, but not too heavy, and then gives tongue-in-cheek, step-by-step advice on achieving architectural fame. Their suggestions for those who would be famous require the plundering of old remaindered architectural and design books and catalogues for 'the least fashionable and so most shocking of all styles' which can be used for imagery by means of Photoshop software. This activity must be fronted by a 'punchy, arty' name, dispensing with the words 'urban' or 'studio', and, above all, a considerable amount of robust mystique. 'Remember, you won't have to design a building for at least ten years. And in this time you will live off your mystique, so make it good. Mystique is what you say, and the way that you say it… Mystique should also suggest revolutionary politics and French philosophy.' Any written statements issued should 'make outlandish claims; tell them everything they know is wrong'. Fame seekers should also 'be prepared to have a radical opinion on anything that may crop up in conversation'.

Since 1991, when FAT – an acronym for Fashion Architecture Taste – first came together as a collective of artists and architects, ostensibly to make an Archigram-style magazine, it has changed its line-up a few times. FAT is now led by a trio of architects: Sean Griffiths and Sam Jacob, both regular media correspondents as well as practitioners, and Charles Holland; Griffiths was a founder member, with Jacob and Holland joining in 1994 and 1996 respectively. Despite the changes in personnel, FAT's mission statement to promote a wider 'array of taste cultures' or accepted aesthetic preferences, has remained the same. FAT's aim has been to banish the self-referential abstractions of modernism and to counter their failure to engage in a culture outside architecture. Not everyone likes FAT's taste cultures, even when they get the point of their arguments and enjoy their knowing and well-observed humour. However, in the last few years the practice has surprised its critics and proved to be not a suspected 'wild card' in the UK's architectural scene but a highly professional outfit now building social housing, a school and other public building schemes in the UK and the Netherlands, all in line with their idiom, of course. 'We all trained as architects but architecture accounts for only thirty to forty per cent of what we do,' Sean Griffiths told me in 2001. Now that percentage must be more like ninety per cent.

Cross-fertilizing architecture with art and other disciplines has enabled FAT provocatively to reclaim the representational power of architecture and its public impact. Well versed in architectural history, and articulate in writing and speaking polemically and humorously about it in relation to their ethos, FAT is an alternative voice that the UK's architectural culture would be all the poorer without.

The flow of models, two-dimensional façades, miniatures and site-specific artworks from FAT constitutes a consistent body of work which has challenged the perception of architecture as abstract. Their onslaught on the closed nature of its language aimed to raise the lowly status of surface decoration as mere pastiche. For a while it looked as though they were following their own tongue-in-cheek advice on how to achieve architectural stardom rather too closely, for while FAT are propelled by the 'idea of architecture as a media in itself and that it has a culture', as Sam Jacob puts it, he freely admits that their earliest projects were cut-and-paste programmes. For example, a design for The Brunel Rooms, a nightclub in Swindon (1995–96), merged a running track, swimming pool and suburban allotment. In 1998 they described their conversion of the Scala cinema in London's King's Cross (1998) as 'aircraft hangar meets hunting lodge'.

Some of the projects allowed for more of a test-bed than others. While Neon House,[1] a neon sign of a house with a pitched roof, is about reconciling the sign with the content, the interior of the Dutch advertising agency Kessels Kramer in Amsterdam (1998) is a cornucopia of disparate objects and architectural elements drawing on suburban and football imagery. The triple-height space features a garden shed, picnic tables, a lifeguard's tower, some of them models, others life-size, but chopped up and represented at a distorted scale. 'It's not a complete representation like Disneyland as there's not enough of it, but the collages allow architecture to function as a piece of communication,' explains Sean Griffiths.

Meanwhile, a different, more civic aspect of FAT's work was developing in London's streets and parks. Rather than being academic Situationist exercises in urban exploration, these were well-judged collaborations with other artists, designers and, above all, with the public. In 1993 Adsite exploited the display cases of 200 bus shelters, creating a dispersed gallery across London. For Picnic, another project, artists, architects, photographers and designers gathered with their work in a London park, making an 'art territory' in response to the Criminal Justice

'We are greatly interested in studying the modern world's mannerisms, attitudes, contradictions and prospects… Most importantly, we work in the culture bunker, rather than the ivory tower.'

> <u>Brunel Rooms nightclub and bar</u>, Swindon, 1995-96 (top left and bottom); <u>Scala</u>, King's Cross, London, 1998-99; (top right) conversion of cinema into a nightclub, live venue and bar

> <u>Kessels Kramer</u>, advertising agency offices, Amsterdam, the Netherlands, 1998; (left) view from turret; (centre top) TV altar; (centre bottom) view at ground level

Act of 1994, which defined a group of more than twenty people in public as a 'trespassory assembly'.

For <u>Home Ideals</u> (1997), FAT gravitated towards the issue of public desire for ways to enhance their homes and local community, inviting the residents of an Islington street to make a collaborative work with an artist to be illustrated on one side of a For Sale placard outside their house; the reverse featured the artist's work. The cultural identity of place came under scrutiny at <u>Holly Street</u>, a social housing estate in Hackney, east London, with a project called Utopia Revisited (1998). The residents, soon to be rehoused elsewhere as the estate was due for demolition, were invited to commemorate personal events with FAT. They also created personal visions of housing, challenging the original utopian ideas embodied in what had become a discredited housing type in the UK. The results sparked <u>Camo House</u> (1998), a series of speculations on the coding of space, which reworks a very ordinary house with a pitched roof with an 'alien' camouflage pattern to illustrate the potential of surface decoration as opposed to truth to materials or construction. FAT's slogan at the time, 'taste not space', argued that 'taste is the point where architecture engages with issues of class, value and hence is the moment that architecture becomes politicized'.

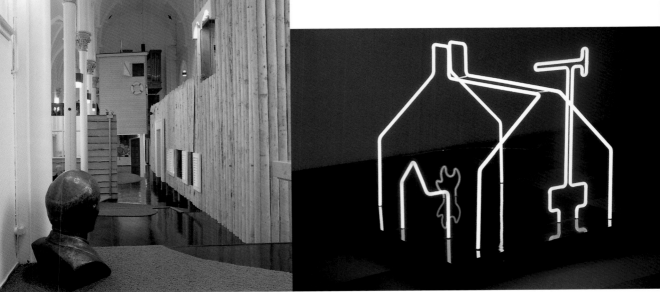

> <u>Neon House</u>, installation in 'Kill the Modernist Within' exhibition, CUBE Gallery, Manchester, 1999-2000 (bottom right)

> <u>Taste not Space</u>, installation in 'Kill the Modernist Within' exhibition, CUBE Gallery, Manchester, 1999-2000 (top);
<u>Home Ideals</u>, installation for Islington International Arts Festival, 1997 (bottom left)

FAT maintain that taste is the radical issue rather than 'the spatial gymnastics favoured by the mainstream architectural avant garde', and more engaging to a wider culture.

Keen to express his personal taste in built form, Griffiths went on to design and build his own house in Garner Street in Hackney, east London (2002), making a cultural statement that architecture – like music, fashion, graphics and interior design – can reformat itself. The house sets up a play between two- and three-dimensional architecture. Its light blue weatherboarding façade (actually a cement-based, man-made material to comply with fire regulations) carries a number of representational layers at various scales, ranging from a 'toy' house, to a miniature skyscraper, to a Dutch gable. At the same time it loosely refers to the general urban condition evoked by the American TV series *South Park*, more generically to suburbia, and also to Pop Art in its flattened, cartoon-like language. The main bedroom is set up as a miniature house-in-house, visible through a large grid of 18 cut-out windows. References are absorbed in the details: the American fridge alcove is styled as a kind of organ; there is heart-shaped balustrading on the staircases. The different programmes combined in the house – office, family house, separate flat – wrap around and distort each other. At every turn the visitor finds himself smiling at the companionable moulding of vernacular and art-based architectural references into one another.

'We are interested in making work that explores the experiences, contradictions and possibilities of the modern world, finding tactics and solutions that are simultaneously conceptually interesting and aesthetically engaging,' FAT have said about the broader identity they have sought for architecture. If David Adjaye sets great store by enigmatic 'fiction-making', drawing on art-driven desires projected in space, FAT's narratives spatialize the unreal yet compelling aspects of larger-than-life popular culture.

It was not surprising that FAT began receiving commissions from the Netherlands, a country that is having its own debates about taste cultures and styles of living. Brought in by Crimson, the group of Dutch architectural historians and urban consultants, in 2002, to contribute to 'WIMBY! Welcome to my backyard', a project aimed at the transformation of Hoogvliet, a post-war satellite town near Rotterdam, FAT found collaborators with a common love of the popular and the vernacular, sharing their idea that, as Griffiths puts it, 'architecture is not about function but about communication'. 'Trying to generate a civic architecture out of things not usually considered part of it', as Jacob has described it, they proposed a hall, landscape and collection of ancillary structures, 'a place for the local Antillian community to party and

> <u>Camo House</u>, a camouflaged concept house, 1997 (bottom centre left and right);
<u>Adsite</u>, one of the two hundred bus shelter art works installed across London, 1993 (bottom right)

barbecue, for pensioners to play bingo, local kids to play speed metal, a cross-programmed hobby ghetto – on a tight budget'. Surface water drainage is destined to become a boating lake surrounding a pet cemetery island, in a landscape referring to 'both the idyllic community of the village green and the tough planning pragmatism of the Wild West town grid'.

In 2002, the client behind Kessels Kramer involved FAT in a second Dutch commission, St Lucas, an applied arts school in Boxtel near Eindhoven. 'Rethinking the school has been a masterplanning exercise,' says Griffiths. 'Its agglomeration of buildings dates back to the 1950s and was originally a convent. It is very utilitarian, bits clash, and the circulation spaces are left over and need to be more logical.' FAT's initial presentation to the Dutch planning committee provoked a degree of wariness as their approach seemed to evoke the idea of a film set. 'It develops as landscape elements,' says Griffiths. 'I wouldn't call it a film set,' he adds, explaining that it invokes Louis Kahn's idea that one should build around ruins, although FAT, in a Pop-Gothic inversion, are building 'ruins around buildings', producing a series of screens and surface treatments with horizontal and vertical elements in brightly coloured terrazzo. 'We've invented a fake history,' says Griffiths. Ugly-beautiful becomes a flexible notion when subjected to FAT's reformulation of architectural identity, which they say is about legibility, clarity and directness as well as combining disparate aesthetic tactics.

FAT's additive collage urbanism – playing games with scale and exploring different ways of treating façades – is now developing in two directions. One is the witty or tongue-in-cheek signature statement, such as the bicycle surveillance unit at Scheveningen in The Hague (2003), a monument with a tiny house on top. The other involves bigger, more process-driven projects that are shaped by the reality of ongoing client liaison and public consultation.

Two housing commissions promise to propel FAT into a position of wider recognition. In 2004 they won a competition to refurbish Tanner Point, a 1960s tower block on the Brookes Estate in Newham. Their heads full of documentary footage of Nigel Henderson staking out Bethnal Green for the Mass Observation group in the 1940s, they pledged to bring diversity to high-rise living. Their brief was to make sure that entire floors could be rearranged, while leaving the structural frame untouched. Breaking with the idea of cell-like accommodation, they introduced communal play areas and courtyards, even a mini-enterprise zone in the form of a small office. Naturally the façade is transformed, loosely taking on the appearance – although not this time in Photoshop mode – of a romantic Bavarian castle. Jacob explains that the idea is not to create architectural

> St Lucas, masterplan of art school campus, extension and refurbishment of buildings, Boxtel, the Netherlands, 2002-; (left) entrance view; (top right) sketch of entrance; (centre bottom) courtyard

fantasy but to 'make somewhere with a more direct connection with place that is open to direct interpretation'. The designs for the balconies reflect the choices of the inhabitants. Jacob insists FAT's instincts are closer to the Arts and Crafts movement than to the fake cities of Jon Jerde, and consequently their design does not try to determine a falsely integrated social group. 'In terms of how people could occupy the project, we are encouraging small ghettos in a tower block rather than equalizing everything.'

In early May 2003 the developer Urban Splash announced that it had appointed FAT to create a development of twenty units of social housing as part of the masterplan designed by Will Alsop for New Islington, an area of Manchester. The panel of judges was made up of future residents being rehoused by the scheme as well as representatives of Urban Splash and the national regeneration agency English Partnerships (created in 1999). Urban Splash's development director Nick Johnson said that FAT had been selected for its 'common sense and straightforward approach' to the challenge of dealing with the 'clear conflict between the traditional architecture the people on the site want and the world-class architecture we want to deliver'. As Jacob puts it, 'the residents liked our design'. Taking inspiration from residents' existing houses, 'we treated each one almost as an individual client', says Griffiths. The L-shaped houses, laid out in pairs, respond to the requirement for a well-planned use of space, private gardens and balconies, and represent, Griffiths feels, 'much more bespoke a design

> bicycle surveillance unit, Scheveningen, the Hague, 2003; (bottom right) a monument with a miniature house on top

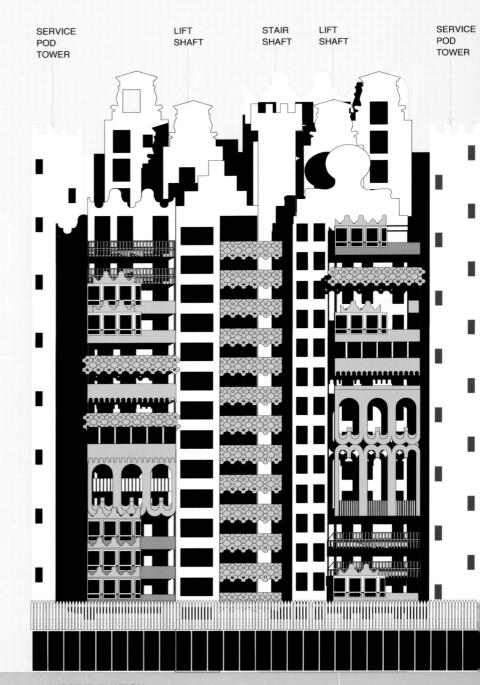

SERVICE
POD
TOWER

LIFT
SHAFT

STAIR
SHAFT

LIFT
SHAFT

SERVICE
POD
TOWER

WEST ELEVATION

> Tanner Point on the <u>Brookes Estate</u>, refurbishment and extension of a tower block, Newham, east London, 2004-; (left and centre right)
west elevation, axonometric; <u>Hoogvliet Heerlijkheid</u>, the study of a garden, Rotterdam, the Netherlands, 2002- (top right)

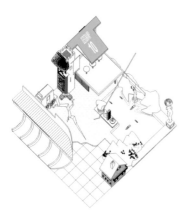

than would be associated with social housing'. The abstracted house shapes of the façades are designed to stand out against Alsop's taller housing blocks behind. They are not unlike Griffiths' Garner Street house, only with a slightly more baroque character, and clad in brick slips. A pinboard construction allows residents to add their own components, such as birdboxes and hanging baskets, so that the houses are the antithesis of a repetitive solution, even though their appearance suggests an anti-architectural identity. 'Most architects see a house as an object composed in a certain formal way,' says Griffiths. 'I see housing as a process that unfolds over time while retaining its individuality.'

'Bespoke' design with a narrative about taste is what FAT is all about. When designing a system of road markings for Bristol (2004) in conjunction with graphic designers GTF, they – like William Morris, whom Jacob cites as an influence – layered pattern over purely abstract elements. On top of block colour, lines and half tones this created graphic densities, and at the same time indicated distinctions like park and pavements, public and private space. Like muf (p. 194), FAT is acutely aware of values and connections that are excluded in contemporary public cultural life. By tapping into what Griffiths calls 'the chemistry of cities, they are finding ways of triggering, allowing things to emerge'.

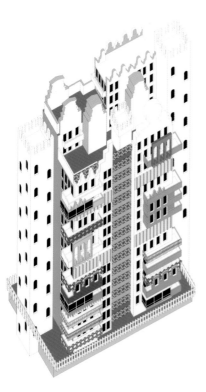

1. Installation in 'Kill the Modernist Within' exhibition, CUBE Gallery, Manchester, 1999–2000.

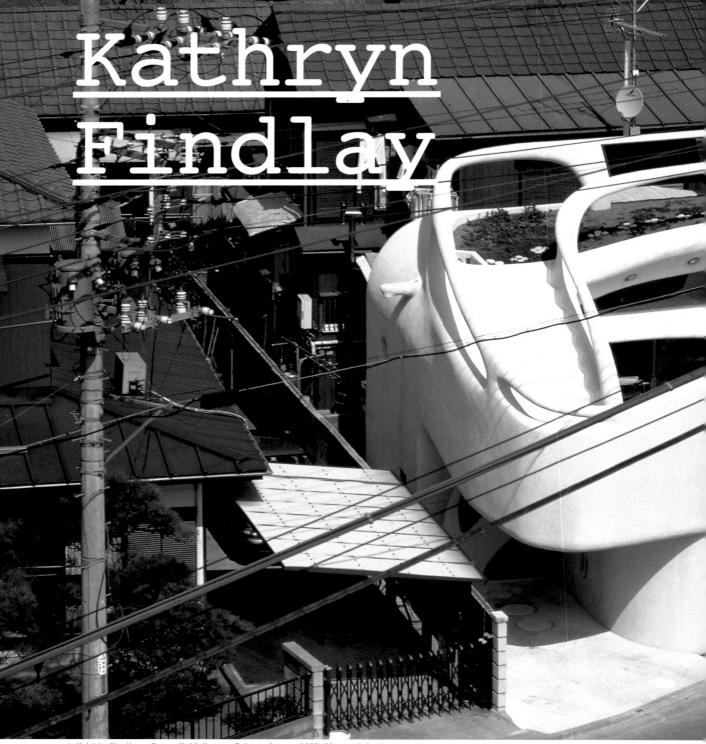

Kathryn Findlay

> Ushida Findlay: <u>Truss Wall House</u>, Tokyo, Japan, 1992-93; aerial view

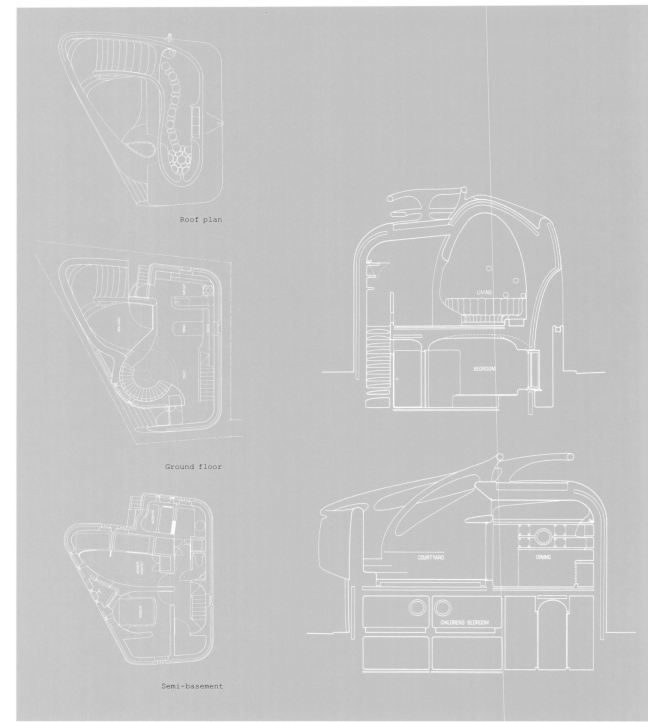

Roof plan

Ground floor

Semi-basement

LIVING

BEDROOM

COURTYARD

DINING

CHILDRENS BEDROOM

> Ushida Findlay: <u>Truss Wall House</u>, Tokyo, Japan, 1992-93; (left, from top to bottom) plans of roof, ground and semi-basement floors; (centre, top and bottom) sections; (right) dining area

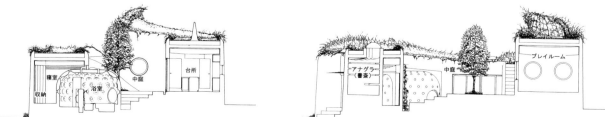

> Ushida Findlay: <u>Soft and Hairy House</u>, Baraki, Japan, 1992-94; (left) the house, hidden under the landscape, has an open internal courtyard with a blue pod-shaped bathroom wedged in the corner; (right) interior of the bathroom with circular window; (bottom) sections

Kathryn Findlay is an architect known for her ability to create organically shaped environments that are intimate, playful and poetic; and a little rarefied. The agenda behind them, as Findlay, who is Scottish, explains, has to do with 'making spaces and finding out what architecture can be', starting on the inside and working with the lie of the land or the path of the sun, rather than creating a structure or shell and filling it in. Each design, therefore, is closely attuned to nature.

Findlay first set up in practice with her former Japanese partner Eisaku Ushida as Ushida Findlay in Tokyo in 1987, after both worked for Arata Isozaki for some years. Ushida Findlay was a prolific firm, realizing a number of highly regarded buildings in Japan, including the Truss Wall House in Tokyo (1992–93), the Soft and Hairy House in Baraki (1992–94), and the Polyphony House in Osaka (1995–97). In 1997 Findlay moved back to London and set up Ushida Findlay in the city with the aim of launching herself in the UK. The practice, which has since been retitled Kathryn Findlay (in 2004), became known early on for its successful – not surprisingly more conventionally shaped – design at the <u>Homes for the Future</u> development at Glasgow Green, the flagship scheme of Glasgow's Year of Architecture and Design in 1999.

Her ten years in Japan deeply informed Findlay's approach to design. A Japanese reading of form and materials and their relationship to nature permeates her work. 'Japanese culture designs with all the senses in mind: people get inspiration from sound, scent, and texture, and combine it uniquely.' Her interest in landscape inspires her to design in layers; and instead of hard-edged elements, she makes the boundaries of her buildings ambiguous and permeable.

The design of <u>Truss Wall House</u> (1992–93) expresses a sense of flow linking exterior and interior. In common with the practice's other buildings, it is a permeable structure, porous even. It began as an ambition to reinvent the rationale behind the construction of a concrete compound curve. On a small urban plot, and influenced by the local landscape which forms a protective enclosure, it has a double skin wall that moderates heat, ventilation and noise pollution. Light comes in from a glazed courtyard, through a top light shaped like a tear-drop, and in the bedroom via glass blocks. Taking advantage of the fact that in Japanese construction the architect is able to go on site and make things, the team made cobbles out of balloons filled with mortar. Expressive buildings can be lumpen and heavy, but here the lines are clean as well as innovative.

By contrast, the roughly rendered walls of <u>Soft and Hairy House</u> (1992–94) look as if they have been pulled directly from the ground. The parapet is hidden under a shaggy fringe of topsoil. 'Architecture as

programme is limiting; that is why with the Soft and Hairy House we wanted to retain a sense of the permaculture. Architecture is fixed, high performance, but I am interested in what is a material, and what is a boundary for something else,' Findlay explains. The fluidity expressed in the design of the Soft and Hairy House emphasizes this priority. Although largely hidden from exterior view, it, like the Truss Wall House, has a continuity in landscape from interior to exterior: 'its form is defined by the constant interplay of the two elements', says Findlay. Appearing more like a landscape with walls made out of cloth, it questions materiality. The bathroom is an upside down landscape, penetrated by glass blocks, some of which contain convex mirrors through which light permeates. Like a blue egg-shaped blob, it has a glazing line going over it, dividing it in half. The visitor is showered with light.

Like the assemblages of the Surrealists, Findlay is interested in juxtaposing normal, everyday things – glass blocks, grass, curtains – creating what she calls a 'slippage' in understanding in order to give 'new meaning, refreshing people's view of where they are in the world'. She is greatly concerned with the smaller scale, micro-issues of place, as well as with how space is housed within a landscape or terrain, but above all with the creation of a relationship between everything.

> Kathryn Findlay Laboratory at University of Tokyo, Architecture Department, with Tomoko Taguchi and Takakuni Yukawa: <u>Kasahara Amenity Hall</u>, Gifu prefecture, Japan, 1999-2000; (left) foyer; (right) ceramic-tiled skin of the building, with its protective 'arm'

'Everything should go beyond form: it's about the
experience, the relationship between things.
Form frames things, but shape is not a means in
itself. I am interested in making a skin that
allows things to change.'

> Ushida Findlay: <u>Pool House</u>, England, 2000-1; (top) white Barrisol rubber and timber finned ceiling with glazed top light; (bottom and right) the building's thatch roof overhanging the glass box of the swimming pool

The daughter of a sheep farmer, Findlay became interested in landscape at a very early age. 'I don't see space as delineated by walls, but by routes and paths through landscape. It's easy to see spatial divisions, something that you box in, but harder to institute a route and then excavate. I've always seen architecture as the making of a landscape, trying to concretize or solidify flow. Everything should go beyond form: it's about the experience, the relationship between things. Form frames things, but shape is not a means in itself. I am interested in making a skin that allows things to change.'

When generating new architecture, the use of CAD techniques can mean that a building derives its significance largely from its skin, because a limitless number of alternatives, for instance, continuous surfaces, can be designed well before the structural engineer decides whether they are buildable. Findlay's buildings are not heavily reliant on CAD in this way but she uses it for 'spatial concepts for which the crafting is important. I love the crafting as well as the conceiving of building: the skin of a building can act as an armature. Space and skin have to be interdependent. The skin itself must be encoded with information about the structure and its environment. We always try to be multi-coded.' For Findlay, the skin of her buildings becomes 'a chameleon – it is its structure, its envelope, and its filter to minimize energy use. It is the materiality that comes that is the thing, and how it goes from being abstract material to serving a purpose in the world'.

The Kasahara Amenity Hall (1999–2000) in the Gifu prefecture of Japan demonstrates this very well. It is an amorphous envelope extending to form a protective 'arm' shading the building from the sun, with glazing to provide passive ventilation. The town of Kasahara is largely dedicated to making tiles, and the hall uses small circular ceramic tiles to form the surface of its external skin. It has also become a popular civic meeting point in what was once a relatively conservative town. The clients wanted a building with low maintenance costs that was environmentally friendly. Findlay responded by making the building fully reflect its purpose through its form. The back wall is a diagram of design derived from the sun's path, creating a passive solar system which responds to each season. The sun's rays project onto a thick thermal wall and go under the floor, and then the heat rises up through ducts and keeps the wall warm. In winter, when the sun is low, the design allows the sun to penetrate the building, but in summer, when it is high, the eaves prevent it from coming in, keeping the spaces cool so cool air can be circulated under the floor. 'I'm interested in making architecture a diagram of something that's scientifically there, of tracing the forces of something you can't see, which are always manifest,' Findlay says. She includes some representational elements – the lines on the floor look like air flows, the bars on the windows isobars – but unlike many architects she does not rely on representation to make architecture.

After working on a number of projects in the UK and in the Middle East, Findlay has been able to maintain the 'expressive, overt side of her work, just subverting it a little bit'. The Pool House (2000–1) in England draws on her cultural experiences in Japan, which she applies in an ingenious way. It was a commission for a swimming pool next to a Grade II listed Tudor manor house with Queen Anne and Arts and Crafts additions. Findlay created a simple structure of steel and stone, with glazed walls looking out onto a planted garden. But it is the roof that demonstrates Findlay's skills in connecting elements. She wanted to create something tactile and organic next to the 16th-century stone wall, and had previously researched Japanese thatch while Associate Professor at the University of Tokyo. Thatch, which is so tactile and easy to sculpt, was introduced into the scheme as a roofing material. The Japanese practice of *shibamune* involves fixing the thatch by clumping the soil, weaving it with straw and then planting it, so that the plants become the binding. Keen to take a traditional technique and use it in a new way, Findlay inserted a glazed top light surrounded by planters buried in the thatch which allowed light through and eliminated the possibility of waterlogging. As light streams in from the glazing, it bounces off the roof dips, which are created from a layer of Barrisol – stretched rubber painted white to protect it from moisture penetration. Findlay's marriage of organic design and traditional thatching techniques gives the impression, particularly at night, of something of great

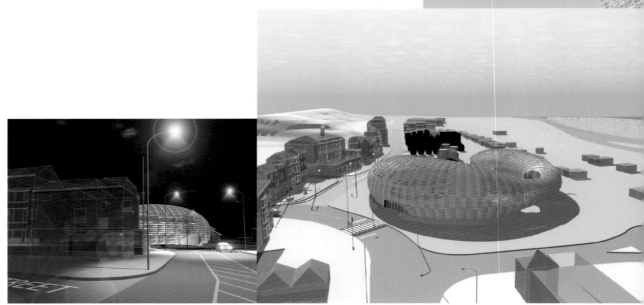

> Ushida Findlay: Hastings Visitor Centre, Kent, 2003; perspectives of the building in the seaside town showing its ribbed construction

> Ushida Findlay: <u>Beach House</u>, Doha, Qatar, 2002; (top) perspective of the building; (bottom left) aerial view of model; (bottom right) visualizations

solidity floating over something curved, light and delicate, of an alluring dematerialization.

The RIBA award-winning design of <u>Grafton New Hall</u> (2001) also explores the fusing of building and landscape. The commission was for a new 2,322 square-metre country house, to the west of the original site of Grafton Hall in Cheshire. Set in over 40 hectares of land, Findlay's scheme breaks with the English country house tradition of dominating the landscape and instead embraces nature. It is compatible with the UK government's PPG7 planning rules which allow new houses in the countryside to be built provided that they are outstanding in terms of architecture and landscape design and enhance the setting.

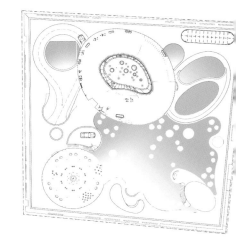

Given the conservative thinking about country house design in the UK, Findlay was very surprised that the developers chose her practice in competition. Their intention was for a speculative design for a notional buyer, allowing Findlay to conceive it freely as a new design model of its type. The proposed building is a low-lying shape with a dome-shaped hub and starfish arms to be constructed in sandstone and explores the notion of a sanctuary integrated with nature. The four long fingers of its design extend into the meadow, creating a series of ridges and furrows that echo the contours of the landscape and allow the building's scale, orientation and mass to be informed by the location. The building is oriented so that the internal pattern of daily activities can loosely follow the path of the sun; each finger houses a different type of living area: sleeping (east), leisure and eating (south), poolside space (west) and guest quarters (north) in a sequence of flowing spaces.

In 2003 the practice was commissioned to design a <u>Visitor Centre</u> for Hastings. The project was cancelled prior to construction due to the client's lack of funds, but it was to have been a viewing platform informing people about locations on all points of the compass. For Findlay, a landmark building must fit in as well as stand out, so she drew on local influences – the shiplap of the boats, the distinctive tall, thin net huts clad with timber slats and marine life. Her scheme was a ribbed or dia-ribbed construction, something that could breathe and also enclose a public place. It was a very site specific design, but not in the sense of replicating other forms; instead it 'embodied lots of things that are already there'.

The singular and bespoke nature of Findlay's designs has in recent years proved highly attractive to a number of prestigious clients in Doha, the capital of Qatar. If Truss Wall House offered a solid, curved structure like something you would eat out of, <u>Villa Doha</u> (2002–5), for a prominent art collector, whose site looks onto the corniche of the bay on Qatar's

> Ushida Findlay: <u>Villa Doha</u>, Doha, Qatar, 2002-5: (top left) site plan; (top right) model; (bottom left) interior perspective; (bottom right) rendering of structure

> Ushida Findlay: <u>Al Koot Costume and Textiles Museum</u>, Doha, Qatar, 2002–; (top left) perspective of lower ground meeting space with perforated roof; (top right) perspective/model of the Museum in a converted fort

coastline, belongs to the same family of building types. Known for being someone with an acute eye, the client wanted a building that was as much a precious object with sculptural qualities as his collection of ancient Egyptian art. It was also to be a private hub from which to view the city's architectural gems, including the National Library and I. M. Pei's Islamic Museum which incorporates the client's offices. Findlay's design sits like a giant pebble on a plinth, with a shallow mirrored pool of water at its heart. A sequence of capacious interlocking spaces, 8,000 square metres in total, including semi-private and private quarters, are grouped around a large void. Plans and sections demonstrate how Findlay made this flowing set of differentiated spaces. The evocative nature of her starfish concept for Grafton Hall impressed another client in Qatar, who commissioned the Beach House (2002). Building and landscape are again engaged in a compelling dialogue; and the house is an energy-efficient domestic environment.

Ambitious plans for public architecture in Qatar include the Al Koot Costume and Textiles Museum in a converted fort in the middle of Doha, for which Findlay was commissioned in 2002. Her design proposes a square plan with an internal courtyard, a 3,000 square-metre footprint, to be built largely underground. The visitor looks up from the lower ground to a perforated roof over the courtyard he or she can walk on, which has a grid for flooring and ceiling patterns relating to Islamic patterns. As at the Truss Wall House, the design takes something solid – in this case rows of vertical threads – and subtracts from it. The threads are perforated steel columns, glowing with light, which support the structure. Clustered in varying densities, they create a geometric laced effect of overlocking geometries. But this building is not about form at all: the theme is filtered and sieved light.

Findlay has one of the most alluring approaches to architecture to emerge from the UK in a long time. The recent bad luck of a series of project cancellations, including the Hastings Visitor Centre, has shown the speculative client environment in the UK to be somewhat dogged by wishful thinking in financial terms. This is a shame because, as with other mostly bespoke examples of exceptional contemporary architecture, Findlay's work revolutionizes the contours of daily life. Commentators point out the rare consistency with which the architect has maintained the original spirit and approach of her student work over nearly twenty-five years. Asked to make wider analogies between her way of designing and other practitioners in the UK cultural scene, she identifies the concept of starting with what you could build and then extracting from it and compares this to the work of celebrated British artist Rachel Whiteread. Findlay takes on and exploits the forces of something you cannot see which are always manifest.

> (bottom) perspective of Grafton New Hall, Cheshire, 2001; a scheme for a new country house

Foreign Office Architects

> <u>Yokohama International Port Terminal</u>, Yokohama, Japan, 1994-2002; sea-side elevation, where the terminal's steel structure of stacked longitudinal girders supporting the roof plaza houses the Osanbashi events hall, traversally glazed without vertical elements

> <u>Yokohama International Port Terminal</u>, Yokohama, Japan, 1994-2002; (left) the roof plaza's Ipe wood surface of fan-shaped slats with V-shaped fencing and projections providing shade; (top right) traffic plaza

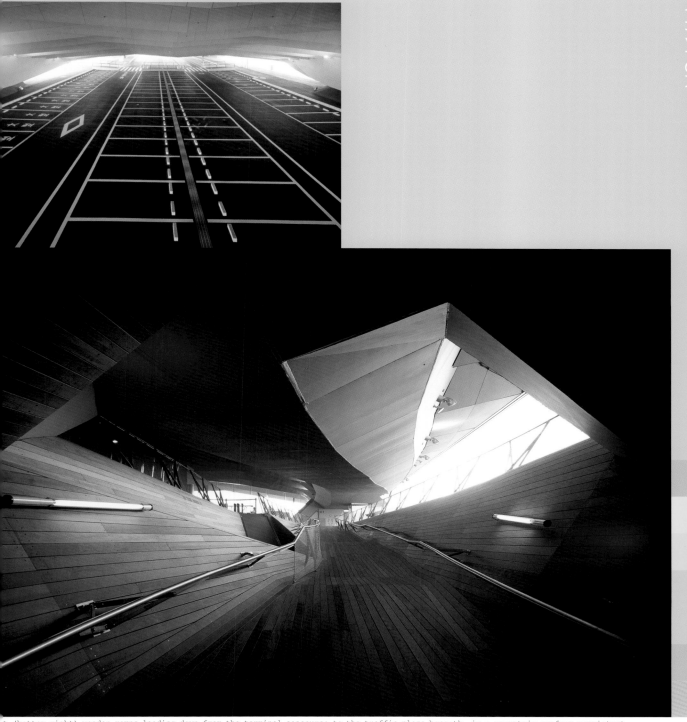

> (bottom right) wooden ramps leading down from the terminal concourse to the traffic plaza beneath, in a geometric surface consistent with that of the roof plaza

'External forces are much greater now, and we've had to engage with these by revising some of our precepts. We are excited about going back to metaphors and analogues. Before we were trying to resist them. That doesn't diminish our interest in techniques and devices. Yokohama has been successful but we are not interested in repeating it. We must be committed to experimentation and differentiation as well as achieving an internal consistency in our work.'[1]

> <u>Yokohama International Port Terminal</u>, Yokohama, Japan, 1994-2002; (left) the folded triangular plane structure of the domestic terminal concourse; (top right) the glass curtain wall extending to the eaves; (bottom right) steel-folded plates of the terminal structure

Foreign Office Architects have established a worldwide brand. With their name predicated on a conceptual approach to foreignness, and a relative freedom from local orders due to their status as outsiders, FOA have, since they were founded twelve years ago, achieved one of the widest global reaches of any UK architectural practices of their generation. They are also known to 'grow' or 'breed' their architecture from a close reading of local conditions, likening the process of realizing a project to the cultivation of wine or vegetables. FOA are interested in scientific metaphors, seeing their experiments within different cultures as species with a complex DNA that can mutate and are permeable by outside influences. Their research-based work is rigorous in its commitment to the development of disciplinary techniques, and allows them to flourish in diverse environments as well as broadening the range of technical possibilities well beyond conventional architectural methods.

The practice was catapulted into the international limelight in 1994, when it beat 660 global contenders to win the competition for the Yokohama International Port Terminal. The £150 million building was completed in 2002, after a three-year period of construction encompassing what FOA call 'a very steep learning curve', which was accelerated by the city becoming a destination for the FIFA World Cup. In 2003, FOA won its first major project in the UK, the £22 million BBC White City Music Centre in London's Shepherd's Bush.

FOA's directors, Alejandro Zaera Polo, who was born in Madrid, and Farshid Moussavi, from Shiraz, Iran, met while studying for their Masters degrees in architecture at the Harvard Graduate School of Design. They chose London as a base to establish their practice in 1992 after a year working at OMA (Office for Metropolitan Architecture) in Rotterdam. Exposure to the Dutch architectural discourse no doubt encouraged FOA's subsequent publishing activities: Zaera Polo had long since contributed to *El Croquis* and other magazines, and FOA produced 'The Yokohama Project' in 2002, an exhaustive account of the making of the terminal building; an issue of *2G*[2] included their essays 'Foaism' and the 'FOA Code Remix'; *Phylogenesis: FOA's Ark*[3], published in 2003, was a small hardback with the austere appearance of a prayer book.

Intrigued by nomadism, they maintain a high degree of international mobility, travelling and setting up local teams to guide their various projects. Zaera Polo is also Dean of the Berlage Institute, Rotterdam, while Moussavi is Professor at Akademie der Bildenden Künste, Vienna. During the Yokohama project, which involved 'making the geometry of the competition design feasible as a manufacturing system' by adopting a largely prefabricated production process, they lived close to the site office for nearly two years. Kunio Watanabe, who led SDG, the structural engineers, virtually camped out in their office.

FOA's work across continents not only fuels their identity but has created a body of work that represents a multi-national urbanism which develops architecture's critical capacity to produce new alternatives. They have described their work in the following way: 'there are subjects in the discourse of modernism that have just gained a new lease of life. We live in a culture that is increasingly globalized, which means that the values of individuality, or specificity, or language, or idiosyncrasy need to be reviewed in the light of processes that require trans-cultural and trans-subjective operativity.'

If the modernists gave the impression that they could solve society's problems and the American new urbanists had a hunch that utopia could be reborn, at least in suburbia, FOA are architects of cultural multiplicity. They disavow the relevance of a single utopian vision and focus instead on detectable patterns in society in order to 'disassemble the great paradigms of references into chains of small local decisions', as Zaera Polo describes it. From these processes, rather than predetermined ideas linked to existing social codes, they find the means to invent new typologies and morphologies promoting the hybridization of space.

FOA's approach to architecture is all about re-evaluation. They are concerned to expand and transform architecture as a discipline, building its arsenal of tools and potential for morphological mediation. As students at the Graduate School of Design at Harvard, they were exposed to a generation of architectural tutors who were convinced that theory – especially film theory, cultural studies and art criticism – was empowering. In comparison with theory, they regarded actual construction of buildings as compromising, and far less profitable than film making, art and IT. Zaera Polo and Moussavi profoundly disagreed with this view and believed that it could only contribute to the diminishment of architectural production. For them, complexity theory offered more scope for application, due to the fact that it was visually based and focused on the organization of matter rather than discourse and, therefore, was more closely linked to architecture. Theory wedded to practice is at the heart of FOA's thinking and shapes every aspect of their work. It is 'a relationship in which theory and practice are no longer understood either in opposition or in a complementary, dialectical relationship, but rather as a complex continuum in which both forms of knowledge operate as devices capable of effectively transforming reality', states Zaera Polo.

> <u>Yokohama International Port Terminal</u>, Yokohama, Japan, 1994-2002; (top left) the undulating contours of the roof plaza; (bottom left) aerial view

During the duo's seven year period (1993–2000) as Masters of Diploma Unit 5 at London's Architectural Association, they fostered a 'laboratory' that served as an engine of 'experimental production', researching and exploiting 'the potentials of a technical repertoire'. Unusual in its commitment to a single discipline rather than to multidisciplinary activity, it was, as Zaera Polo explains, 'built up on a mix of Jacobin radical faith in the transformation of reality with a Calvinistic commitment to production and rigour'. The unit became an extension to FOA, feeding the practice with ideas and people, many of whom went on to become Sherpas in the team making Yokohama. Zaera Polo typifies their ethos of working as building a 'cultural synthesis' through the demands of the project, the input of group members and the series of techniques it provokes. These included architectural services, such as project management, estimation, surveys, and modelling by means of artificial intelligence, all of which FOA want to see exploited to help the discipline evolve. By 'researching the instrumental to make the discipline grow', Zaera Polo feels architects can 'integrate the emerging economic, cultural and social structures'. FOA see no point in going outside the discipline and trying to operate as bad sociologists while neglecting to improve the technical equipment needed to meet today's stringent political and cultural demands. But FOA do feel that 'architecture, more than the other arts, cannot exist outside the processes of economic, cultural and urban transformation.'

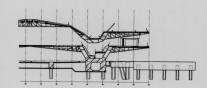

For FOA, the design process at its best is a process of creating knowledge. Their experience at Yokohama bears this out. An intense period of research focused on the material organizational and construction processes, but many of the technical procedures were kept open-ended to allow for the development of new solutions. 'We didn't have a predetermined image of the project,' says Zaera Polo, 'the image that emerges is always unexpected.' When they began, he explains, 'orders and rules, processes and laws provided the starting point for constructing the project'. Now they integrate these with natural and bodily metaphors – representational carriers that communicate the project – which they resisted earlier on. The power of external forces, including the demand by urban stakeholders for schemes from which they can make political capital, is not to be underestimated. The way FOA conceptualize their buildings as species reveals how much they like consistency as well as natural evolution; however, they are less interested in physical appearance than in the advantages of adapting the 'species' for different uses. The results – as shown at Yokohama – are unexpectedly fresh because they were not developed from conventional processes of imaging, collaging and structural juxtaposition.

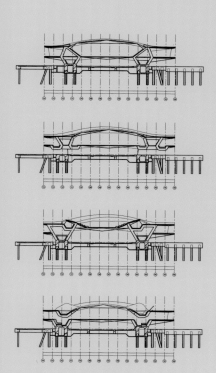

> (top to bottom) cross-section DD detail; cross-sections AA, BB, CC, DD

The idea of architecture as the result of scientific and organic growth, rather than as a representation of nature with a formal approach to infrastructure, allows it to transcend typological norms and break down 'the opposition between the rational and the organic'. Intentionally unhindered by conventional making processes, the architecture forms itself as a new topographic condition. FOA space is flowing, ever-changing, non-Cartesian – an enigmatic hybrid of differences.

FOA celebrated their ten year anniversary in 2003 by grouping their projects in the *Phylogenesis* exhibition and book as a personal classification of their differences rather than of their similarities. What was built up created a morphological taxonomy of categories, often bifurcated (their technical haiku for Yokohama, for instance, was a ground-multiple, face-constant-pierced-contingent-axial), and by such means the historical or aesthetic trappings of typologies were challenged by their exclusion. The success of FOA's approach can be measured by the degree to which it synthesizes their understanding of contemporary conditions and identities. Reading the environment of Yokohama in terms of past expectations of architectural language, to say nothing of traditional port terminals, is way off the mark. An organization of high complexity, Yokohama's 'genetic code' draws on the Japanese garden, especially in its use of wood and vegetal textures, as well as origami-style folded surfaces. The project's DNA also embraces the techniques of shipbuilding, for example in the complex forms of the steel plates that were shipped to the site ready constructed.

Although it was conceived as 'a generic maritime interface', the Yokohama Port Terminal can also be experienced as an encounter with the 'classic and the baroque' (Moussavi). It is a spacious (49,000 square metres), barrier-free, anti-monumental extension of Yamashita Park into the bay, 'a penetration of the ocean by the city'. The terminal and public leisure facilities are interwoven in an open environment that avoids the linear convention of pier circulation. It represents a strong alternative to transport building typologies; the building appears as a body with apertures that function as a spatial interface, definitely not a scenography scaffolded into three-dimensional reality; even the chain-link mesh of the barriers on the plaza was conceived with a transparency of surface in mind. The gently sloping surfaces, with ramp or lift access, create a fluid continuity across levels and dispense with the need for stairs. This makes it easy to navigate the multi-use hall spaces and the two direct curves with their warped pattern in Ipe wood of the rooftop plaza and visitors' deck, an artificial landscape which offers a new type of public garden and a place for play or quiet reflection. 'It's not an on-off, in-out mechanism, but one with a series of loops; not a gate but a territory, a multi-directional space,' Zaera Polo explains. 'Mobility is not exclusive

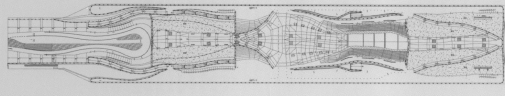

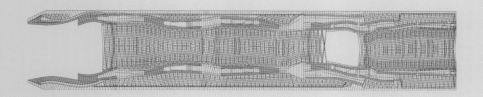

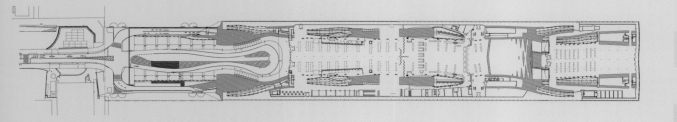

> <u>Yokohama International Port Terminal</u>, Yokohama, Japan, 1994-2002; (top) tip of pier from above showing roof plaza; (bottom, from top) roof plaza plan, terminal concourse roof plan, terminal concourse plan

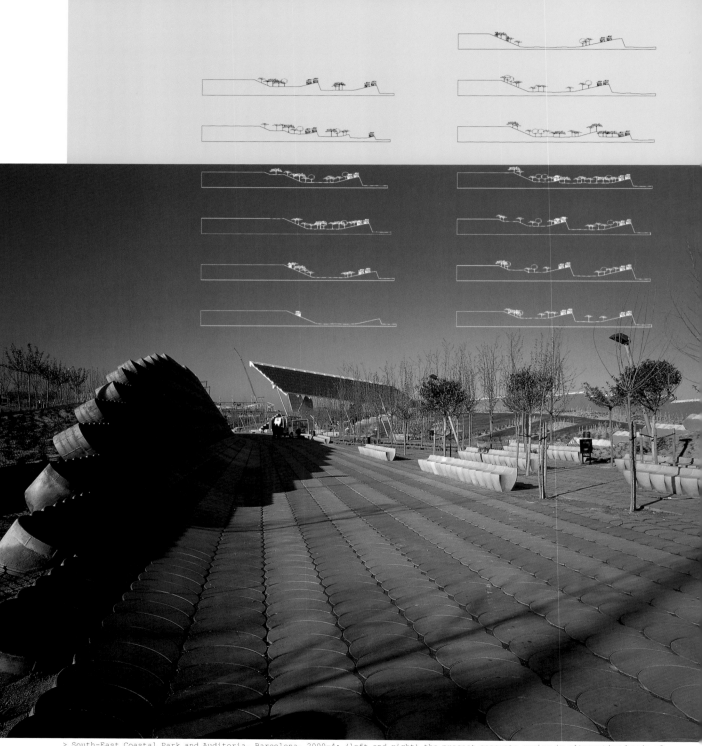

> <u>South-East Coastal Park and Auditoria</u>, Barcelona, 2000-4; (left and right) the precast concrete paving in alternating bands of colour rises into dune-like elevations; (top left) sections

to transportation buildings,' adds Moussavi; 'cities are increasingly about infrastructure. Mobility has made the spaces we occupy less and less static, and more and more dynamic.'

Unlike conventional architecture, the bifurcated surface of the continuous ground of Yokohama folds into itself, creating a 430 metre long, 70 metre wide, 15 metre high structure made from longitudinal girders that stack up. Instead of emphasizing the structural differentiation of walls, columns and floors, each piece is multi-purpose, and even the glazed lobbies, softly corrugated like curtains, do away with the need for structural mullions. 'The result is a hybridization of given types of space and programme through the distinct tectonic system of the folded surface,' explains Moussavi. Such a distribution of the loads through the surfaces themselves, 'moving them diagonally to the ground', made the design one of 'geological asymmetry capable of modification during construction', as well as addressing the lateral impact of seismic shifts that Japanese geology is prone to.

FOA mastered the complexity of their project, but from an early stage their concern lay with 'the actualization of the potential of building technology', rather than optimal solutions to technical problems. Many innovative aspects (for instance, using hydraulic lifts to limit the appearance of vertical elements, and not employing mullions to fix the glass) overrode conventional building regulations, and needed approval from a special tribunal. This process-related construction rationale for Yokohama was a gift for FOA's talented A-team of young architects. An early estimate by the client's project manager proposed that thirty to forty architects would be needed for Yokohama, but FOA adopted a Japanese ethos of working free of segmentation. More like Microsoft beginning life in a garage than the top-down corporate structure of many practices, the non-hierarchical FOA team worked with the fervour of jazz musicians or computer hackers, eliminating nugatory processes or purely managerial staff.

A loose and yet rigorous arrangement also characterizes a scheme like the undulating 7-hectare <u>South-East Coastal Park and Auditoria</u>, part of the new infrastructure created by the City of Barcelona in 2004 for the area of reclaimed land to the south-east of the Diagonal. Instead of resorting to what Zaera Polo calls 'contradiction as a form of complexity' and a direct reproduction of 'the picturesque qualities of nature', FOA's artificial topographies 'exploit complexity through coherence and consistency', blending the natural and the artificial into a complex organization. The sand dunes triggered FOA's design and became the 'material mediator', creating a natural, irregular shape of terrain able to accommodate auditoria, with slopes to protect from sea breezes.

Rhythmic 'conveyor belt' pavements of disc-shaped precast concrete forms, laid out in alternating colour bands, could be adjusted without cutting on site. A network of circuits, with different grades of paths and zones based on an analysis of various sporting activities and their topographic contexts, caters for the various activities planned for the site – walking, running, cycling, skateboarding, performance and relaxation.

FOA's sensitivity towards landscape and urban growth has made them a key part of the team working on the London 2012 Olympic bid, in particular the masterplan for the 600-hectare Lower Lea Valley, with EDAW, HOK Sport, Allies & Morrison and Fluid. The plans released in November 2004 showed the Olympic village based around a new park, with many of the facilities set low within a sinuous landscape surface, and as many as thirty-seven bridges across the waterways that bisect the site. FOA's proposed design for the main stadium took its inspiration from the human form, with the roof wrapping around the venue like supporting muscles. However, instead of the strategy typical of many Olympic villages, where the stadiums and facilities are a series of look-at-me objects, here the landscape and buildings have equal value, with an emphasis on integrating pathways, bridges and green spaces. 'We are creating something that will grow out of the specific conditions and form of the Lea Valley. This will be part of the lasting legacy for the local community,' says Zaera Polo, arguing that the redevelopment process should not be sanitized for the sake of a potential Olympic spectacle. In fulfilling London Mayor Ken Livingstone's ambitious plans for regenerating the area, which included 35–50,000 new housing units, it is important, FOA believe, to reveal the magnificent power of this 'back-of-house' part of London, with its topography of canals, locks, roads, tracks, sewers and infill land.

An ability to judge the potential impact of built form and a facility for designing infrastructurally are qualities that FOA combine with an advanced understanding of cities as centres of interconnected economic and political eco-systems in which spatial change can never be uniform. Projects of urban renewal frequently involve intermediate conditions that are neither wholly urban nor suburban. This issue is being addressed at D38 Parque Empresarial en la Zona Franca (2002–7), a new high-rise office complex in a part of Barcelona that is being renewed, which FOA are designing with Arata Isozaki. 'We intend not only to provide office space but a new, high quality public environment that constitutes a credible urban scenario for the city's future,' explains Zaera Polo. There are two key ingredients: a continuous and a differentiated environment, rather than a series of icons, in which a new typology of office space is developed. 'We have designed a campus of interlocking gardens covered by building masses, rather than making enclosed air-conditioned

> Bluemoon aparthotel, Groningen, the Netherlands, 1999-2000; elevation of steel cloth panels, adjustable from totally open to closed

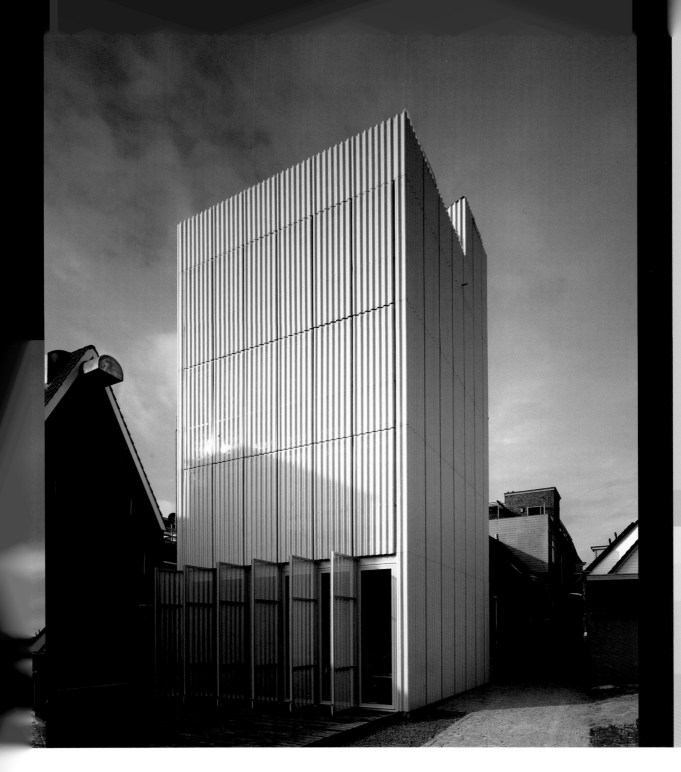

> <u>BBC Music Centre</u>, White City, west London, 2003-; (top left) A continuous band envelops the two main halls; (top right) cross-section perspective of the two halls on either side of the musicians' gallery, the top floors house offices and a canteen

lobbies as in northern European office buildings,' says Zaera Polo. Instead the lobbies will be open, with the buildings acting as canopies at different levels. Their design allows the buildings to respond to changing demands for a variety of types of working environments. FOA have devised it as a Tetris game, with a play on a 52 metre x 52 metre x 52 metre cube. FOA anticipate that it will 'operate in a similar way to that in which a Gothic building or a Mediterranean village grew', explains Moussavi. 'The final design will be produced by the interplay between a series of rules and parameters for things like maximum heights, percentages of site coverage for footprint and cantilevered volumes', as well as market forces.

The Bundle Tower, a 1,300,000 square-metre high-rise structure, is a new prototype that operates with the building massing rather than with just the distribution of the structure. To avoid excessively deep workspaces heavily dependent on artificial light and mechanically controlled ventilation, the complex is constructed as a bundle of interconnected towers 500 metres high. These provide a flexible floor space: 18 metre diameter tubes buttress each other every 36 metres. It was commissioned in 2002 for an exhibition of proposals for Ground Zero by the New York gallery owner Max Protetch. The idea of a group of towers linked and buttressing each other occurred in a number of the entries shortlisted for exhibition. FOA went on to develop their prototype, with its idea of self-buttressing towers – which was not at that stage a site-specific proposal – with their partners at United Architects[4], a multidisciplinary organization of architects, under the motto of 'United We Stand', for the actual Ground Zero competition in 2002 staged by the Lower Manhattan Development Corporation (LMDC) and the New York Port Authority. A mixed-use design incorporating the Ground Zero memorial and train/bus infrastructure, 'it synthesized new alternatives for the well-tested urban typologies: the skyline as an automatic result of either homogenizing rules or the politics of laissez-faire; the high-rise building as a vertical extension of a footprint; and the ground and the underground, the public space and the infrastructure as neatly dissected realms,' says Zaera Polo. Not only did the group exercise show that high-level collaboration is important to the way FOA work and can be extended by scaling up internationally, but their final placing in the competition shortlist (of nine proposals from seven groups) endorsed the practice's ability to design significant urban schemes.

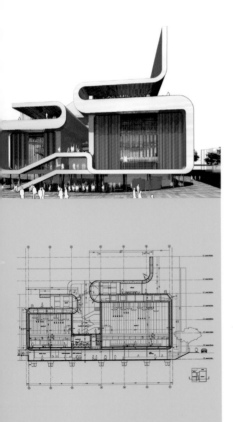

> (bottom, left to right) longitudinal section; longitudinal sections through main hall and musicians' gallery; cross section

> <u>D38 Parque Empresarial en la Zona Franca</u>, high-rise office complex, Barcelona, Spain, 2002-7; (top) model showing the campus with a continuous structure of buildings and interlocking gardens

Perhaps because of Yokohama's undulating landscape, FOA are associated with low lying 'ground conditions'. Their scheme for the South Bank Centre's Jubilee Gardens, London, competition in 2001 (which was not pursued by the client due to site ownership problems) is one example; La Rioja Technology Transfer Centre on the outskirts of Logroño in Spain (2003–5), facing an internal garden on one side, a landscape with views of agricultural nurseries on the other, is another. Their scheme for the Novartis park above a car park on the edge of a large urban research campus in Basel, Switzerland (a 2003 competition entry), typifies FOA's desire to assert a continuity between the natural and the artificial, overcoming the distinction between outside and inside, in its proposition for a functionally and spatially differentiated hybrid environment.

Amidst this crop of more subtle propositions, the conspicuous folded structure of the BBC Music Centre on the corporation's White City campus in west London, a £22 million competition win from 2003, may seem an anomaly. The design of the intentionally iconic Centre, which is to be a community and public resource, features a continuous band that envelops the two main studios (one for the BBC Symphony Orchestra, Concert Orchestra and Symphony Chorus, and designed for audiences of up to 600 people, the other for rehearsal and recording purposes) of the building, which has a compact plan, enclosing public spaces, including a foyer and gallery, that are divided by an acoustic buffer. Space is arranged as screens or diffusers, promoting continuity between the musicians' studios and the urban context beyond. By breaking the mass into two volumes, the series of interconnected plazas transcend any role as server space. Part of the band is the triple-layered glass window-screen on the south side which will be treated as a broadcasting device, with a layer of dichromatic 3M Radiant Mirror film (or a similar film) that changes colour, heightening its impression of interactivity. A grid of LED lights will reproduce the music through an audio scan that converts it into digital patterns of colour and light. This maximizes the building's transparency, creating a kind of theatre where music is produced.

The differentiated identity of the building evolves not from a CAD image but from the concept of music as a linear structure due to its physical notation or registration. By playing with the generative system of the Centre's function in this way, the design creates a dynamic instrument of a building that is closely related to the needs of the resident musicians and is the result of extensive consultations with them. The design aims not to produce a literal representation of music or nature in physical form, but a complex organization, the outcome of a morphogenetic process free of arbitrary techniques.

> La Rioja Technology Transfer Centre, near Logroño, Spain, 2003-5; (middle) perspective of the low-slung, two-storey building in the landscape; (bottom) the building's linear structure, with classrooms and corridors organized along a spine

Conventions of what constitutes exterior and what interior in urban space are, therefore, frequently redefined in many FOA projects. The scheme for Torrevieja's 650-seat municipal theatre and auditorium (due for completion in December 2005) near Alicante, Spain, operates like an incision into a solid mass, say FOA. It exploits the plot's limited space by raising the limestone clad auditorium so that the public plaza can penetrate the space below, becoming a foyer that sits beneath the cantilevered mass of the building.

Reconfigurability is another recurring theme in FOA's work. It appears in its scheme for the Bluemoon aparthotel (1999–2000) in the inner city of Groningen, in the north of the Netherlands, historically a site of maritime traffic. The idea of a 7 metre x 7 metre four-storey tower, with three open-plan suites, and clad in insulated silver fabric, was inspired by the concept of hotel occupancy as nomadic. Like a tent or sleeping bag, the steel cloth cladding wraps the building in perforated steel panels that are adjustable from total enclosure to total openness. This allows residents to 'reconfigure their dens to suit their needs in a way similar to the zipping and unzipping of a sleeping bag', say FOA. It will be interesting to see whether FOA's future urban housing in Barcelona and Madrid will continue to explore concepts of adaptability of the building envelope, to break down received notions of domestic typologies.

FOA 'don't oppose reality by making visionary statements but by trying to find possibilities within it'. They promote architectural experimentation not as an avant-garde formalist 'disturbance', but through the re-evaluation of technical and disciplinary procedures. The musical analogy they offer places them not so much with the random openness of John Cage's work but the complex algorithmic formulae and structures of Pierre Boulez's compositions. FOA also use techniques and parameters to produce new models 'able to cope with more dynamic processes, differentiated distributions and complex organizations'. This is what makes FOA's response to context so powerful.

1. Comments from a lecture given by Alejandro Zaera Polo and Farshid Moussavi at the Architectural Association, London, 11 October 2004.
2. Foreign Office Architects, 2G, n.16, 2000/IV, Editorial Gustavo Gili, SA, Barcelona.
3. Phylogenesis: FOA's Ark, ICA, London 2003 and Actar, Barcelona, 2000.
4. Greg Lynn Form, Kevin Kennon Architects, Reiser & Umemoto and UN Studio.

> Torrevieja Municipal Theatre and Auditorium, near Alicante, Spain, 2000-5; (top) perspective of the cantilevered building in the public plaza; (bottom right) the folded plane walls of the auditorium; The Bundle Tower, 2002; (bottom left) a high-rise prototype

Gollifer Langston

> <u>Sunderland Glass Centre</u>, 1994-98; view from the edge of the glass roof towards the North Sea

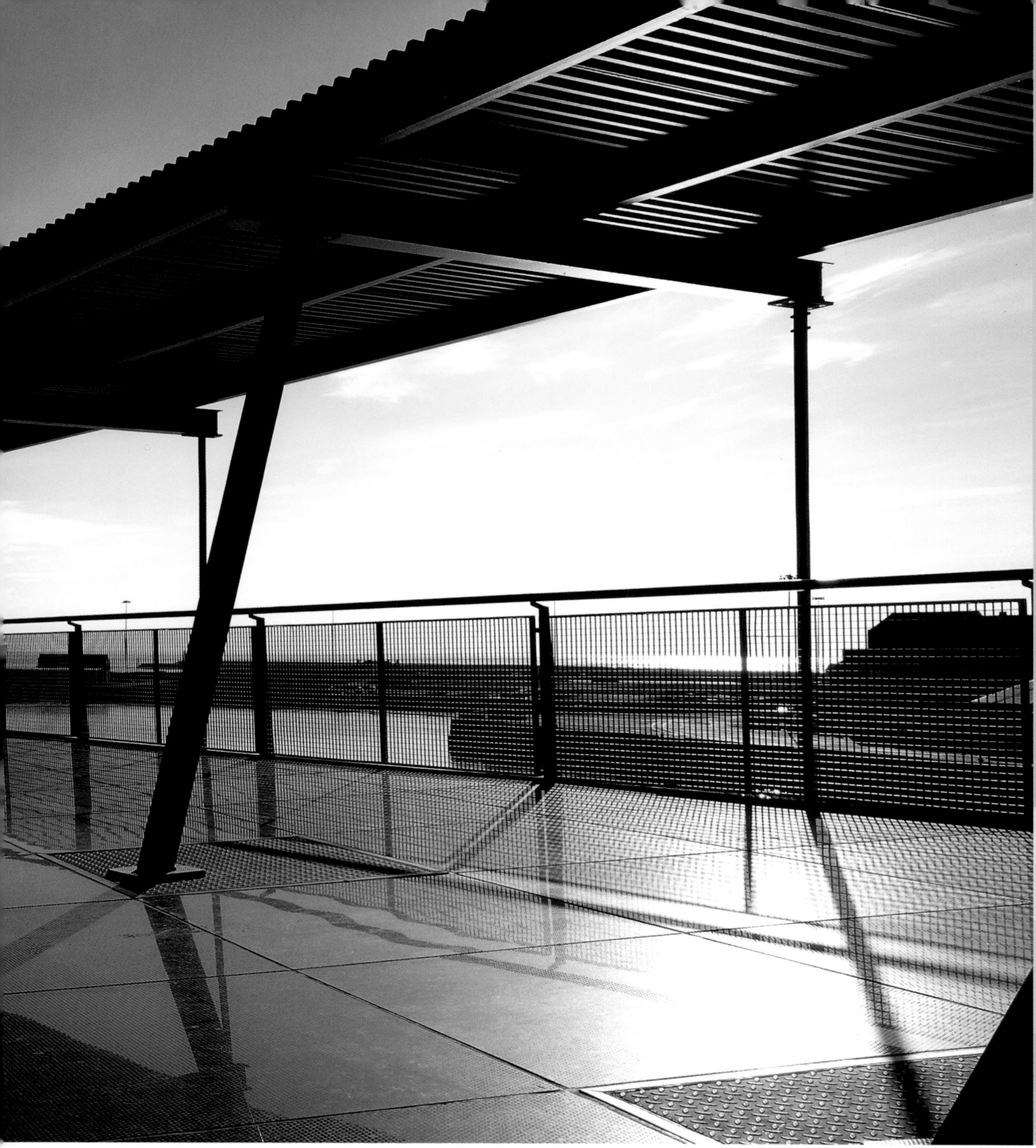

> <u>Sunderland Glass Centre</u>, 1994-98; (left) riverside with shading screens and seminar pod beneath main roof

'In architecture you have to be able to work on all levels. It needs to be pragmatic and spontaneous, calm and loud at the same time, because life is that complicated.'

> (above) view from restaurant out over River Wear; (top) view of building from opposite river bank

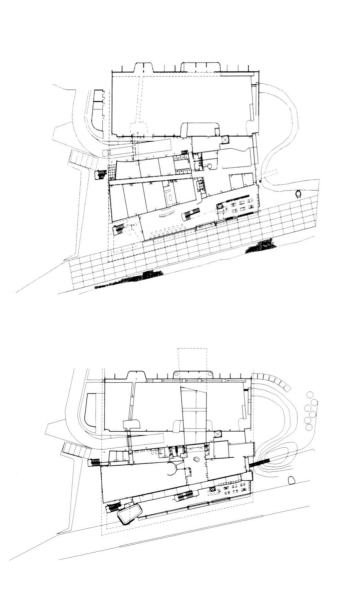

> <u>Sunderland Glass Centre</u>, 1994-98; (top left) ground floor plan: factory, workshops, restaurant and shop; (bottom left) upper level plan: exhibition, administration and main reception

The accolade of Millennium Product status was recently bestowed on Gollifer Langston's first building, resulting from Prime Minister Tony Blair's challenge to UK businesses in 1997 to nominate 2,000 world-ranking new products and services. The results embraced fields as diverse as agriculture, automotive design, entertainment and the environment. The Sunderland Glass Centre, completed in 1998, won over the judges with its simple and innovative solution, a rare but well-integrated mix of public and industrial facilities. Gollifer Langston's schemes for a number of inner City Learning Centres[1], an initiative by the Department for Education and Skills (DfES, 1999), can also be regarded as setting benchmarks, their designs reflecting the impact of social and technological changes on the process of formal learning. Although these kinds of fresh typological interpretations have not achieved the same level of media attention as the Millennium initiatives, work by practices like Gollifer Langston represents a major cultural investment in the reinvention and promotion of public cultural and educational facilities and their resources in the UK.

The CLCs, as they are known – secondary schools supplemented by information and communication technology (ICT) facilities – reflect a radical rethinking of educational institutions. Visiting Gollifer Langston's first two completed projects, pragmatism is one evident hallmark of their approach. But it is their flair for non-hierarchical spatial arrangements, for a new mix of functions, that distinguishes them from many practices. 'We've been lucky as most of our projects have been for clients who decided they wanted to break the mould,' explains Andy Gollifer, who co-founded the practice with Mark Langston in 1994.

Gollifer, a Liverpudlian who studied under architect John Miller at the Royal College of Art in the 1980s, can see the pitfalls in using formal architectural language if addressing social change is the objective. He cites 'modernism [that] is too polite. In architecture you have to be able to work on all levels. It needs to be pragmatic and spontaneous, calm and loud at the same time, because life is that complicated.'

The practice was just one year old when it won the competition for the National Glass Centre in Sunderland in 1995. Work began two years later, as soon as the funding was in place. A £9.6 million building, it was commissioned by the Tyne and Wear Development Corporation, part funded by the European Regional Development Fund (ERDF), and made possible by a grant from the National Lottery. It catapulted the architects into the headlines, although they have had a lower profile since.

Sited on a disused dock area on the edge of the banks of the River Wear, the centre responds to its context with a steel-framed structure set on a

> <u>Platform 1 City Learning Centre</u>, King's Cross, London, 2001-3; the building at dusk: its curtain wall glazed façade has digital lettering

sloping site that gives a new sense of place to a lost piece of riverside. It is a building with an innovative and complex building typology. 'It compresses all its disparate functions within one envelope and explores the possibilities of them sitting side by side. It was much more interesting to combine both public and work spaces,' explains Andy Gollifer. 'The point [of the building] was to say, we've lost all the traditional industries but glass production is still going strong, and here is its symbolic heart under one roof. We tried to get the transparency in.' The factory coexists with a series of independent workshops for smaller scale designer glass production, café, restaurant, foyer and other public facilities, all on the ground floor. Gallery spaces, a seminar pod, upper foyer on the upper floor are connected by a ramp and set in a double-height space under one glazed roof.

The relationship between structure, façade and river is very clean: the façade is glass, hung from the front columns which also support the front walkways and shading. The façade, which was designed with Arup, gives a high degree of openness to the view; all the public elements are positioned close to the river, so visitors can see into the workshops and outside from wherever they are within what feels like a covered walkway.

Battle McCarthy designed the natural ventilation towers and earth tube for natural cooling, and heat recycling from factory to public areas. Although it is an industrial building, and as such a big container, the building's character is that of a factory, not a shed. A shed implies something that makes little concession to its context, whereas the Centre is very site-specific, 'seeking to give a new sense of place to a lost piece of riverside'.

The King's Cross and South Camden Community Learning Centres in north London are two of a second wave of City Learning Centres. The DfES plans to build thirty CLCs in inner city areas around the country, and Gollifer Langston's designs serve as a benchmark for others to follow. The King's Cross Centre is devoted to language learning, while South Camden has a more general focus on IT. Both centres use IT as a core tool, so making IT approachable was a vital aspect of the designs; so, too, was making the buildings a physical focus for a local community in which a wealth of different languages are understood.

A vital theme that Gollifer Langston render physical in both projects is the radical effect that technology has had on the nature of school building, directly impacting on how space is used and what type of spaces are needed, to say nothing of ventilation requirements and

> <u>Platform 1 City Learning Centre</u>, King's Cross, London, 2001-3; (left) main entrance with cantilevered steel frame; (top right) ground floor learning area looking towards reception; (bottom right) double-height reception

suitability of materials used. 'The reinvention comes from the brief,' says Gollifer.

While King's Cross was a new-build scheme next to an existing school, South Camden was an entire site of buildings, some from the 1970s and 1980s, located in an area that is the focus of regeneration. The existing facilities were fragmented, and the architects wanted to 'reinforce the context' and create a sense of security and connection. First they undertook development planning work: 'Looking at the whole, it was a question of identifying where the difficulties were and then knitting the spaces back together,' Gollifer explains. 'There was a desire on the client side to avoid imposing a grand statement.'

For South Camden, the practice responded to changing needs – increasing numbers, altered demographics and a revised curriculum. It also became involved in fundraising for the new building. The Centre has IT, design and multimedia facilities for use by primary and secondary schools as well as local community members. A separate building, which makes use of the same curtain wall system as the Glass Centre in Sunderland, has a large hall with dining facilities. 'Transparency, an immediate contact with the exterior space, and the revealing of activity is important,' says Langston. The need to give informal working and interactive learning methods a context is addressed in the ground floor educational spaces, which are styled like a bar or restaurant and linked by a metal staircase to more self-contained work areas upstairs.

The main building is set up from its street elevation, a massively long structure which twists the façade that is punctured with holes with a common entrance point. As a result light comes in but the views out are limited. 'It's an inward looking space. It's nice to have a slightly glimpsed view of the outside,' says Gollifer. The same feature appears in some of the meeting room walls, a device that connects street and working space.

An emphasis on accessibility in language and use of industrial materials is also built into the design at the King's Cross CLC building, which opens up on its public side with a new forecourt shaded by two existing plane trees. Its facilities are arranged around a double-height space that can be accessed from the school behind. This area functions as a reception and open-plan learning area, with computers and mobile furniture; but it also includes a recording studio. The more contemplative areas – the library and classrooms – are on the floor above, with the library visually accessible through glazed panels. This juxtaposition 'makes for a much more dynamic feeling to the space', says Gollifer. 'It's important to enjoy different things happening side by side.' Carefully

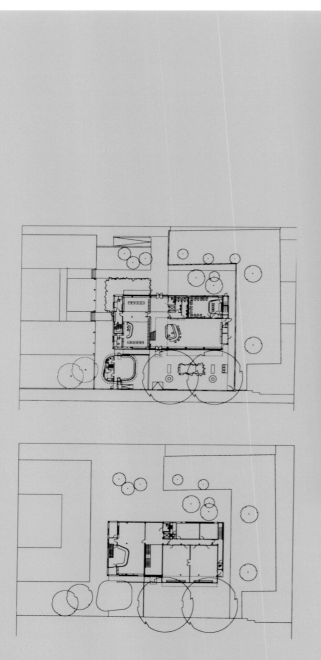

> <u>Platform 1 City Learning Centre</u>, King's Cross, London, 2001-3; (left, top to bottom) ground floor plan, first floor plan; (right) polycarbonate clad crèche to the left of the entrance

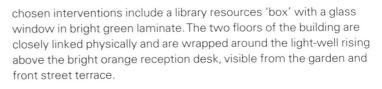

chosen interventions include a library resources 'box' with a glass window in bright green laminate. The two floors of the building are closely linked physically and are wrapped around the light-well rising above the bright orange reception desk, visible from the garden and front street terrace.

The building is a simple form clad in fibre cement panels, with curtain wall glazing with black Lignacite blocks inside. Its transparency is emphasized at night. A glass shelter above the entrance, with a cantilevered steel frame, echoes the language of the Sunderland Glass Centre, itself a big steel frame. To the left of the entrance is a timber-framed crèche in corrugated polycarbonate. Adding to the building's presence, digital 'manifestation' dots on the glazing form letters announcing its purpose. Gollifer Langston believe that 'detail must enhance the constructional nature of a building'. Both the CLCs have what the practice define as an environmental strategy. This includes exposed concrete rather than suspended ceilings. 'We enjoy the rawness and unfinished quality of industrial materials.' They also favour it for environmental reasons because the concrete frame contributes to the building's cooling by acting as a heat sink. 'The case made to the client is that by using a construction material unadorned you save on another material. That helps them to accept the aesthetic,' says Langston. Snowcrash acoustic panels with a felt finish, suspended from the ceiling, counteract the ongoing noise that an open plan space creates.

Now the practice is designing an extension to house performing arts teaching at <u>Acland Burghley School</u> in Camden, a concrete slab building by architects HKPA that Gollifer feels might be a Brutalist milestone, but one that he is prepared to deal with. Studying architecture at Bristol University in the mid-1980s, 'everyone was force-fed Corb [Le Corbusier]; his ideas were a kind of gospel in those days; but the positive aspect stays with you,' he says. The practice draws on Corbusier's 'real rigour' and simplicity, the focus on 'the architect's route through the building that's inherent, guided by colours and walls', and his treatment of space without flat walls. Gollifer cites an influential precedent for the recording studio of the King's Cross CLC which breaks up the typology's typical regularity. It was the ground-breaking <u>Metropolis</u>, a suite designed by Powell-Tuck Connor and Orefelt in the late 1980s which Gollifer oversaw as project architect. Just as the aura surrounding the performance and recording of music has changed, a new architecture was needed to house these activities. The mixing desk has become the centre of operations and studios now have access to daylight, features of both the music centre at King's Cross and the scheme for Acland Burghley.

> <u>601fx film company headquarters</u>, Soho, London, 1994; perforated metal screens in main studio

> <u>Camden City Learning Centre</u>, London, 1999-2002; (top left) plan of South Camden School showing the new Learning Centre; (bottom left) entrance to double-height foyer; (right) front elevation with perforated concrete panels and transparent ground floor area

The practice's design for <u>601fx</u> (1994) in Dean Street, Soho, central London, a film company specializing in computer-generated special effects, deals with space in response to new creative uses in a similar way to Metropolis. 'It allows the views between different activities to open up. As with music, the technology for producing film has changed so it's no longer in a darkened room using a 21-inch monitor.' Instead the environment is light and bright. They exploit the façade with perforated metal panels that control light and become translucent, and mirrors to increase the appearance of depth. These operate like a series of screens: 'It's about what you reveal or not. When you take things out of boxes you have to think of other ways to define space by subtle change,' says Gollifer. 'We are quite European in being unselfconscious about the materials we use. We live and work in a culture where things have to be dressed, coated and finely tuned. Buildings become weighed down, or overwrought. There's a need for refreshingly resolved solutions, and a different kind of respect for context.' Both he and Langston believe that they have developed 'their language from their circumstances'. They have worked almost exclusively with 'newer institutions' and on schemes like recording studios in a period characterized by change. 'More functions, and different functions are coming in – things that have not previously felt so accessible to people – blurring the boundaries.'

'It's a bit of a contemporary obsession that everything should be accessible,' says Gollifer, putting the emphasis on this politically correct buzzword that covers everything from the Internet to New Labour's policies for education and health centres, to drive-in McDonald's and reality television. He cites the 'endless plateau' of the Italian architectural practice Superstudio (founded in 1966) as a good metaphor for an accessible place that is not specific, which can be anything from a family house to a picnic space. They proposed this as an alternative to a subtly controlled place where you are guided by everything. In the Glass Centre the practice clearly tries to hold on to a quality of plural reality to help people read it. To realize the openness of their design, they take the 'plateau' and make a hole in it, and include a ramp to take you somewhere. Similarly, for a building like King's Cross to promise free access for a multitude of functions, its architecture 'should have the same spirit. We are giving public access to a process'.

1 Part of the Excellence in Cities (EiC) programme of support launched in 1999 for deprived secondary schools in urban areas.

Klein
Dytham
architecture

> <u>Leaf Chapel</u>, Kobuchizawa, Japan, 2004; a wedding chapel beside a pond; the canopy is punctured with holes plugged
with lenses, and it lifts at the end of each ceremony

（KDa）

> <u>Cat's Eyes</u> façade and entrance, Foret department store, Harajuku, Tokyo, Japan, 2002; façade covered in tiny reflectors

HARAJUKU'S
BRIGHTEST
ピカピカ
SPOT

34m
WIDE

HAPPY

FREE
EXPRESSION

apan, 1999 (top and bottom right) pretzel-shaped hoarding in silver balloon fabric

> <u>Rin-Rin</u>, Harajuku, Tokyo, Japan, 2000-1; (left and bottom right) street showcases in front of Laforet department store; <u>Leaf Chapel</u>, Kobuchizawa, Japan, 2004; (top right) interior of the wedding chapel with a hydraulically controlled wall

Just before the economic bubble burst in Japan, hopeful young architects Mark Dytham and Astrid Klein left London for Tokyo. It was 1988, and their plan after graduating from the Royal College of Art was to 'get to the roots of modern architecture and its huge Japanese influences', and to find some work. At that time, rapid increases in land values in Japan had come to a halt and the country was struggling to deal with the hangover marking the end of its period of massive growth. But the pair were not deterred by such macrocosmic worries, or concerned that penetrating the local scene would be a tall order without a command of the language. Busking on three-month travel scholarships, on arrival they immediately telephoned the big architectural names. Toyo Ito, for whom they later worked on a masterplan for Tokyo Bay, helped them to get their first job, designing a hair salon in Ginza. In 1990 they founded Klein Dytham in the city they made their home. This led to a series of commissions for interiors, and their first building, in 1996, the Idée Workstation, a furniture showroom, was followed by further small buildings and public installations that increasingly captured media attention.

At that time, after ten years or more of 'bubble trouble' – the financial crisis in Japan during the 1990s – coupled with a decreasing birth rate and a top heavy 'silvering' population, architects were rediscovering the need to think small.

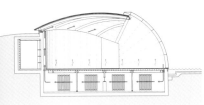

> (far right) exploded diagram of Leaf Chapel structure, and section

Despite the fact that there was a falling away of public projects and work for the larger corporate firms had declined, Dytham believes that the recession actually encouraged the emergence of a new generation of young designers. After all, the outbreak of punk in the UK in the late 1970s came from an unpromising economic climate. With fewer big commissions available in Japan, KDa feel that there have been more 'hustling opportunities for young architects', obliging them to think creatively about different ways to employ their skills. 'It's now more to do with ideas than materials,' they say.

Reflecting the reality of Tokyo as a great place to experiment, KDa's body of work is highly responsive to the eclecticism of the cityscape; they immerse themselves with childlike relish in its ever-renewing culture of graphics, products and vending machines. This exploratory scavenging of context and appropriation of cheap and indigenous materials, such as compressed bamboo and 'sonic mesh' (from aerospace technology), often places elements in unexpected contexts, for instance car reflectors on façades of buildings, which they call 'dislocation'. They were one of the first young architectural practices to mediate their cultural environment by featuring elements of it on their website, such as their favourite fetishes, including a Japanese dog walking machine and 'Canned', their choice from the myriad of canned drink concepts pumped into the local market every year. Every year they send out often hilarious self-assembled or designed Christmas cards (those for 2000 included a Y2K compliant, bug-free Japanese handwarmer sachet). Their wide-ranging design output also includes products, for example a new kind of digital camera and furniture for architect Toyo Ito's Lyric Hall in Nagaoka.

KDa's passion for commenting on society in a playful way has included an installation of plastic objects costing 100 yen in the main plaza of the International Tokyo Forum and 2.7 metre-high structures made of suspended shopping bags included in 'Jam Tokyo London', an exhibition held in the huge Tokyo Opera City. Gummi-bath, a freestanding blue Technogel (polyurethane) bathroom tiled with a duck motif, was a more sensual concept than most bathroom designs and installed in the grey space of one of the main piazzas in Milan in 2002. This prototype led on to sinks made of soap, where you simply rub the sides. 'It's got to be understandable, with some kind of connection back to architecture.' While their work epitomizes Marshall McLuhan's epigram, 'the medium is the message', many architects would be wary of playing so directly with consumer culture, for fear of being subsumed by another language; but KDa do not worry about the dividing line: 'We're not afraid of retail and advertising. We're turned on by it. A lot of architecture is too serious. Architecture can be seen as a new form of advertising.'

50

> Beacon Communications advertising agency, Meguro, Tokyo, Japan, 2002; sketch and view of media viewing area with stepped seating

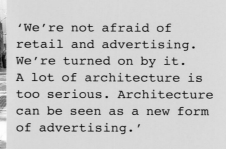

'We're not afraid of
retail and advertising.
We're turned on by it.
A lot of architecture is
too serious. Architecture
can be seen as a new form
of advertising.'

> <u>Green Green Screen</u>, Omotesando Avenue, Tokyo, Japan, 2003; (top) a construction screen with greenery in front of Tadao Ando's mixed-use development; (bottom) twelve metres long directors' table; at the rear, a ribbon of meeting rooms and viewing areas acts as a ceiling strip

> <u>Idée Workstation furniture showroom</u>, Shimouma, Tokyo, Japan, 1996; (left and right) polycarbonate façade layered with transparent coloured film

KDa have always enjoyed Tokyo's love affair with technology, while at the same time hating its predictable robotic efficiency. The city's culture struck them as strongly visual and image-conscious: they noticed people in the street constantly checking their appearance in reflections or mirrors, a common sight in subway stations. They inserted video screens into the interiors of Video Sento, a project to reinvent the venerable Japanese public-private space of the *sento*, or bathhouse, as if to create a mimetic game in a bid to appropriate for the younger generation the *sento*'s scenic traditional decor of panoramic landscapes.

KDa's architecture is about performance as well as a kind of stealthy activity within the city. As a creative tactic but also as a means of survival, their adoption of the culture of advertising – billboards, hoardings, and other eye-catching devices on the street – has been an improvisational means for making architecture. A Japanese lifestyle magazine recently gave Rem Koolhaas credit for bringing 'art into architecture without the public really noticing', and KDa do something similar in stretching the micro-language of brands, and transforming the street environment into an arena of spontaneous activity. 'Fast, quick projects are the norm in Japanese culture. We won't be sued in fifty years if the roof leaks,' say KDa. Their buildings and projects offer simple, expressive strength as an architectural rationale, rather than longevity. The Idée Workstation building (1996) in Shimouma, Tokyo, somewhat reminiscent of a 1950s' gas station, with its polycarbonate façade layered with transparent coloured film, looks like a product to be consumed; at night it reads as a Japanese lantern.

In Idée, KDa fused the communicational power of a digital screen with a billboard. Two more recent, unmissable street installations got the public asking, is it architecture or advertising? Pika-Pika (1999) was a huge temporary hoarding for a developer, positioned in front of a building site at Jingumae in Tokyo on top of the construction fence. Designed to cause a stir by 'building the most ridiculous thing we could', it took the form of a giant pretzel, a 34 metre-long bulbous silver lilo made from inflatable, high-performance balloon fabric. Installed for two weeks, it stopped traffic and was featured on television. Wonderwall, for Virgin (2000), a 20 metre-long red interactive billboard in central Tokyo, created the physical focus for a competition by demanding that participants crowd the front of the site to enter via their I-Mode Internet phones.

The power of performance pervades their working culture. From the second half of the 1990s, KDa based themselves in a converted taxi garage they called Deluxe, a ground floor studio in Azabu-Juban. Deluxe improvised as a 'crossover' space for exhibitions, performances and parties. From the beginning they worked alongside UK graphic and multimedia designers Namaiki, a team of sound designers and the Tokyo Brewing Company. The 'big crazy churn' of Deluxe's events programme gave them a strong cultural identity, subsequently augmented by KDa's unmissable projects elsewhere in the city.

Tokyo can be hard for Westerners to establish roots in: KDa created their own cultural meeting point, one that was highly popular and multicultural. In 2003 they launched SuperDeluxe, an events space backed by the brewing venture, building on its success. The move left their studio free for work, and created a new centre of activity close to another of their projects, the café (2003) within the new Mori Art Museum in the Roppongi Hills complex which is located on the fifty-second floor, a space punctuated by lollipop mirrors giving a 'glimpse – albeit sometimes artistically "distorted" – of panoramic views of the city even when you are sitting with your back to it', as Klein explains.

KDa have found their métier in the reinvention of space, and this has extended to the streets of Tokyo. Green Green Screen (2003), a 274 metre-long construction screen occupies Omotesando Avenue, the city's Champs Elysées, which will stay there for three years while Tadao Ando's mixed-use development reaches completion behind it. The building replaces the Donjunkai social housing which dates back to the 1920s. 'The building was known for its endearing greenery,' says Klein. Green Green Screen has its own particular verdancy: 'Our wall shows the passage of time, with thirteen different types of evergreen ivy, plants and grass growing from felt pockets attached to the screen.' The different shades of green create a pattern like a barcode along the entire length. Graphic wallpaper on the theme of leaves and plants is interspersed among the real green in an info-eco mosaic; yet more stripes of varying width include 'high end advertising'. Interestingly, Rem Koolhaas also included advertising in his 2003 publication *Content*. The screen does not have an overwhelming presence, it aims to draw the spectator in: 'When it is viewed obliquely by people walking alongside the screen its planting appears to be continuous hedge.'

It is not just because KDa's streetscape projects are 'expensive stuff' that Dytham feels they reach a level above the commercialism of the street. Rin-Rin (2000–1) in particular provokes the question: Is it architecture, streetscape, or media? Commissioned by Laforet, a Tokyo department store at Harajuku, to design changing billboards in front of the façade, KDa came up with a 70 metre-long ribbon of stainless steel showcases in pastry cutter shapes, like trees in a cartoon. This 'little forest', an artful monument, refurbishes the entrance area, drawing on the memory of a row of trees that was cut down to make way for a new subway line. An urban intervention in miniature, KDa have created an

> Klein Dytham Architects with Toshio Iwai, Bloomberg ICE, Marunouchi, Tokyo, Japan, 2003; (left) an interactive info-lounge

open boundary between the store and the street. While passing customers stop to enjoy a brief, intimate look to check their make-up, Rin-Rin's curves of reflective steel playfully distort their images. In a city without a grid, where the boundaries are not clear, its deformed surfaces insert an interactive design language. A glass strip of floor extends the display onto the pavement. At night, echoing the changing visual and textual data on buildings' display systems, it lights up in different colours. Working closely with the brand's objectives, KDa have brought out the artistic potential of public space.

KDa's design for <u>Foret</u> (2002), Laforet's sister store 100 metres down the road, takes advantage of Tokyo's vibrancy at night, reformatting and reflecting it back via thousands of tiny 'delineator' road reflectors fixed onto a bright green façade. Because delineators reflect light back to its source at whatever angle it enters the lens, even a camera flash can light up the whole façade, as if it has been turned on and off in an instant. In the entrance area, visitors tread on a surface of white glassbead paint normally used for zebra crossings, and encased solar powered LEDs dot the floor, flashing in the dark.

At <u>Beacon</u> (2002), at Meguro in Tokyo, a new advertising agency created out of a merger of three firms, with 300 staff to

> <u>Mori Art Museum café</u>, Roppongi Hills, Tokyo, Japan, 2003; (right) lollipop mirrors give panoramic views of the city

accommodate over four floors, communication was key. A 60 metre-long 'ribbon' connects all the rooms on each floor – a mixture of meeting and multipurpose areas – acting as a ceiling in some rooms, wall in another, an amphitheatre in another. Sometimes the 'ribbon' is glazed in, elsewhere left open, allowing the space to spill out into the main office. The directors are given one 12 metre-long table where they sit with the company president at the end of one floor, breaking down the formality of the management area. Apart from specifying 150 furniture types, KDa came up with 1,000 types of fabric, including a fake pink snakeskin that appears scanned as wallpaper.

Offered the opportunity to interpret world famous financial news agency Bloomberg's activities at its headquarters in Marunouchi, behind Tokyo Station, KDa created the <u>Bloomberg ICE</u> (interactive communicative experience, 2003), a 'smart' info-lounge, with Toshio Iwai, a leading Japanese interface designer. They wanted to inject something that had never existed in this working environment: the ICE installation is suspended like a large stalactite, a digital screen on which FTSE and NASDAQ financial data becomes ticker tape, with digital shadows that rise and fall according to market levels. When infra-red sensors behind the 5 metre x 3.5 metre glass wall detect a visitor's presence, the data begins to interact with his or her movements, as a shadow, wave, harp or volleyball, depending on which play option he or she chooses. While Wonderwall was one of KDa's earliest stabs at making an interactive game spatial, ICE promotes the personalization of space through an engaging interface elegantly installed to react to the body as a biofeedback mechanism. It might even constitute a new environmental genre, an alternative on-premises version of the amusement arcade or pachinko parlour typically found in Japan's main cities; and it is one that has proved very popular. Innocent yet knowing as a design, it defies the boundaries between office and street, work and play, data and body.

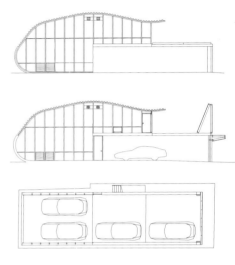

KDa have increasingly embraced tectonic form, always in an ingenious way. Schemes such as the <u>Vroom!</u> garage building, outside Tokyo in the Aichi Prefecture, which was completed in 1999, have an improvised structural logic to their design. The clients, a real estate dealer and his wife, with a collection of top marque Italian and German cars to house, gave KDa a narrow strip of roadside land to work with, which 'cost less than their Maserati', says Dytham. The resulting structure has concrete walls and floors. Instead of conventional columns and beams, window mullions act as a lighter column support beneath the roof. The building's shapely curves not only emulate the form of a car, but the profiled steel roof is itself a beam supported on the window frames, just like a car's structure. It is also convertible, and cranks up within thirty seconds to create a new frontage, transforming the building's perceived scale on

> <u>Vroom! garage</u>, Aichi Prefecture, Japan, 1999; (left, from top to bottom) sections showing the profiled steel roof which emulates that of a car and garage door closed and cranked up to open, plan; (bottom, left and right) the garage's three-part frontage when closed

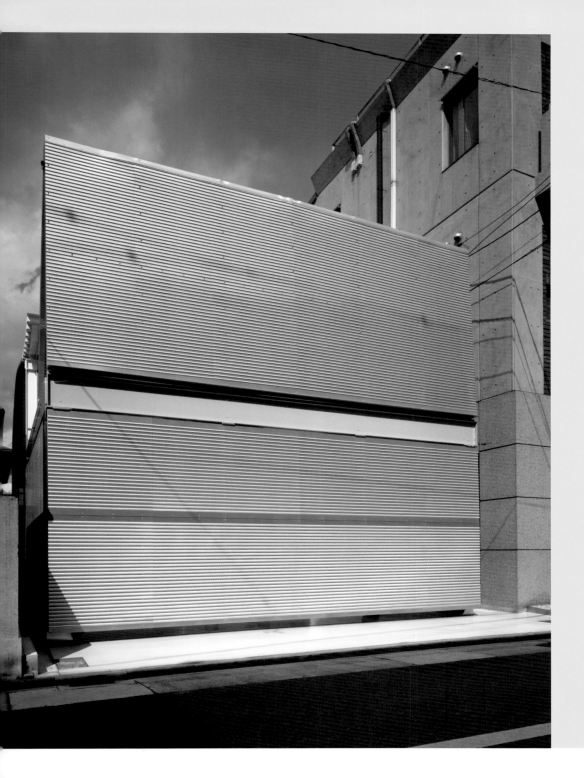

the street while screening the upper floor study area. Adjustability is also the formula behind the <u>Leaf Chapel</u> (2004), a wedding chapel in the green setting of Kobuchizawa, Yamanashi, with views of the southern Japanese Alps and Mount Fuji. The structure is made of two 'leaves' – one glass, one steel – with a hydraulic mechanism, which together form a mobile 'veil' that lifts silently at the end of the ceremony. A 6 millimetre steel sheet with 250 millimetre ribs, its fabric scrim, punctured by 4,700 holes each plugged by an acrylic lens, appears like a veil of lace. Light filtering through the lenses projects the veil's pattern onto the fabric inside, in shifting forms as the sun turns. When it is open, the veil could be a water plant blooming in the pond in front of the chapel; when closed, an analogy with a field of swaying flowers comes to mind. At night, it becomes a huge yet delicate lantern. Leaf Chapel rivals nature with KDa's typical delight in performance.

<u>Undercover Lab</u> (2001) uses the more typically architectural balancing act of the cantilever for its impact. It is a building tucked away in the back streets of Harajuku on a 12 metre x 12 metre site at the end of a 10 metre-long driveway; but KDa's design made a virtue of the lack of architectural context. 'The aesthetic comes from the strangeness of the site.' A black cantilevered structure hovers over the narrow entry like an anonymous shipping container hanging in the air. Its shape gives its clients – a fashion company – a press showroom with a catwalk and 20 metre-long hanger rail. A discreetly placed building, the cantilever reaches towards the street, allowing five cars to be parked on the site beneath its overhang. In a typical KDa scenographic sleight of hand, this enigmatic construction manages to command attention even though the main part of the building, including a studio and office, is set back 10 metres. To add to the strangeness, KDa use rather English-looking bricks on the end wall, while inside it is concrete with the formwork left on.

In common with the younger generation of Japanese architects, like Atelier BowWow, Atelier 1, Mikan Gumi, and, in the UK, FAT, KDa work on a deeply collaborative basis across a range of media. However, they are unique in developing construction hoardings as a form of architecture, and these works have become a leitmotif for them, generating many new commissions including housing. KDa's modus operandi is based on acute powers of cultural observation, which makes them well-suited to urban design in other contexts. Dytham says that their events programme offers an intravenous drip of inspiration, joking that 'without this machine, the energy disappears from our work'. Playspace or no playspace, the fact that KDa thrived in one of the worst recessions in the industrialized world says a lot about their attitude, which is not over-precious about design. With everything they do, 'there is a spirit, but not a style'.

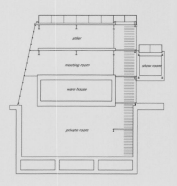

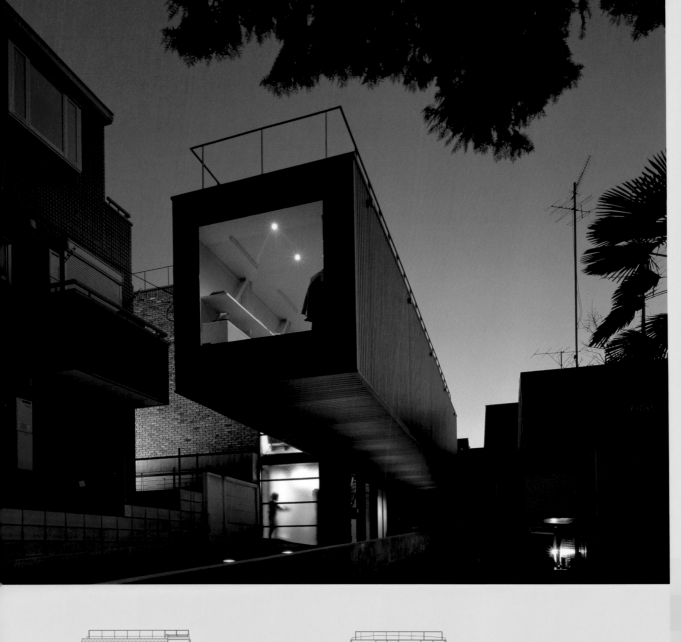

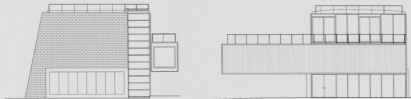

> (top) the cantilevered showroom reaches towards the main street; (bottom, left to right) section through building: front elevation, side elevation

muf

> <u>Hypocaust building</u>, St Albans, 2001-4; façade in glass fibre reinforced concrete and oyster shell aggregate, with a tilted steel mirrored soffit giving glimpsed views from outside and inside the building

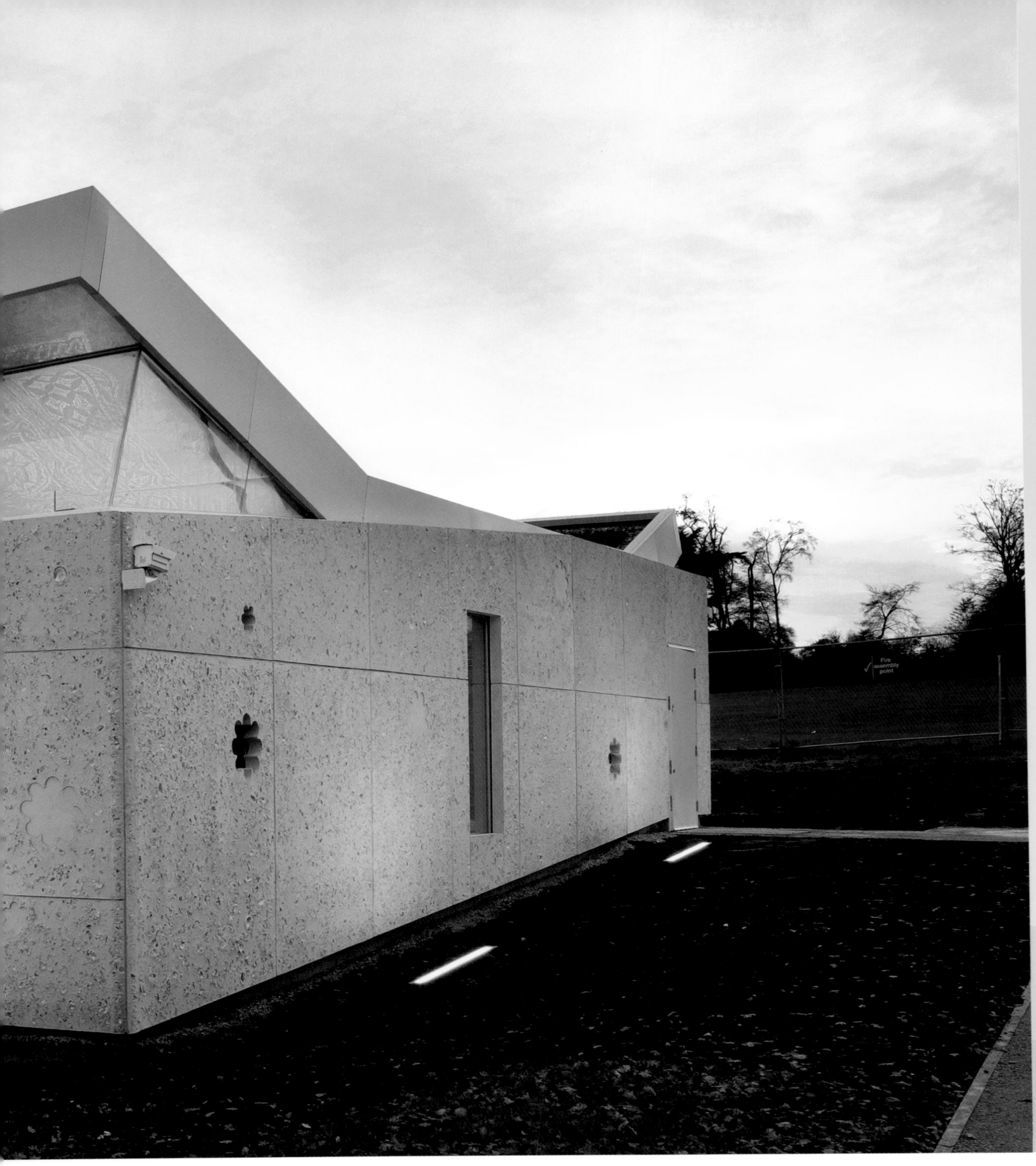
Fire
assembly
point

> <u>Hypocaust building</u>, St Albans, 2001-4; (top left) interior with viewing deck around the in-situ Roman mosaic; (bottom left) detail of the concrete and oyster shell aggregate wall with punched window openings; (right) the tilted mirror soffit at one side of the building

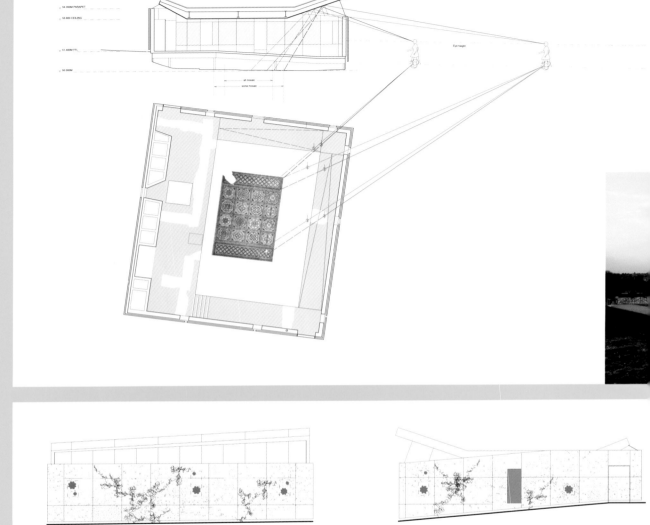

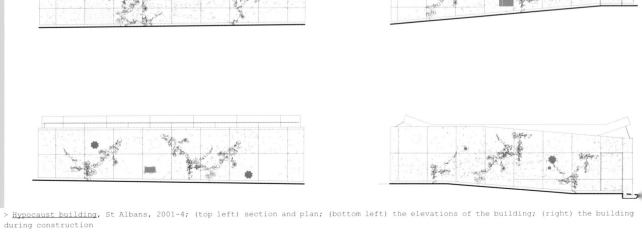

> <u>Hypocaust building</u>, St Albans, 2001-4; (top left) section and plan; (bottom left) the elevations of the building; (right) the building during construction

muf is a group of architects and artists that works with public bodies – borough councils, art and social trusts, often in the form of complex multi-agency structures – to maximize assets and advocate design across a broad range of urban design and strategies, public art, building and interior projects. muf is committed to revealing 'the interdependence between the built and the lived, between physical and social infrastructures'[1], questioning and re-evaluating the cultural identity of public space to make it more democratic, opening up the world of the normative, the official and the institutional so that imagined, unofficial outcomes for everyday lives can coexist with them.

Liza Fior, Katherine Clarke, Cathy Hawley, Ashley McCormick, Mark Lemanski, Vic Baine, Anastasia Saward and Indu Ramaswamy run muf collaboratively. They no longer teach so they live by the work produced by their studio, which was established by Fior, Clarke and architect Juliet Bidgood in 1994, and benefited from the collaboration of the late architect Katherine Vaughan Williams (Shonfield; 1954–2003) whose input gave lucid shape to their thinking. Modern Urban Fabric is what their provocative acronym stands for. It served them well early on in getting attention. By drawing on their hybrid identity as architects and artists, muf aim to produce innovative solutions that create better relationships between the social, spatial and economic infrastructures of the public realm. Their building projects mediate between content and context in a way that creates a dynamic, experiential relationship between interior and exterior, viewer and viewed. An early exhibition, 'Purity and Tolerance' (1995), held at the Architecture Foundation's home at the foot of The Economist Building in London, featuring a reflective white latex ceiling stretched across the gallery which expanded in the heat generated by people at the opening, took steps towards fulfilling these criteria, and made a powerful statement about architecture as immersion in an experience rather than as distanced objects.

To achieve their goals they deliberately widen the scope of the brief, pushing it into new formats, staging live events and video works as part of the process that unveils public desires, and making space for the coexistence of their social agendas. Many muf projects include the canvassing of local residents for their opinions prior to establishing a full set of priorities. Shared Ground (1998), a scheme of urban improvements – a new, wide pavement of in situ aggregate (local Thames shingle), furniture, signage and planting for Southwark Council – over a one-kilometre stretch of Southwark Street in London, was preceded by a public consultation documented on video: *100 Desires*. Made by Clarke, it coalesced the 'shared ground' of expectations and interests concerning the private and public domains of the street, and was intended to help shape the parameters of the design. Work included negotiations with property owners to invest in the longer term design quality of the public landscape of the street (pavements, street furniture, choice of building materials). One of the results was a shift from car to pedestrian identity, including tactile paving for the partially sighted.

Video in conjunction with urban projects has the capacity to 'turn bits of the city inside out and displace them'; it is a 'medium that makes space a parallel universe', says Clarke. A key project in which muf used video to demonstrate the interdependence between physical and social infrastructures was their SureStart on the Ocean project (2000), a government-funded scheme for the Ocean Estate in Stepney, east London. The glazed façade of their design for a playspace for the under-fours and their carers, which doubles up as a meeting room, is veiled from public view by texts in Bengali and English applied in gold and scarlet lettering. Artist Sue Ayrton's film *At Home*, depicting babies living on the estate in their domestic environments, was projected onto the façade during construction at night, a time of unofficial curfew for the women and small children who live on the estate. The intention of the project was to reverse the interior-based nature of the lives of occupants and take away the stigma associated with community provision. 'We're never working in a homogeneous situation,' says Fior. 'Our work is an attempt to create another reality.' Although the process involves a degree of utopia, they are 'quite awake to the limits', adds Fior.

Security, Mobility and Pleasure is an urban design framework that muf carried out for West Ham and Plaistow, east London, in 2001. It was funded by the New Deal for Communities (NDC), a central government programme of strategies which has the physical environment of deprived communities as one of its areas of focus. muf proposed designs for environmental improvements, but also practical plans for their maintenance and funding. They involved all sections of the community in their consultation before designing green links and open spaces, arguing successfully for greater investment in boundaries (e.g. lighting, planting, signage and pavement treatments) and two safe 'home zones' (residential areas where pedestrians take priority over cars). To overcome the tendency towards fragmentation in parts of the neighbourhood, they developed The Mounding over the Greenway crossing in 2003, a 6 metre-high step-free ramped route linking public spaces and existing and new amenities. This doubles up as an informal amphitheatre, with the seating facing a recreation ground. In the Rudolph Road home zone, the hard landscape is interrupted by soft hillocks allowing for a variety of uses.

> muf with artist Sue Ayrton, SureStart on the Ocean, a playspace on the Ocean estate, Stepney, east London, 2000; (top left and bottom left) doubling up as a meeting room, the playspace has texts in Bengali and English on its windows

> (right) Sue Ayrton's film *At Home* projected onto the façade of the building during construction

> <u>Garden</u>, Camden Arts Centre (remodelled by Tony Fretton), 2003-4; (top left) plan of site showing Centre and garden with the curved shape of paving area; (bottom left and right) paving includes overlaid elements indicating the forms of former houses on the site

Asking questions about a specific piece of land, such as what it is used for and what is of value, was central to <u>My Dream Today: Your Dream Tomorrow</u>, a community garden for Thurrock Council on the Broadway Estate at Tilbury (2003–4), developed with the local residents and a multi-agency team put together by the Council. The design is an undulating landscape of shared and discrete spaces for horse riding, including a formal dressage arena, play, with spaces for the under-fives, and relaxation, incorporating steps for meeting people. The edges of the garden are secured against joy-riding with barriers of planted gabions as a continuation of the landscape, rather than structures with a language of fenced enclosure. As with so many of their projects, muf staged an event involving the future users of the garden, this time a gymkhana with local children.

A common theme, then, in many of muf's works is the idea of shared ground for a variety of constituencies. Clarke agrees that their agenda includes 'a whole set of invisible relationships – it's not just about architecture. Our work is concerned with how power is brought to bear on the subject. Who does or doesn't have it, and how individuals can intervene. Who is excluded and who is integrated, and how to bring pleasure into this context. Place in the city is not a fixed issue, but fluid.'

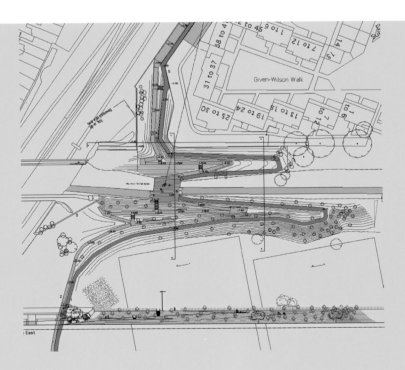

> <u>Security, Mobility and Pleasure</u>, urban framework for West Ham and Plaistow, east London, 2001-2; (top); proposals for environmental improvements included (middle) 'home zones' like <u>Tibbenham Square Walk</u>; and (bottom) <u>Mounding over the Greenway</u> crossing

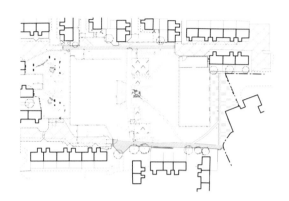

> <u>My Dream Today: Your Dream Tomorrow</u>, community garden, Broadway Estate, Tilbury, 2003-; (top left) site plan; (top middle, top right and bottom) landscape reconfigured to create areas for horse riding, play and relaxation

Since the privatization of public space in the Eighties and Nineties, we have seen the 'culturalization' or gentrification of space, muf argue. Their community-based work tries to acknowledge and channel the tensions existing 'between people and the multiple and contested understanding of place in cities' into the creation of new possibilities.

Even when working on a modest scale muf maintain their commitment to redefining the use for a space. They designed the <u>garden at the Camden Arts Centre</u>, which was remodelled in 2003 by architect Tony Fretton. Fretton's design opened up the space at ground level, and the garden, formerly a Second World War bomb site, had a wild quality that muf wanted to retain. They incorporated the idea of a terrace laid out like the footprint of the Victorian houses that used to be there. Three different domestic spaces were marked out, bringing the local historical context to the surface.

At Port Patrick in Dumfries and Galloway, muf's <u>Beach at the End of the Line </u>(2002–3) made the derelict edge of the harbour into a space for play and relaxation. The natural order of the cliffs, rocks and sea was intersected by a distorted grid laid out in grass, paving and play equipment in order, says Fior, to 'reveal the give and take between natural forces and the imposed order of human inhabitants'. Etched into the back of a 30 metre-long bench edging the south-facing cliff, a timeline traces the personal, local and national history of the site. History and its context was a theme of the <u>Hypocaust building</u> at St

'Place in the city is not a fixed issue, but fluid… Our work is concerned with how power is brought to bear on the subject. Who does or doesn't have it, and how individuals can intervene. Who is excluded and who is integrated, and how to bring pleasure into this context.'

> <u>Shared Ground</u>, a pilot scheme of urban improvements along a one kilometre stretch of street for Southwark, south London, 1997; (top) new paving surfaces, benches and signage

Albans (1999–2004), a pavilion set in a park showcasing a Roman mosaic and hypocaust above the excavated Roman city of Verulamium. One of their first new-build projects, it exemplifies muf's capacity for incorporating innovative environmentally sound structural solutions using low technology within sensitive contexts. The single-storey 14.6 metre x 13 metre steel frame building, designed with structural engineers Atelier 1, has a cranked up roof creating a glazed clerestory strip internally mirrored on the soffit to reflect glimpses of the surroundings, and a floor stained like marble cake to show the position of the Roman walls. The façade is made of glass-reinforced concrete cladding, 30 millimetres thick, with an aggregate of crushed wild oyster shells that – not unlike Japanese architect Tadao Ando and his concrete – muf spent time experimenting with. It gives a pearlescent sheen, and with its rosette-shaped window openings punctuating the sides, the building is very responsive to the landscape. With the mirroring device, and the frieze-like exterior which refers to Roman mosaic decoration, the building resembles a jewellery box. The structure's intentionally thin cladding and micro-piles minimize disturbance to the ground. Grassing the roof further gives the impression that the structure has been lifted out of the ground, although unlike a historic artefact its identity is that of a contemporary meeting place.

Contemporary urban environments demand that architects think imaginatively beyond the confines of plastic form. muf expand the traditional boundaries of the architectural profession through interventions that challenge the underinvested, neglected and divisive nature of public space. By way of extensive public consultation, they strive to make an environment that can be seen by the community to reflect a wider sense of ownership; and by revealing things that usually remain hidden or marginalized, they achieve robustness in form and function and contribute a new sense of security and of pleasure. All of their public projects are in this sense redemptive and provoke a positive response to their rhetorical question: 'If the sense of who we are is in part dependent on where we are, then does being in a place, however transitory, generate a sense of ownership of that place, however momentary?'

1 'This is what we do – a muf manual', Ellipsis, London, 2001.

> 'Purity and Tolerance', exhibition at the Architecture Foundation, St James's, central London, 1995; the exhibition featured a white latex ceiling

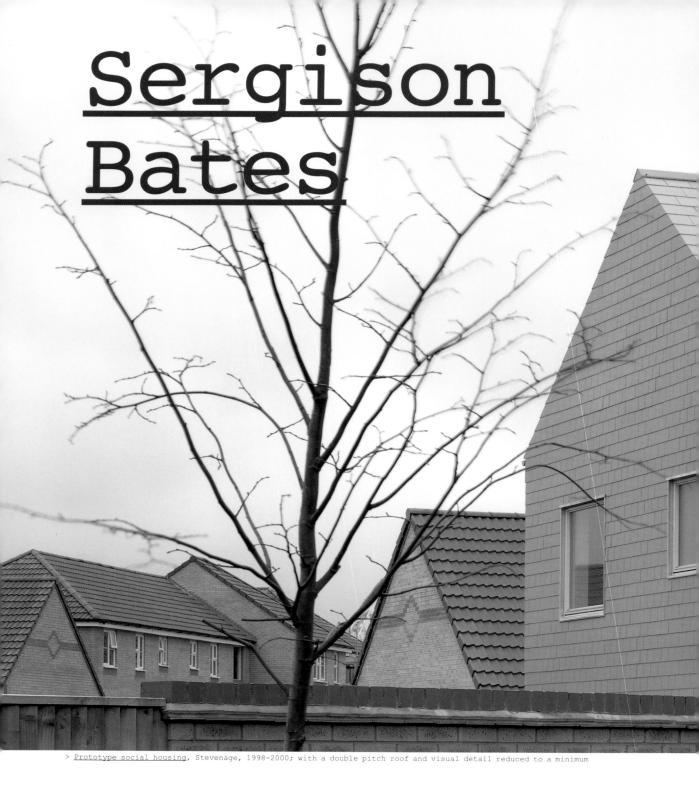

Sergison
Bates

> <u>Prototype social housing</u>, Stevenage, 1998-2000; with a double pitch roof and visual detail reduced to a minimum

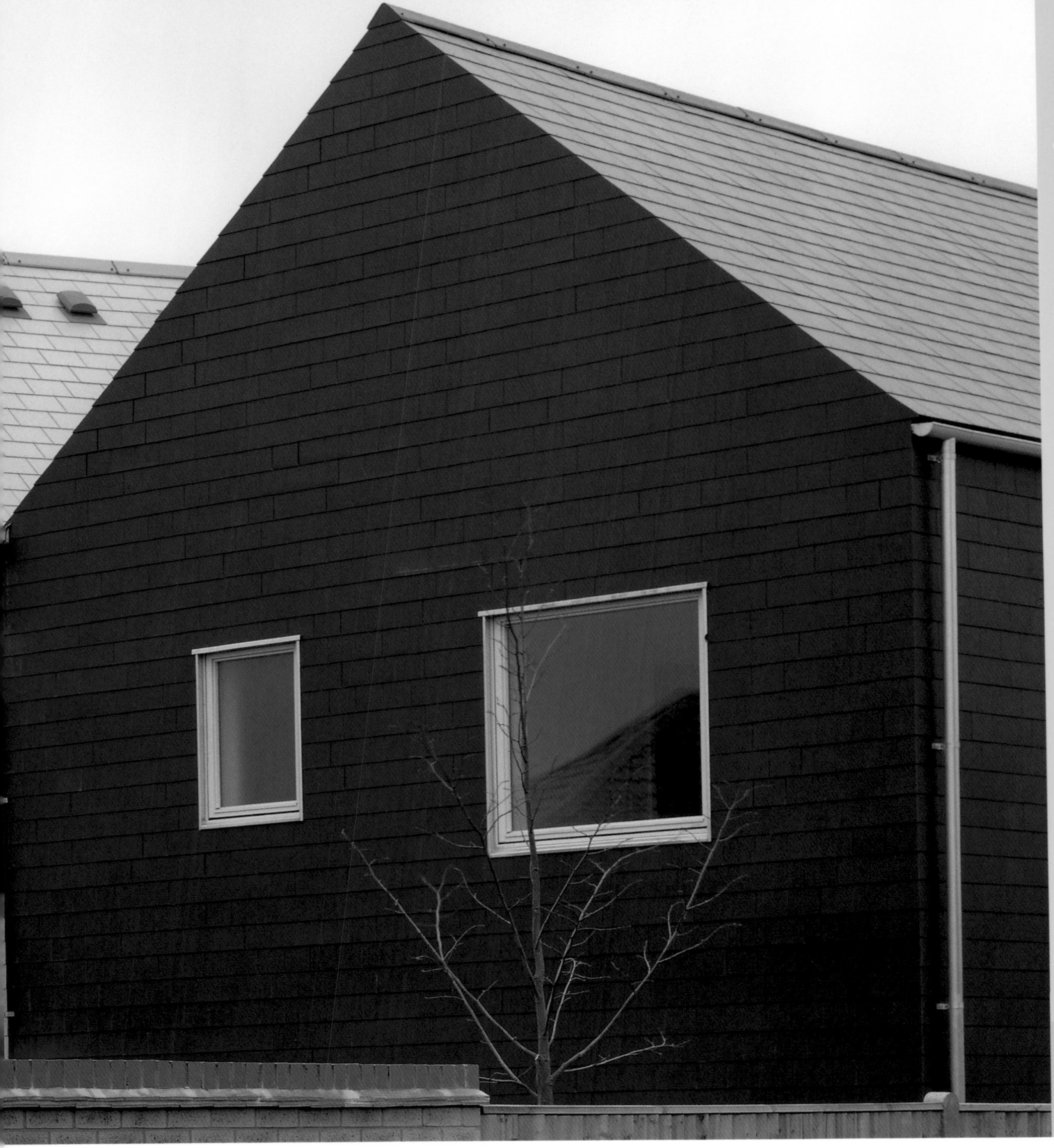

Sergison Bates are spurred on by a number of concerns that certain of their luminary elders, who prefer a promiscuity in expressiveness informed by a rich palette of materials, simply cannot relate to. Their abiding strengths lie in their strategic use of a reductive language of materials and construction techniques in projects predominantly in the public sector, such as housing and schools. The firm's engagement with a larger scale of major urban framework design reinforces its position in the contemporary climate of committed urban regeneration in the UK.

Working at many different scales, Sergison Bates's scrupulously detailed study of the everyday has led them to the 'recognition that our environment is made up of very small pieces and that by consciously effecting change at an incidental scale, a much greater impact is felt'. This analysis was documented in two papers that appear in their book, *Papers*, self-published in 2001, Bates's 'A way to work' and Sergison's 'A view of the way things are', originally written in 1996. The first piece 'looked in detail at the way cities are made and at the associative qualities of an urban condition', explains Sergison. The second discussed the fact that city centres are the result of ever-changing pieces of infrastructure, and are less capable of absorbing large-scale change than their peripheries'.

They 'seek an authenticity in construction where the nature and intensity of material is expressed directly and with rigour'. However, rather than being dogmatic about how a structural solution can be achieved, they deliberately conceptualize construction, lending it the means to express the presence of a space. What matters to them is the experience created by the use of a particular wood or type of masonry, quite subliminally in some cases. This is far from the classic UK high-tech approach that can rely on the fetishistic power of details for its appearance of technical virtuosity. Sergison Bates prefer to use single materials, such as polycarbonate panel as cladding, to simplify the architectural form and bring about 'an ambiguity between its principal components, like the merging of the wall with the roof and ground'. Construction is layered and its components act as mediators between the fabric of the building and the human activity that goes on inside it. Layering is also a feature of *Papers*, which has five covers made of art paper, each a different colour, ranging from earth to grey.

They talk of combining looseness and precision, rationality and emotion to achieve hybrid solutions. 'We need to be obsessed with construction in order to be loose about it, and to make work that engages with what is there – with the real and the ordinary,' say Bates and Sergison. Accordingly they work from the specific and universal conditions they observe, aware that composition and spatial relationships can be

manipulated to heighten ambiguity and also to add humour. Minimalism and Pop Art, for instance Bruce Nauman's *Dream Passage* (1983), and the socio-realist work of the photographer Tony Ray-Jones, are important influences, particularly in the way that they encourage new ways of seeing the commonplace.

Sergison Bates have long since been fascinated by dwelling habits. They talk of considering the discreet qualities found in habitation that are 'ephemeral, in constant flux, individual and human'; but they do not intend to load their design with symbolic ornamentation in homage of these qualities. Instead, they engage in association, mediating idea and place by giving attention to the ordinary, even mundane, elements of built form that are 'touched, handled and brushed against' every day, for instance, internal linings, architraves, skirtings and shutters. All of these architectural details are regarded as opportunities to create spatial presence. So one side of an architrave might be widened to accommodate a light switch, while a skirting board is extended upwards to make a dado lining; in each case the usual consistency of application is disrupted in favour of a specific expression and to facilitate ease of use.

The influence of the work of Alison and Peter Smithson, and their resounding message of a new reinterpretation of orthodox modernism, was an early 'call to order' for the practice, initially derived from the duo's copious writings. As intellectually motivated architects able to combine writing and building, the Smithsons were the consummate role models for Sergison Bates. They are also inspired by the work of the Portuguese architect Alvaro Siza, identifying with his sense of context, which aims to reveal rather than transform meaning. There is a kinship between their

> Prototype social housing, Stevenage, 1998-2000; front façade with adjacent front doors; (top right) construction drawing

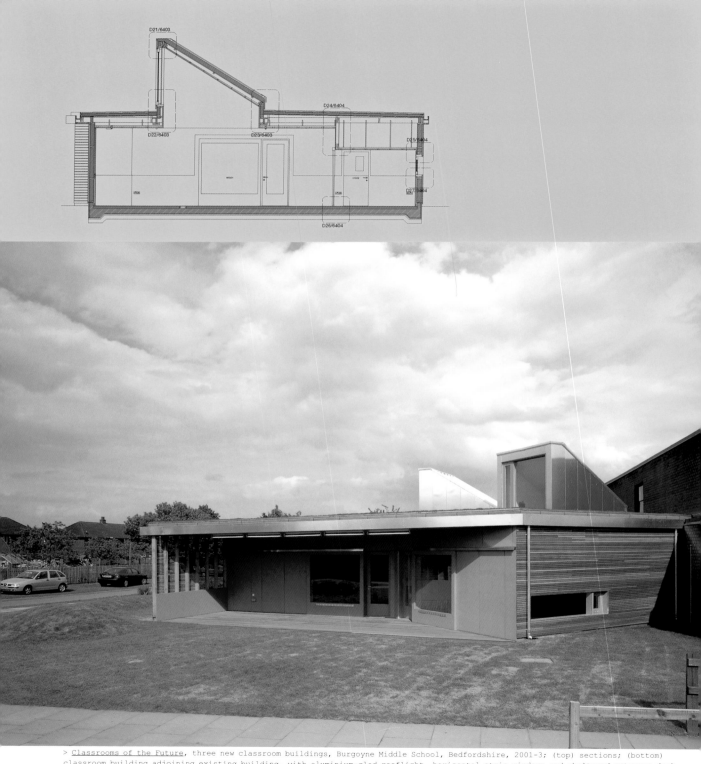

> <u>Classrooms of the Future</u>, three new classroom buildings, Burgoyne Middle School, Bedfordshire, 2001-3; (top) sections; (bottom) classroom building adjoining existing building, with aluminium-clad rooflight, horizontal strip windows and sheltered entrance deck

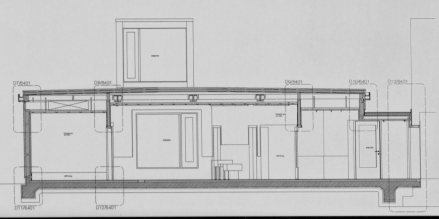

> <u>Maple Tree Lower School</u>, a nursery school, Bedfordshire, 2001-3 (above)

> <u>Sandy Upper School</u>, Bedfordshire, 2001-3; (top, from left to right) classroom interior, timber-clad façade with horizontal strip windows, sheltered entrance; <u>Burgoyne Middle School</u>, Bedfordshire, 2001-3; (bottom) timber rainscreen clad wall

attitude to construction and Siza's formal approach to buildings, as seen, for example, in his Galicia museum in Santiago de Compostela, Spain (1988–93), or Quinta da Malagueira low-cost housing in Evora, Portugal (1977), for SAAL, the national housing association, in which all non-essentials are removed.

There is a quiet subversion, but most noticeably a consistency, running through all the architects' projects. A concern to use the minimum number of materials and to use a reductive architectural language is prevalent. Timber as a basis of structure is widespread. For instance, Triboard and Pyroc feature in recently built public and private sector schemes in Wandsworth (housing and offices) and Tilbury (housing, see below). Detail throughout is suppressed into defined moments, not unlike Peter Zumthor's design for the baths at Vals, where underneath the surface a lot is going on to achieve simplicity.

Sergison Bates's schemes also work strongly with the idea of the horizontal section and a looseness of plan. For example, on quite a complex site like Wandsworth (see p. 218), the housing aligns itself to the faceted geometries of the building. When they were commissioned by Bedfordshire County Council as part of the £13 million Department for Education and Skills' 'Classrooms of the Future' scheme to design three new school buildings (2001–3) – <u>Maple Tree Lower</u>, <u>Burgoyne Middle</u> and <u>Sandy Upper</u> (infant, junior and secondary schools respectively) – they were faced with a very complex site in terms of orientation. As a result, the plan was arranged to achieve an asymmetrical form. The scheme afforded Sergison Bates considerable freedom in spatial organization: the brief was not fully formulated at the outset, and the practice worked closely with the schools' headteachers on its development. Encouraged by them to make a circular classroom, the three spaces each ended up as hexagons. The architects tried to strike a balance between the fact that it was intended as a pilot project for a prototype and the specific needs of each school by developing a number of elements that were repeatable. In plan, each of the three school buildings consists of a central, top-lit room with ancillary spaces and a covered entrance, timber-framed walls, timber rainscreen cladding and a mix of horizontal windows and floor-to-ceiling sliding doors with brightly coloured frames.

Earlier work by the practice shows that they prefer individual rather than replicated solutions. With their three 'Classrooms of the Future', for which repeatable solutions that are also sustainable were desirable, they have created a formal language of architecture and typology that is adaptable and identifiable rather than standardized. Pursuing their personal need for authenticity and legibility in construction, the floor

'We need to be obsessed with construction in order to be loose about it, and to make work that engages with what is there — the real and the ordinary.'

> <u>Assisted self-build housing</u>, Tilbury, Essex, 2001-2; (above) west façade, with veranda, of apartment building and raised boardwalk

decking is also used as a rainscreen; junctions are treated in different ways, and soffits are left partly unpainted. The three new school buildings also reflect the architects' interest in conceptualizing construction through the treatment of cladding as a wrapping; and colour is used in a painterly way to create individually identifiable spaces.

The architects' assisted <u>self-build housing at Tilbury</u>, Essex (2001–2), within the Thames Gateway, is just as direct: there is nothing about the construction that is not fulfilling a function, yet the design achieves a strong overall presence. Located in the run-down and troubled 1960s' Broadway housing estate, it was the initial part of a regeneration programme. Replacing a patch of disused open ground at the edge of the site, it consists of an apartment building raised off the ground on feet with a landscaped courtyard. The intention was to develop affordable housing through a building and apartment typology that would appeal to young people and not replicate the terrace typology predominant in the area. The east façade has a formal frontage, while the west is more informal, with a timber verandah and overhanging roof looking onto a courtyard. The architects compare this scheme to the condominiums often found in social housing on the west coast of the USA. Choosing self-build, and engaging relatively untutored young locals to construct the project – not a common way to realize housing – certainly challenged the normative processes of construction, the identity of the context, and

> (top) plan; (bottom) view of first-floor veranda

gave them an added impetus to source original facing materials designed to exploit and highlight the simplicity of frame construction.

Sergison Bates's scheme for <u>housing, studios and offices in Wandsworth</u>, London (1999–2003), involved refurbishing, extending and adding density to an existing paint factory building. Wandsworth Workshops was built in the 1930s and stands alongside the bedraggled beds of the River Wandle, opposite a supermarket and close to the town centre. The architects added a timber-framed single-storey extension to the existing roof. Supported on a steel transfer structure, the new building includes eleven apartments, some live/work units, a medical centre and a café, and creates a continuous, mat-like structure on the gently faceted form of the existing structure. The apartments are reached via timber-decked covered walkways with a consistent grain of pine; each one has an open-air courtyard, pre-galvanized aluminium sheeting on the openings, canopies and mail boxes as well as Douglas fir doors and window frames. The hermetic nature of the dwellings is played off against the communal atmosphere of the walkways.

All the joinery is at 90 degrees, with no mitred elements. Each apartment has a simple room arrangement around a central hall, with living rooms and bedrooms opening onto covered balconies. At the southern end of the site is a new apartment building. The concrete flat slab and column structure is faceted in plan: it follows the boundary of the site and continues the undulating form of the existing workshop buildings.

The architects' concern with what they call 'reduced form-making, based on the familiar images of buildings', is evident in their design for a <u>public house</u> in Walsall in the West Midlands (1998) in collaboration with Caruso St John and alongside the Walsall Art Gallery by Caruso St John. Once again they use linings and claddings to lend the building expression through their layering, material, volume, and, above all, associative power. The façades of the building are clad in facing materials which balance colour with texture and reinforce the volume of the whole rather than the detail of each part. Its shed-like form gives it a similar appearance to neighbouring warehouses and superstores. The inclusion of an outsized enclosing roof, adjusted in line with the footprint of the site, creates a fairly unusual set of proportions conveying its public identity without recourse to historical precedents.

The commission for a <u>prototype house</u> for the William Sutton Trust, built in Stevenage (1998–2000), was an opportunity for the architects to speculate on the image of the ubiquitous 'semi'. Reinforcing the form by reducing joins and overlaps between materials and surfaces to a minimum, they make the roof and wall cladding continuous and freely

> <u>Housing, studios and offices</u>, Wandsworth, south London, 1999-2003; (left) exterior of the former paint factory showing the new single storey of apartments on the top floor; (top right) street elevation; (bottom right) the timber-decked and walled apartment walkways

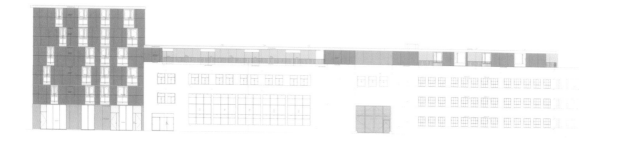

arrange the windows to allow walls and roof to appear part of a seamless flow. Rather in the manner of the strategy for the public house in Walsall, in which the whole volume is reinforced instead of individual details, this tactic applies a language of protection, a metaphorical stance that promotes the 'dwelling' experience of a house.

Like many of their peers, the architects are experiencing a shift in the kind of work being taken on, moving on to a number of medium-scale public and cultural projects. In 2004 they won two commissions in Belgium as a result of the 'Open Oproep' (open call) procurement process led by the Vlaams Bouwmeester, the Flemish Government Architect. One is a dramatic arts and audio-visual department for the Hoger School (University), requiring the conversion of a former chocolate factory in Brussels; the other is a library at Blankenberge on the Flemish coast, to be created by adapting and expanding an old school building.

The architects' involvement with masterplanning has taken them on 'a huge learning curve'. In Switzerland, where the duo are visiting professors at ETH, the Swiss Federal Institute of Technology, in Zurich, they have found that there is wide acceptance that architects should be involved in masterplanning. However, when it comes to a wider acceptance of masterplanning as part of architecture back at home, 'architects in the UK haven't yet fully found the way to do this, creating the instruments to make the decisions', says Bates. Much, he feels, hangs upon the inclination of the particular political infrastructure presiding over a project. However, Sergison Bates's strategy and framework plan for Woolwich, south London, in collaboration with East was positively received. It was 'a blueprint for accelerated regeneration, new housing and jobs and major investment by the public and private sector', as Bates says, and led on to the commission to masterplan the riverside Woolwich Royal Arsenal site (2003), which is destined to be predominantly residential with commercial and leisure facilities.

An early project from 1997 demonstrates that Sergison Bates's conceptual approach to social mediation can be extended to a larger scale of complexity. They were asked to consult on the future contextual framework of the Sittingbourne Settlements in Kent. Working with East again, they analyzed the grain of the landscape and traced the land's history, in particular the way it had become enclosed, back to the time of the Enclosure Acts and other changes in agriculture 200 years ago. They observed as they did so that 'pattern making in the English landscape seems very in tune with national characteristics', says Sergison. 'A sense of negotiation and systems that are capable of absorbing variations is present.' As a result of this research, the architects introduced an enabling infrastructure, a loose matrix of organizing strips

> Sergison Bates with Caruso St John, public house, Walsall, West Midlands, 1997-98; (bottom left) interior with graphics by Jane Chipchase; (bottom middle) next to Caruso St John's New Art Gallery, the shed-like form of the pub's roof

that can be topographically arranged to assist development on earth bunds (causeways) half a storey high which delineated, protected and serviced land through drainage. The bunds were intended to become what they call 'soft integrators: fingers of green', easing the natural demands of the site. Rather than proposing a uniform layout for the siting of 550 houses required for the site, their system envisaged the development of an 'edge town' that would make nature easily accessible from individual houses.

In their Sittingbourne Settlements scheme, the duo were proposing to extend the limits of an existing and well-established suburban condition. They have also written of their more general interest in breaking with 'the myth of the vernacular'. Their housing design output to date offers a series of specific design alternatives that are 'closer representations of the vernacular than the current reliance on replicating the appearance of the past'. More significantly, their agenda extends to the advocacy of 'shattering the image of suburbia to make way for the real demands of sustainability, cultural engagement and social opportunity' which they remain singularly and idiosyncratically true to.

> <u>Hoger School</u>, Brussels, 2004; (top) model of the dramatic arts and audio-visual department;
Sergison Bates with East: model of <u>Sittingbourne Settlements</u> conceptual framework, 1997 (right)

S333

> <u>Schots 1 and 2</u>, CiBoGa Terrain, Groningen, the Netherlands, 1997-2003; volumetric landscape: Schots 1 seen from sloped court of Schots 2

> <u>Schots 1 and 2</u>, CiBoGa Terrain, Groningen, the Netherlands, 1997-2003; (left) sloped landscape and terraces of Schots 2

> (right) first floor interior court of Schots 1

> <u>Schots 1 and 2</u>, CiBoGa Terrain, Groningen, the Netherlands, 1997-2003; (left) shopping street between Schots 1 and 2; (middle) vertical green landscape wall; (far right) first five floor plans

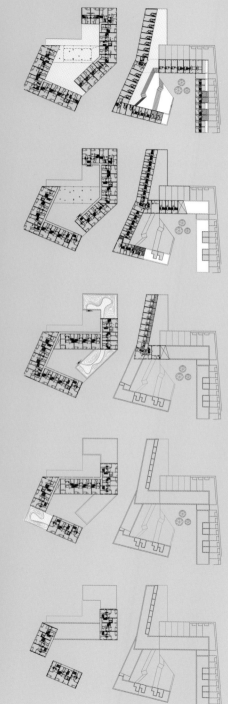

'The multi-layering of activities and landscape offer an alternative to the interiorized, hermetic world of the traditional urban block.'

In its commitment to speculation about urban processes and to building, S333 is one of the most internationally active architectural practices among a small number in Europe that are predominantly responsible for a slow paradigm shift in architecture towards a new way of reading urban reality. A multidisciplinary studio of architects and urbanists, led by Dominic Papa, Jonathan Woodroffe, Chris Moller and Burton Hamfelt, S333 generates operating strategies that draw on architecture, landscape and urbanism, infrastructural design and socio-economics. Current commissions are located as far apart as Singapore and Bergen, Norway. Determined to 'rediscover architecture within contemporary cultural conditions', as Papa puts it, rather than being over concerned with representing reality through physical form, S333's interest 'in manipulating programme to create a sense of place is driven by social concerns, and treats form as a verb rather than a noun', says Woodroffe.

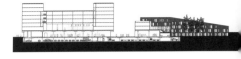

The practice was formed in London as a strategic think-tank in 1990, at the height of the recession, out of a shared wish to generate debate about contemporary urbanism in Europe. Operating in the early days by organizing workshops, publications and competitions, S333 has since then substantially bridged the gap between architecture and urban design through its multi-scalar activities. Right at the outset, in 1991, it beat 600 entrants to win an international competition for the revitalization of the 27 hectare city centre of Samarkand in Uzbekistan. Bordered by four distinctly varied urban conditions, Samarkand offered itself as an experiment in alternative masterplanning techniques. 'Instead of specifying zones, the plan simply set up a system of routes through the site, linking back to the surrounding fabric,' says Moller. 'Between the empty spaces of the future city centre, the site was free to be developed following market requirements, and rather than showing one urban scenario, we suggested many.' However, before the mayor's plans could be realized, the Soviet Union collapsed, and the project was scrapped.

A more robust architectural scene awaited them in the Netherlands, where the practice decamped in 1994 after winning the Europan 3 international housing competition for Groningen's Circus site. The exposure aroused by this project led more recently to commissions for medium density housing in Beaumont Quarter, Auckland, New Zealand (completed in 2004), Oldham, Manchester (urban plan, 2004) and for mixed-use social housing by the Toynbee Housing Association on the Tarling Estate at Shadwell in east London (the competition was won in 2000 in collaboration with architects Stock Woolstencroft). Tarling resulted from a competition to transform a post-Second World War estate with poorly defined public spaces into an urban setting: the

> Schots 1 and 2, CiBoGa Terrain, Groningen, the Netherlands, 1997-2003; (from top) two cross-sections through shopping street, long section through Schots 1, long section through Schots 2

> S333 in association with Studio of Pacific Architecture: <u>Beaumont Quarter</u>, inner city housing, Auckland, New Zealand, 2001-5; (top) view from 'Leap Frogs' to 'ZigZags', two of the housing types; (bottom, left to right) 'Cliff Hanger', 'Leap Frog', 'Saddle Bag' and 'ZigZag'

> <u>Bloembollenhof Vijfhuizen</u>, Vijfhuizen, the Netherlands, 1998-2003 (phase 2, 2005); housing type 2: 3 in 1, three-bedroom house

challenge that S333 took on was to provide spatial diversity, reinventing terraced housing.

S333 frequently finds itself labelled 'Dutch', but now that the public sector bodies behind Thames Gateway, a major urban regeneration project in east London, have given Dutch architects and planners West 8 and Maxwan a key masterplanning role, S333 is in a good position to take advantage of this fluidity in intellectual trading based around the regeneration of place. Their strategy is a tactically productive one that plays on political and cultural exchange across national boundaries.

Another of S333's early commissions was the 1995 project for the city of Zaanstad in the Netherlands, an urban development study for a 20-hectare site around Zaandam railway station. As part of their plan, S333 proposed to transform a 4-hectare waste dump into a 'Dutch Mountain', a recreational park incorporating land art in a meshwork of paths and multi-coloured, angled gardens. The park gave S333 the ideal opportunity to create a variety of conditions for open public space, from calm and sheltered to rugged and windy. 'It highlights the challenges inherent in designing a living organism that is in a continual state of change. Whether it is soil settlement, weather conditions or planting cycles, design concepts have to accommodate this flux,' explains Hamfelt.

CiBoGa Terrain in Groningen, S333's 1994 winning scheme for Europan 3, embodies a modus operandi that as in so many of their projects uses analysis of the site as the generator of ideas. Groningen's local authorities were well known for inviting architects such as Daniel Libeskind, Zaha Hadid and Rem Koolhaas to build in the city, but had failed to find a new way of perceiving this particular site. The 14 hectare zone of CiBoGa is in the north-eastern former industrial area of the city, which follows the curve of the original medieval walls. Once the site of a circus, freight storage and gas works, it was a nebulous area which the city council at first hoped to capitalize on by creating an edge condition with offices. Later, once the national government agreed to provide €12 million to depollute the area, it came to see CiBoGa as a potential residential area. From the 1970s onwards, alongside an interest in masterplans, the compact city plan increasingly came back into favour in the Netherlands as well as the UK. In their design for CiBoGa, the S333 architects were able to combine compactness while triggering an ecological rebirth of the whole area, creating a reborn edge city that previously would doubtless have been dismissed.

The competition, entitled 'At Home in the City – Urbanizing Residential Neighbourhoods', requested proposals for the design of a new living environment, specifying that the architects should 'rethink the

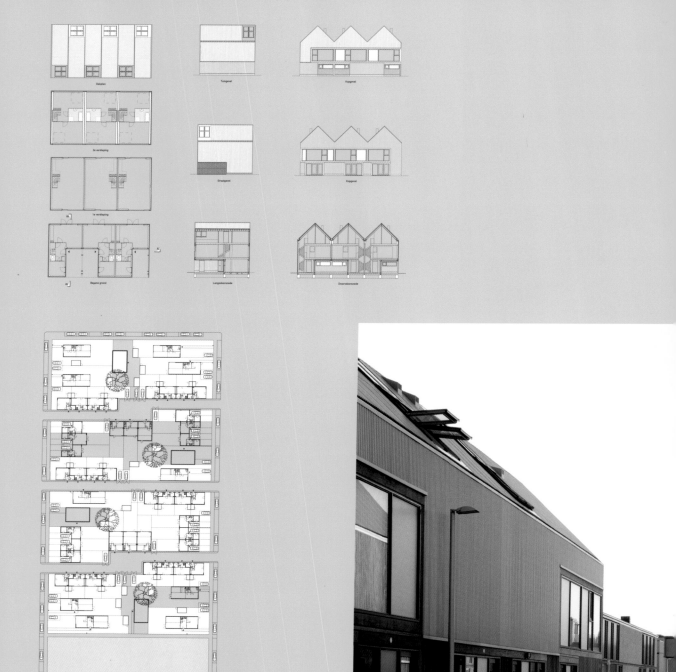

> <u>Bloembollenhof Vijfhuizen</u>, Vijfhuizen, the Netherlands, 1998-2003 (phase 2, 2005); (top left) housing type 2; (bottom left) site plan;
(top right) view down one of the new lanes; (bottom right) view from interior through first-floor living room

relationship between the city's private and public spaces and the spatial scaling from domestic intimacy to urban collectivity'. S333 responded to the fact that the developers wanted a high density of residential units, while the city wanted to establish an ecological corridor through the site to connect the park to the west and the canal to the east. In response to these conflicting demands, S333 set about creating what Papa calls 'a three-dimensional overlapping of programme and landscape elements'.

During the developmental stages, the city's department of urban planning expanded the remit, asking S333 to draw up a masterplan for the entire CiBoGa site, to include 1,000 housing units, 1,000 parking spaces and 30,000 square metres of mixed use and recreational areas. In response, S333 undertook intensive studies, forums and typological research, working with other architects to explore contemporary living and working patterns, issues of time-share, security and privacy. On-site workshops were run with Foreign Office Architects, Professor John Frazer and architects Battle McCarthy, and members of the Architectural Association's Housing and Urbanism Unit mapped movement and spatial links. Research projects by environmental engineers, and workshops with developers and local business groups, explored the potential conflicts of the new commercial programmes and leisure-based facilities on the adjacent urban fabric. Working with the city's ecologists, and with landscape architects, S333 also examined how initiatives in ecological sustainability could direct the development of a critical mass of housing.

It is likely that no other Europan win has resulted in such an intensely prolonged and public-involving form of scrutiny. Focused on the theme of social change – in this case flexibility in living patterns – the project centred on the fact that 'urban dwellers, in establishing new parameters for the use of public and private space, are promoting spatial usage that is more time-based, aligned to individual work/living patterns, mobility and their own personal choice', explains Papa. CiBoGa is intended to help break with the time-honoured tradition in the West of leaving the city for the suburbs and countryside for more living space.

S333 was also commissioned to design the first two urban blocks as *schotsen* (icebergs), described by Papa as 'a compact building volume eroded by views and "desire lines" that negotiate between the public and private realms'. With three levels oriented in different directions to take advantage of the sun, the composition was clearly defined by movement flows, sight-lines and the wish for oblique open public spaces rather than the kind of geometric restraint that working in a historic centre would have imposed. Shops and housing entrances are all at ground level, and houses and apartments are in U- and L-shaped blocks oriented at the middle level around a courtyard, with private roof terraces and gardens on top. 'Unlike the tradition in Britain of architecture focusing on itself, Schots 1 and 2 do not form an isolated object but rather respond to their surroundings,' Papa explains. It is not a self-contained, isolated suburb or edge condition, but a new hybrid type of living environment in an area with very limited housing provision. The housing and shops have density, but they do not prevent openness and high-quality public and collective space, so that the site acts as a link between the park to the west and the canal area to the east. A series of galvanized steel steps with gravelled tray surfaces (*taluds* in Dutch) lead up to three large terraces that provide more intimate areas.

While the far rarer incursion into mixed use in the UK so often gets developers and local councils nervous about aesthetics and siting, the *schotsen* (completed in the summer of 2003) not only innovatively mix housing and retail but also incorporate a range of terrace houses, courtyard blocks and apartment towers. The scheme represents an important architectural response to increasingly shifting and fragmenting patterns of living in the city: residents can move between the rented dwellings as their aspirations, family size and finances change.

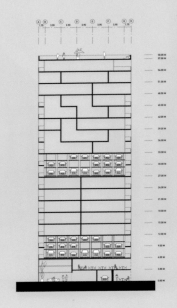

Each *schots* is overlaid by a surface landscape interweaving with the architecture: large areas of ivy, patios, flat-glazed roof gardens, ramped surfaces, courtyards and playgrounds lend variety and promote biodiversity. 'The multi-layering of activities and landscape offer an alternative to the interiorized and hermetic world of the traditional urban block,' explains Papa. 'Context, nature and urban ecology re-position themselves here as generating forces in the re-evaluation of the role of housing within cities.' Cars are banned from the site (only fifty per cent of the housing units may have a parking space on the perimeter, and public transport has been boosted), pedestrian routes link the park and the canal, integrating the scheme within the overall urban landscape.

As a result of the team's research into housing typologies, energy alternatives and ecological issues, the CiBoGa scheme won recognition as a national pilot scheme for sustainable urban renewal. While in the UK the trend is to use marketing imagery to sell shell and core space, in Groningen the collaborative ethos established by the city council, development consortium client and S333 brought about an innovative design approach in which far more emphasis was placed on the project's organization and strategic development, delaying emphasis on the final aesthetic form.

In 1988 the Dutch government launched VINEX, a much vaunted policy paper on housing in the context of regional planning, with a rota of new sites assigned for up to one million dwellings to be built by 2005.

> <u>La Ville Forêt</u>, 1,700 housing units and 50,000 square-metre mixed-use community, Grenoble, France, 2000–; (top and bottom left) sections; (top right) visualization from mid-level parking system and terrace pool; (bottom right) diagram of typological variations

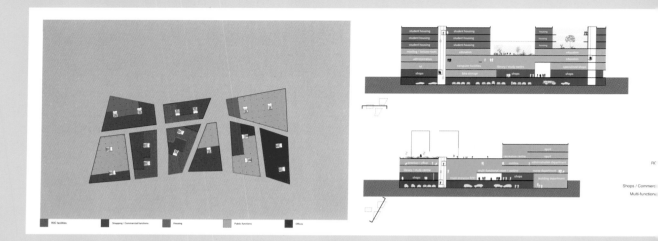

> <u>ROCvA CAN</u> (Regional Opleidings Centrum Amsterdam Noord), urban study for a 30,000-square-metre community college, Amsterdam, the Netherlands, 2002; (top left) integration of community college within urban plan; (top right) multi-functional sections

Developments were largely determined by competition, with a policy of including quotas of young practices on shortlists; in short, there was a tried and tested mentoring system which the UK lacked. S333 found in the Netherlands fertile pre-conditions for applying their methodology. Their competition win for the village of Vijfhuizen, also in the Netherlands, gave them the chance to go further in answering a vital question that applies to all VINEX developments: How do you avoid the creation of a monoculture, and open up the possibilities for complexity? The housing programme at the 1.2 hectare site of Vijfhuizen, near Schiphol Airport (1998–2002), adds 700 new dwellings to the village. Its design is based on the premise that the expansion of communities does not have to lead to sprawl: the suburb can be reinvented.

S333's strategy for Vijfhuizen created 'a regular irregularity' through the redistribution of collective space, introducing a higher than usual diversity of housing types; for example, the double-fronted house type is given work/live spaces with an alternative front, side and back door access, as well as varied garden orientation. The architects created 'plug-ins', roof extensions or additional ground floor rooms so people could customize their houses. Land use has been considered carefully, with lanes through the site and the redistribution of public space; new short cuts and parking positions introduced; and areas for expansion, leasing and other services allowed for. 'We re-configured the site as an active field, a system with order, rules and limitations from which the arrangement of the housing could ultimately emerge,' says Hamfelt.

Both the scheme for Vijfhuizen and their three-stage urban design for the 6 hectare centre of Nieuw Vennep (2000–3) are situated in the Haarlemmemeer polder, to the south-east of Amsterdam, close to Schiphol Airport. Their implementation strategy for the development, phasing, and investment for the new centre was based on a sequence of large and small 'urban rooms', serving as starting points for the arrangement of public space and a mix of buildings, 280 new houses, 625 parking spaces and 22,500 square metres of retail and commercial space. A series of workshops enabled local residents directly to influence and contribute material to the development plan, the third and final stage in the project. In working on this project, it was becoming increasingly clear to the practice that there was 'a need to begin developing tools and methods to help facilitate negotiation between different interests and stakeholders, with the ambition of reaching a broader collective', says Moller. He describes how for the workshops 'we invented and built a game, rather like Monopoly, with rules, pieces and monetary restrictions specific to the constraints of the project. This allowed the workshop participants to begin to engage in the complexities of the plan, "playing out" a series of potential development

> Dutch Mountain, transformation of waste landfill into a recreational public park, Zaanstad, the Netherlands, 1997–; (left) model; (above) site plan

scenarios.' S333's urban scenarios address issues of social segregation, and new forms of intensification, bringing into close focus the limiting ways in which land has previously been used. The elements which the practice propose building into the fabric of an intensive mixed-use scheme, such as CiBoGa, offer a series of densities in an urban development not just a single model of intensity.

S333 feel that we need to talk in terms of urban intensity not density, so that housing design is seen as part of a variety of provision for a community, including schools, infrastructure and social services. An intensive approach to a site also needs to be seen as an urban ecology, understanding the interrelationships between these different layers of the city. Their strategy for <u>La Ville Forêt</u>, a housing scheme for the city of Grenoble in France (2000), makes this way of thinking a priority. The result of an invited competition, it establishes a set of programmatic layers that create a new density and flexible blueprint for a prospective community. The prospect of a continuing exodus to the suburbs, bringing with it urban sprawl without real growth, is addressed on the level of a highly dynamic yet open-ended conception of programme. 'The project speculates on just who these inhabitants are and on what kind of strategies and formalizations could be developed from such a condition,' says Hamfelt. The design proposed a wide range of housing typologies against a backdrop of the surrounding mountains. It included car parking areas and collective and private gardens; leisure and retail facilities are innovatively stacked in tall structures. The proposal centres on creating a new street life to accommodate these diverse programmes.

The <u>Beaumont Quarter</u> in Auckland, New Zealand, completed in 2005, was another medium density counterproposal to urban sprawl, for which S333, in association with the locally based Studio of Pacific Architecture, drew on the lessons learned from their speculative work at La Ville Fôret. S333's strategy here, as Papa explains, was about 'shaping the conditions under which forms and objects may emerge'. The complex form of the cliff face, combined with regulatory restrictions, created a maximum sectional envelope that changed every metre along the cliff. S333 addressed this by designing four types of houses, playfully named 'Cliff Hanger', 'Leap Frog', 'ZigZag' and 'Saddlebag', clustered to create villa-scale elements (thirty-two cliff dwellings and seventeen terraced houses on the half-hectare site) in forms generated from the vertiginous topography, deploying galvanized metal, wood and corrugated steel and bound together by a boardwalk from the street to the cliff top.

The design process also involved negotiating what Papa has described as the 'conflict between programmatic demands for density, privacy, large interiors, generous outdoor space and stunning views against

> <u>Oldham Beyond</u>, urban regeneration framework, Manchester, 2003-4; (top row) visualizations of <u>Mumps Enterprise</u>, Creative Quarter, Hollinwood; (centre row) <u>Blossom Tree Walk</u>, Featherstall Road, town square; (bottom row) <u>Coliseum</u>, Green Walk, Urban Green Living

environmental issues of acoustic pollution from a nearby motorway'. S333 argued publicly that medium-density housing at Beaumont would liberate some of the finance for resources like a sports club, café and high quality private landscaping. An even more audacious proposal to maximize vertical space was produced in 2004 for Groningen City Council's new 'High Buildings' urban policy, which advocates multi-use at a time when the cost/benefit ratio for the relatively few new high-rises in the Netherlands is being examined closely. However, instead of an iconic form flagrantly rising from an unspecified public realm, where the ground level is completely cleared, S333's towers 'plug' into a proposed urban fabric drawing on cultural and historical conditions at ground level.

In recent years, S333 has acted as a strategic advisor for urban development. In this capacity the team worked on the 2002 commission for the Regional Opleidings Centrum Amsterdam Noord (ROCvA), a community college in the new centre of Amsterdam. It shares a site with the North/South metro station. The design for the college appropriates 'the useful part of' a shopping mall and model of a traditional urban passage to fuse public and educational space. One of several contemporary educational facilities being re-evaluated by young architects, ROCvA, like all S333's projects, investigates the need for diversified daily usage and for freeing the potential of urban typologies and their uses from a state of isolation, as seen in many planning schemes in the past, to realize the potential of contemporary communities.

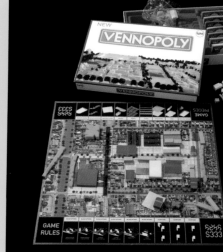

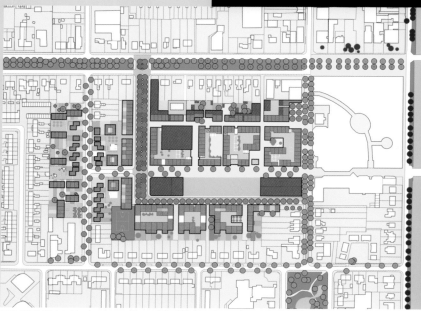

> New Town Centre Nieuw-Vennep, urban development plan for a six-hectare site, with 280 housing units and 22,500 square metres of retail and commercial spaces, Netherlands, 2000-3; (bottom) site plan showing new alternatives evolving from a traditional type

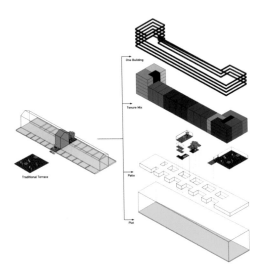

> Vennopoly game designed as interactive tool to engage the public (top left); S333 in association with Stock Woolstencroft: Tarling, Tower Hamlets, 2003-6 (on site);(top right) mixed tenure housing and retail; (bottom) perspective of block 3

Multi-scalar practice

> Sarah Wigglesworth Architects: <u>Stock Orchard Street</u>, house and office, Islington, north London, 1997-2000; front gate of willow hurdles with galvanized steel frame below office wrapped in quilted fibreglass

Urban design in the UK, which in many ways is at least a decade behind in strategies and practices that are commonplace in mainland Europe, has begun a catch-up process in the last few years. Younger architects in particular are passionately committed to bridging that gap. Economically, the country is in a strong position to change its approach to urban design, but success hinges on awareness not just of initiatives creating exemplars but on matching the commitment to reclaim and transform neglected urban space prevalent in the work of younger practices.

It has been questioned whether the English have had the confidence to design cities as well as towns with the brio of their European counterparts. Masterplanning projects in the UK often become embattled terrain between local politicians' and developers' visions. However, younger architects are slowly being recommended for jobs, and their strategies for urban design, masterplanning and urban research increasingly have a holistic approach, with socio-geographic factors given as much emphasis as spatial ones. They also have less desire to propose formal elements in a self-referential way. One drawback to commissioning large practices to undertake major masterplanning jobs is that they often show a lack of sensitivity to specific local cultural issues. In response to the virtual impossibility of devising a convincing masterplan for long-term urban development, localized remedial responses are growing. However, many public and private sector clients do not yet fully recognize the skill and sensitivity with which younger practices bring architecture and urban design together.

The mindset that aims to avoid applying design to an urban area in an abstract fashion is epitomized in the approach to the 2012 Olympic bid, and legacy masterplans evolved for the Lower Lea Valley by EDAW, Allies & Morrison, HOK Sport, Foreign Office Architects (FOA) and Fluid. Their strategy for the Olympic Park has been to avoid a sanitized environment, or one crammed with architectural objects, as in the redesign of Potsdamer Platz in Berlin, and to create a genuine legacy for the residents of the valley, an environment laced with waterways, old railway lines and disused industrial buildings. Like many other dilapidated city areas, this is the habitat of the largely disenfranchised, with forty per cent of its population under twenty-five, and high rates of unemployment. It is ripe for a regeneration initiative.

The developing hybrid practice of landscape urbanism, which focuses on geographic, topographic and climatic realities, including the natural disorder of urban living and the history that is both palpably present and intangible in the cityscape, is starting to make an impact. It offers a real alternative to widespread global urbanization, which enforces sameness and wholesale eradication of the past. The Landscape Urbanism programme at the Architectural Association's Graduate School, run by Eva Castro (co-director of architectural practice Plasma Studio), is one of the most advanced educational proponents of this approach in the UK.

Such hybrid thinking, however, remains a tough field to promote at the level of professional practice. Even a world-renowned landscape architect like Adriaan Geuze, of West 8 in the Netherlands, who has been commissioned to work in the UK on a number of occasions, has admitted that UK clients often have trouble appreciating that his practice straddles architecture and urban design. S333, another practice based in the Netherlands (but founded in the UK), also spends a high percentage of its output on urban studies (ten per cent) and plans (forty per cent), and regularly teams up with similar minded international practices, such as 3RW, with which it is working on a new masterplan for the development of Bergen in Norway. By contrast, most young UK-based practices rarely reach these levels.

New roles for collaborative, research-driven urbanism are slowly growing. Oldham, near Manchester, and Castleford, in Yorkshire, are engaging teams of young architects to

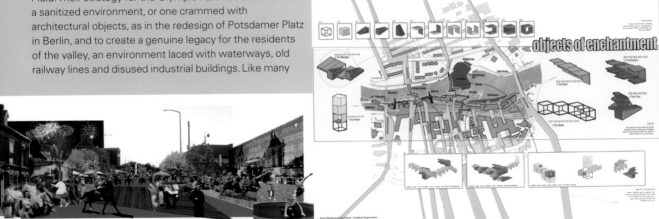

Sarah Wigglesworth Architects: The Castleford Project, Yorkshire, 2004– ; urban scheme connecting the banks of the River Aire and the Ader Navigation Canal to the north with the existing town centre, with decks, shelters, towers and tubs to generate activities

regenerate their town centres. When several practices are brought together to tackle an area, there is a cross-fertilization of data and research that inevitably enriches the final results. The Castleford Project was the world's first televised regeneration project[1], initiated by a consortium of local government urban regeneration agencies and Channel 4/Talkback Productions, who began by filming the cut and thrust of meetings and site visits. Deborah Saunt David Hills Architects (DSDHA) are designing Tittle Cott Bridge and underpass; Sarah Wigglesworth Architects are working on a plan for the town centre's riverside, linking it to the canal to the north and including a series of basic elements, such as decks, shelters and towers, to attract people and activities; Hudson Architects are responsible for market stalls and siting; McDowell + Benedetti are creating a river crossing and new waterfront access to the River Aire; Allen Tod Architects are constructing a new 'play forest', developed with local young people; and US landscape architect Martha Schwartz is engaged on plans for the New Fryston area of the town. To date, the exercise has shown the potential of democratic participation and transparency in dealing with issues to overcome hurdles in urban regeneration represented by conventional practice and broadcast via television to a wider than ever audience.

Strategies for urban improvements have become more inclusive. Tonkin Liu's competition winning design for The Architecture Foundation's Any Old Street, a brief to transform the public space around Old Street in east London, boosts the notion of community ownership by reinventing the open public area outside the shops on the north side of the street as 'a promenade of light' and trees, with a range of ringed bases intended for seating. Co-funded by Islington Council and the New Deal for Communities (NDC) scheme, the initiative began with a public consultation study by muf

architects to ensure that the regeneration plan could be implemented in this location. Tonkin Liu's scheme[2] was judged an outright winner because it was considered to be sufficiently robust to survive the process of implementation. The design reaffirms pedestrian use of the streets in a way that has been deeply informed by close observation of urban centres, in particular the Italian ritual of *passeggiata* by young and old. It occupies a linear space that rises at the end close to the underground station. This versatile scheme could also be used for markets, concerts and festivals; yet it avoids anonymity. The architects stress the need to make the design 'work psychologically with the area'. That also means not being distracted by media criticism of the design's socially inclusive policy, which does not attempt to ban or ostracize the small group of drinkers that meets in front of this roadside sequence of shop fronts. Tonkin Liu applied mapping techniques, which they have long explored with their students at the Architectural Association, to identify the properties of the trees and the potential uses and qualities of the seating elements, rather than cataloguing the people of the area as a precursor to some form of social engineering.

A project about many things happening simultaneously, Any Old Street is direct about what it does. While too many urban designs in the UK are just a collage of elements, this proposes an inclusive system that distinguishes between fast 'traffic' people, who are not locals and who move through the space at speed, and the majority of users who live close by. Including multiple elements that are customized rather than repetitively uniform, the surfaces of the benches suggest the mosaics of Barcelona's successful Parc Güell.

The architects at Fluid[3], part of the London Olympics 2012 masterplanning team, take an incisive approach to design, with activities ranging from urban masterplanning to the design of individual buildings. They have been working for seven years, one of a number of practices that are defining a new approach to urban design,

> Tonkin Liu Architects: Any Old Street, scheme to upgrade the public spaces on Old Street, east London, as an avenue or 'promenade of light', 2004- (left); House 1a, East Finchley, north London, 1998-2001; (centre) timber-framed house; (right) the house at night

making public consultation, dialogue and participation central to the process; and they have broad experience of participatory design projects of all types and sizes, from multi-million pound private sector Single Regeneration Budget (SRB) and New Deal for Communities (NDC) projects to smaller scale schemes. They have worked with many regeneration agencies, including the London Development Agency (LDC), NDC bodies across the UK, the Greater London Authority (GLA), the Architecture Foundation and the New Economics Foundation. As well as acting as consultants to local authority bodies and universities on contemporary urban policy and design, they are working with developer Argent St George on the huge project to regenerate King's Cross in London. Involving Fluid has led to the application of a range of public consultation methods, many activity based, using route mapping, collages, drawings, questionnaires and creative workshops, video or new media to engage people in the regeneration process.

For the London Olympic 2012 masterplan for the Lower Lea Valley, which is a much larger area, Fluid's public consultation work aimed at building a map of social and spatial reality. The comments collected allowed them to identify priorities that are largely invisible but fundamental to the future functioning of an urban community – how best to handle traffic access; how to organize bio-diversity, ensuring that buildings have zero-carbon emissions; and planning heating systems, and compiling an agenda for materials.

Awareness of mapping – first hatched as an architectural technique within academia about ten years ago, and usually not part of a commission by a public or private sector client – is now more widespread and intrinsic to the work of practices like Fluid and S333. Both Tonkin Liu and Fluid are aware that you can go on measuring civic needs indefinitely, trying to understand how a chunk of urban territory could work in the future; at each step of the way, the levels of response, such as concerns about levels of density, or local perceptions of the more frightening elements of an

environment, enable architects to create a map of themes, developing a bottom-up vision of desirable change. It is fundamental work that needs time and cross-party support from central government. The thirty-nine areas of the UK – including cities and coastal towns – allocated NDC funding have been falling apart for thirty years or so: change cannot be instant. Working at West Ham and Plaistow, with McCreanor Lavington through the Architecture Foundation (then directed by Lucy Musgrave, who is now director, with Claire Catterall, of General Public Agency), Fluid has outlined an urban framework plan, helping local people to bid for funds.

It is significant that an initiative like NDC, which is widely recognized as an important decentralized urban regeneration process with a high degree of public consultation – a way of bringing about urban change that parts of Europe have been engaged in for years – has involved so many younger practices. Regeneration needs a younger generation to empower the process with fresh approaches. One such scheme has been Thurrock, a programme of research with a visionary brief for an area of Thames Gateway between Basildon and Dartford, which involved examining land use and development to produce models of regenerated environments with the potential to influence other communities. It was a recent project by the General Public Agency (GPA), which characterized Thurrock as a flat and marshy 'non-place', sixty per cent green belt and with five main urban settlements deserving coordinated development (under the Urban Development Corporation, a non-departmental public body). It required a holistic approach to regeneration, combining house building programmes with long-term thinking. GPA takes a multidisciplinary approach to projects like Thurrock, which are largely about envisioning new environments and creating opportunities that can be central to the cultural identity of a place.

Scottish architect Peter Richardson, who set up Zoo Architects in Glasgow – now known as ZM Architects[4] – was responsible for the £3.3 million Tramway Theatre scheme in

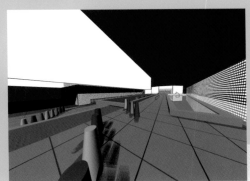

: a programme of improvements to Southwark streetscapes, south London, 1999/2001 (left); Stanford-le-Hope 2015, artist Nils Norman,
osals for Thurrock, Essex 2003– (centre); ZM Architects with artist Eva Merz and skateboarders: Broad Street, Aberdeen, 2003 (right)

the city, and is adamant that it is possible to find innovative ways of looking at the plurality of life, but that it must include a reassessment of how 'problems' are customarily defined. Skateboarders, for instance, are often seen as posing threats to urban civil society because they choose to use 'common-places'[5]. In a group project for Broad Street in Aberdeen, Scotland, Richardson worked with a local councillor, the head of the city's planning department, skateboarders and artist Eva Merz, as well as some of the residents of a city-centre sheltered housing development, to investigate the controversial erection of barriers to prevent skateboarding in front of a prominent building and devise alternatives that would avoid marginalizing skaters who want to be part of the public space. The plan incorporated bollards, ledges and stairs so skateboarders could carry out their 'ollies', 'grinds' and other tricks in close proximity to the rest of city life.

East, an urban design, landscape and architectural practice founded by Mark Brearley and Julian Lewis in 1996, works for a wide range of borough councils and public sector clients and undertook the £1.2 million scheme for environmental improvements to Southwark, south London (1999; 2001). A feature of the scheme was the increased personalization of streets which evolved from public consultation: terrazzo mats outside significant buildings; stainless steel name plates engraved with the names of premises set into the pavements; big steel and timber benches and pole-mounted mirrors. 'We don't design urban situations,' says Lewis, 'we creatively steer them.' 'Urban strategy requires open structures, cross-disciplinary discussions, standing back from aesthetics alone. Places are not conceived with a single focus, nor on the same time scales as familiar objects like buildings or products,' adds Brearley, now working as an urban designer in the Greater London Authority's Architecture and Urbanism Unit.

If streets are invariably bypassed for design improvements, landscape architecture is all too often an afterthought. Informality and differentiation in urban landscapes are qualities valued by Gross.Max, an Edinburgh-based landscape design practice working in laboratory-like conditions where each individual idea is tested to avoid standardized solutions. Gross.Max is moving into the field of urban design by virtue of its diversified yet integrated approach. Founded[6] by the English-Dutch duo Bridget Baines and Eelco Hooftman, and joined more recently by Nigel Sampey (who worked for the Rotterdam practice West 8 between 1995 and 2001), Gross.Max's work embraces public parks, civic squares, housing schemes, as well as land reclamation, structure plans and regional studies. Known for its minimal and architectural approach to landscape design, the practice's work expands the definition of the modernist landscape into something interactive. Building on this with the idea of 'curatorship of the street', devising temporary events for the spaces that the team has designed, Gross.Max has also consistently entered competitions for public spaces alongside long-established practices such as Alsop Architects. The group will soon become more visible in London, after beating Alsop Architects and Hopkins Architects to win a £6 million scheme for Brixton Central Square. Gross.Max is also designing the 1.5 hectare site of Potters Field Park, next to London's City Hall and Tower Bridge. The £8 million pilot streetscape for the Corporation of London, commissioned by the Chief Planner Peter Rees, is being implemented in a phased programme over the next two years. The team has collaborated with Zaha Hadid on large-scale mainland European projects, such as her BMW plant at Leipzig in Germany and Naples railway station, and it is designing a public garden for David Chipperfield's Wakefield Gallery in Yorkshire, with lines of pieces of

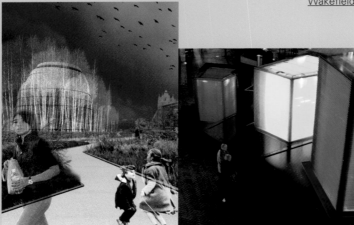

> Gross.Max: Potters Field Park, by the River Thames, London, 2004 (left); The New Bullring, landscape design for Europe's largest retail-led urban regeneration scheme, Birmingham, 2001-3 (centre); Picnics in the Green Belt, 2001; (right) ideas for London's Green Belt

concrete on the flood plain amidst a carpet of plants. The practice is probably best known for the new Bullring public space in the revamped centre of Birmingham, designed for the developers Hammerson and Land Securities. Instead of the bombastic amphitheatre proposed by another practice, the developers recognized that a more subtle approach was needed which would reflect something of the vibrant surfaces of the nearby Selfridges department store designed by Future Systems[7]. Six-metre-high cubes of stacked glass with water running over them, illuminated by the glow of LED lights, limestone plateaux and pine trees, create a playful effect. Gross.Max is not precious: the team likes people to adapt and colonize its spaces. In 2005, its designs for two London squares – St John's Square in Clerkenwell and Lyric Square in Hammersmith – will be unveiled.

Every project has its origin in the site, say Gross.Max. Shying away from a concept of landscape as a colonizing presence, or a pristine contrast to the city, they are interested in intensifying the experience, creating 'atmospheres that can be occupied', as Hooftman puts it. Not so far removed in spirit from the multi-scalar ambitions expressed in Rem Koolhaas's book *S M L XL*[8], their instinct is to intervene in something very small, like a garden or inner-city pocket park, but also regional planning, analyzing each project's entire morphology and materiality. Used to working with multiple stakeholders and grassroots public consultation, they feel that landscape design in the UK became 'increasingly insignificant' at the end of the 20th century, creating 'a whole blind spot' – with the exception of the growing interest in land art dominated by the larger corporate landscape practices. Notable UK exceptions include Martha Schwartz's Exchange Square in Manchester (1996–2000), constructed

on the site of a terrorist bombing. The new synergy between building and landscape, demonstrated by Foreign Office Architects' coastal park on reclaimed ground in Barcelona at the city's new Forum site or its technology park in La Rioja, next to the Iregua river, also in Spain, which promotes the integration of nature and culture, could make headway in the UK, but this depends on the fostering of public opinion.

When it comes to taking a stand in society, younger UK architects' 'midfield'[9] activities, responding to processes of modernization, are mostly channelled via media activities, such as the writing of articles, books and pamphlets; open jury and committee positions within government, educational and cultural bodies; and local community activism; but also on the job, by convincing a client to 'buy' into the bigger picture. The Architecture Foundation[10], directed since its inception in 1991 by Richard Burdett, Lucy Musgrave and Rowan Moore, has lobbied government and the media; it also staged the UK's largest ever series of public forum debates on the future of London, as well as Musgrave's 'Roadshow' initiative to generate creative community planning proposals for derelict or under-used public sites in London. Her 'Creative Spaces: a toolkit for participatory urban design' publication followed[11]. S333 frequently engages at a political level in order to change regulations. Its alternative thinking in Waste Space, a study of 'environmentally hindered zones' in Amsterdam, made the front cover of the Dutch newspaper *Het Parool*. ROC, another client, has invited S333 to act as architectural lawyer, defending its policies on architecture to the city council of Amsterdam. East made 'Picnics in the Green Belt' (2001), a propagandistic web-based study, producing 100 proposals for London's Green Belt, challenging the notion that it is so precious that it should

iall McLaughlin Architects: low-cost housing, Silvertown, east London, 2001-4 (left and centre); Annalie Riches, Silvia Ullmayer and
ti Garibaldo: In-Between house, Stoke Newington, east London, 1999-2004; (right) a terrace house built by the architects

not be used. In 2004, The Office of Subversive Architecture, a group of architects committed to public inclusion in community development, opted for guerrilla activity, converting a disused signal box in Shoreditch into a fake half-timbered suburban dwelling, a common 'dream house' symbol. They staged 'Sideshow', a salon, during the Thames Gateway Forum, a major conference held in London's Docklands for developers and investors. This and the signal box initiative, which bypassed traditional permissions, was a bid to intervene in the built environment and prompt debate about how east London was being regenerated.

Whether via agit-prop events or as part of urban design commissions, penetrating public consciousness and immersing oneself in the culture of the client has become vital in a pluralist culture in which media communications must be accompanied by effective face-to-face means. S333 practises a level of prolonged informal and formal public consultation in the Netherlands, where planning is regarded as an ongoing process. A participative style of architecture has been forged by Will Alsop, who has been engaged in masterplanning for some time, combining fun and design messages through creative workshops and promotional films and video. However, public consultation methods have not been imported from the Continent to the UK; they have been at the heart of the work of indigenous practices like FAT, currently working on two Dutch commissions, and muf, which cut its teeth on mainly public sector schemes supported by government funds for socially deprived areas in the UK. Both practices have public identities as architects-artists, and their style of working adds new functions or experiments with the brief. Collaborative planning processes have become far more common, combating conventional approaches to the public approval process. Charrettes[12], which are intensive work sessions over a period of days harnessing the energies of all interested parties to create and support a feasible plan, re-emerged at the London Architectural Biennale in 2004 and are occasionally staged in the UK by the AIA (the American Institute of Architects).

The notion of community consent is well understood by the best younger practices whose urban plans are innovative yet realistic, rather than visionary or conceived on such a comprehensive level that an area becomes programmed into blandness, leaving little scope for spontaneity. Definitions of architects' core skills are shifting and those that are hard and relate to the production of buildings are increasingly being joined by the soft skills of consultation with the public.

In housing design, the empiricism that the current generation applies to identify a fresh approach to aspects of the contemporary environment is clear to see. Rejecting the utopian perspectives of their predecessors, they tackle problems arising from the physical and wider cultural context to find generous solutions. There is a growing awareness that new building paradigms are needed as energy prices continue to rise. It will be fascinating to see how these new ideas develop as these architects continue to make their presence felt in a home market that is still largely tied to a safe mainstream catalogue of styles.

Avoiding a standardized approach to vernacular styles, architects like Allford Hall Monaghan Morris (AHMM) have created ground-breaking, award-winning schemes on brownfield sites, such as Raines Court in east London. AHMM and de Rijke Marsh Morgan (dRMM)[13] have innovative schemes in progress, as do Alison Brooks Architects (Brooklands Avenue, Cambridge, the last undeveloped brownfield site close to the city centre) and FAT (social housing within New Islington, Manchester, the Government's third designated Millennium Community of high quality, sustainable mixed-use urban developments[14]). These practices are introducing principles of differentiation into spatial layouts and façades without exceeding budgets, as well as wringing flexibility out of tight planning constraints.

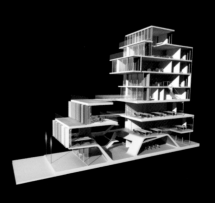

> Piercy Conner: Angel Meadows, Manchester, 2004

Initiatives by younger UK architects are taking shape internationally, too. Foreign Office Architects' most recent foray into housing design (the practice is also engaged in designing housing for a new community on the edge of Valencia in Spain, a group scheme led by architect Vicente Guallart), for a site at the Barcelona Forum, consists of sea-facing units in a triangular-shaped tower with a golden screen façade, a structure that will look like a compass pointing to the south and hold its own among the other buildings on the site. Architects like S333, who are responsible for a number of schemes in the Netherlands as well as in the UK, have also adopted the generalist role previously played by important figures like Eric Lyons, architect of the pioneering Span housing in Blackheath, south London (1957)[15], becoming actively involved in the design, urban planning and landscaping requirements of schemes, and closely associated with their development and marketing.

Social housing has been re-evaluated by a number of architects at the behest of the Peabody Trust. Niall McLaughlin's low-cost housing for Peabody at Silvertown, east London, consisting of twelve 70 square-metre two-bedroom flats with 2.8 metre-high ceilings, uses radiant light dichroic film on the large windows of its façade. The surface changes colour, depending on where you look at it or what time of day or season it is. McLaughlin's scheme and its neighbour by Ash Sakula embody fresh, unorthodox ideas: architects thinking their buildings through not as style statements but from first principles of how people would use and experience them. The prevalence of experimentation by young practices in the field of housing is not so surprising: after all, it is the most personal of projects, a type that is most commonly offered as a commission by an architect's family. The younger generation's commitment to

new models of public and self-build housing recalls the work of architect Walter Segal and his 1970s designs for housing in Lewisham, south London, which were supported by the local council. A cross fertilization between sectors has been facilitated: recent award-winning designs by young architects demonstrated a revisiting by a new generation of a whole raft of ideas reminiscent of those last seen used in an experimental way in social housing in the 1960s but now applied to the high-density private market. In the process, a democratization of belief in high-quality design has taken place: it has begun to be perceived by developers as both affordable and a way of maximizing the potential of sites.

Housing as a social issue has become a hot topic in the UK at last, due to demand far outstripping supply in the areas where people most want to live and work. Deputy Prime Minister John Prescott has committed central government to building 1.1 million new houses in the south-east by 2016, making Thames Gateway a priority for just under half of them. Speed, efficiency of construction methods, such as prefabrication and capacity, are key issues. However, problems relating to location abound: greenfield or urban brownfield sites; the enormous task of making a flood plain like Thames Gateway a sustainable community. In the Thames Gateway, the largest new community development is Barking Riverside, being masterplanned by the Dutch architects and urbanists Maxwan[16], with 12,000 new homes for an anticipated 25,000 residents. Many architects with proven talent as urbanists oppose John Prescott's well-publicized adherence to the idea of formulaic design codes[17], inspired by his visit, in 2003, to Seaside, a model town in Florida, which featured in the film *The Truman Show*. This is due to their potential for artificial homogeneity, applying design codes to building schemes that can hardly be applicable in the UK which has a plethora of highly talented architects whose internationally proven skills in urban design and public consultation mean that individual and contextual rather than fundamentalist approaches can be adopted. These debates about approaches, and arguments about levels of investment in the prefabrication industry, distract from the creative solutions put forward to meet the genuine need for affordable housing in urban areas. The latest schemes are

Piercy Conner: Brookes Road Estate, Newham, London, 2003; (left) regeneration of a 1960s housing estate; Sarah Wigglesworth Architects: ock Orchard Street, house and office, Islington, north London, 1997-2000; (right) main elevation

nearly all urban, and many of them demonstrate the skills of younger architects in working with difficult high density sites, helping to meet the standards in housing aspired to by the design community and the public, which are not yet matched by government commitments.

The ingenious use of low-cost materials to achieve public housing that is ecologically advanced and affordable is well documented in the specialist and consumer media but represents a rich repository of proposals yet to be fully acted upon in the UK. Of the practices profiled in this book, AHMM and DSDHA have designed prefabricated social housing for the Peabody Trust, one of London's largest and oldest housing associations with a strong track record for design quality and innovation. Raines Court, designed by AHMM, is the first Housing Corporation funded modular housing scheme in the UK, an £8.9 million building that investigates the potential of off-site volumetric construction, a risk-taking venture. With its client, AHMM studied the likely long-term benefits of this method, which maximizes volume and floor area – due to the width of the module, new layouts and plan types can be generated. The study resulted in a new project, MoMo, or 'mobile modular' housing, which is being developed with a shipping container manufacturer and has the potential for international application.

The most common route to innovation in housing design by younger practices is self-build. While Sergison Bates's development at Darwin Road, Tilbury, is an assisted scheme under the government's New Deal programme, combining skills training (and a possible prototype solution for other sites), most are for personal occupation. Architects Annalie Riches, Silvia Ullmayer and Barti Garibaldo's In-Between House, a reinvention of the traditional terraced house, goes one stage further, being a 285 square-metre communal project on a site between two rows of houses, for which the planners initially judged that a bungalow was the only suitable building type. However, the government's new density guidelines enabled the architects to create three contrasting, idiosyncratic units within the uniform frame of a terrace, built in a reconstituted timber frame.

The last eight years has seen a proliferation of opportunities to introduce new ideas into house builders' repertoires in both the social and the commercial sectors. In a field with few guarantees that speculative proposals will be built, firms like Alison Brooks Architects have generated ideas that manipulate the programme and draw out the potential of a site without depending on a tabula rasa. Moreover, in this climate of multi-dimensional cultural collaboration, architects have turned into business speculators. One young practice, Piercy Conner, known through competition and housing association commissions

for its skill in designing new housing forms, proposed Microflat, high quality prefabricated housing in pod form with diverse facilities at street level. The concept was first shown at full size occupied by temporary inhabitants in the windows of Selfridges department store in 2002. The practice then took on the challenge of finding a backer and suitable sites: a supermarket parking garage, even the space above a supermarket – tiny, vacant central urban interstitial sites – were ideal for the future occupants of the Microflats, twenty-somethings otherwise unable to live near work. Now there is backing and interest from a local council body that realizes a small housing policy is necessary in a city like London.

The Microflat represents excellent potential for the micro-generation of urban life. Piercy Conner's interest in post-industrial voids and what to do with them, and the sustainable future of city dwelling, is also borne out in the Angel Meadows scheme it submitted to open competition (with Levitt Bernstein and Whitby Bird) for transforming the central district of Manchester into a Sustainable Urban Community in which live/work facilities are complementary. The emphasis is on family-sized units and a dual function to all open areas, countering the inflexible nature of the city's squares. Placed second in this competition, Stuart Piercy and Richard Conner, still in their early thirties, are coming close to winning the larger scale commissions that will allow them to build their concepts. Their winning entry for Brookes Estate, a 1960s' estate in Newham, east London, proposed a modular 'overcoat' to create a new street focus in the form of a modern bay window, offering the scope to create new living spaces as well as an environmental buffer. Adapting existing low-rise homes, it represented a way of recycling the housing on the estate in a refreshed form; yet the local council lost the courage to see it through. The architects represent a discursive type of practice wedded to housing innovation in the context of urban change. This is reflected in their production and communication processes: through the means of rapid prototyping models, a design can be speculatively presented to public and private sector parties, opening up a discussion about test-bed approaches.

Younger architects are more concerned than ever to make housing work for people. The semi-detached house, the terraced house, live/work spaces, social housing, homes for key workers (public service employees such as nurses and teachers) all demand reassessment in the wake of intense social change and escalating property prices. As the trend grows towards self-employment and flexible working patterns, the home expands its identity to become a multi-functional base. Other needs, for instance for single people and live/work units, have joined the demand for high quality dwellings for families. The retreat to the countryside or to suburbia, from London in particular, by middle-class families with children does not make these developments any less pressing. Small, young practices are eager to address the question: How to pull housing away from anachronistic social codes through the application of new processes and reassessment of forms and materials which are the matter of architecture? Finding new spatial solutions, they are extending the discipline's familiar boundaries and its impacts.

The Straw House at Stock Orchard Street, in Islington, north London, designed by Sarah Wigglesworth, of Sarah Wigglesworth Architects and Professor of Architecture at the University of Sheffield, with her partner, Jeremy Till, also Professor of Architecture at Sheffield, aims to be a model of sustainable living, using a number of innovative technologies, some for the first time in an urban setting. A new system of walling incorporates straw bales wrapped around the north-east and north-west elevations, and the first domestic use of gabion walls (steel cases of recycled concrete). Straw is extremely cheap, recyclable and highly insulating, with low embodied energy, explains Wigglesworth, who is beginning to see her designs and strategies being adopted by clients. The bales are quick and easy to build with, a prototype system the architects have developed for wider usage. The office at Straw House, which fronts a railway line, is faced in sandbags for acoustic protection. It is also wrapped in a cloth of insulated silicone-faced fibreglass that creates an antithesis to the corporate modernist identity of the contemporary office: for these architects it represents 'a provisional architecture resisting the demands for eternity, fixity and progress'[18]. This counters 'the security blanket against the realities, disruption and disorder of everyday life' of disciplined making and detailing by predecessors like Mies van der Rohe. It is a blanket that can, with a little thought, be unpicked, taking apart the unsustainable interweaving of the weft of morality with the warp of technology.'[19]

Constructed between 2001 and 2004, the award-winning Straw House is a real work in progress, highly practical and, from the macro- to the micro-scale, an experiment. It was dubbed by *The Guardian* the iconic house of the decade. Like many designs for housing by the architects' peers, it has clearly been conceived to perform a dialogue with its rough urban context rather than assert an identity at the expense of authenticity (the duo describe the street as 'a London backwater…where cars come to die'[20]). As with some of the best UK housing from the 1950s and 1960s, its ethos is not about erasing its context, but intervening in reality, creating an interface between new and old, and a statement about what technology can do in the world without so much being a world unto itself[21].

This vital new form of urbanism being practised by the UK's younger architects stems from an inclusive sensibility that prefers to create a dynamic relationship between building as a formal structure and the multi-faceted environment that surrounds it. Informality and a fresh sense of mutuality rather than hierarchy between elements accommodate a diversity of use and cultural patterns. Architects should be ahead of the game. Few other professionals have the opportunity to gather together such a range of cultural insights spanning technology and construction as well as social patterns. Far from focusing solely on buildings and a world without urbanism, these perspectives give them the tools to unlock the potential of environments, rather than closing them off. It is a wonderful view architects have from the bridge of realities that need attention, and all the signs are that the architects featured in this book are not squandering theirs.

Notes
1. Wakefield Metropolitan District Council, Yorkshire Forward, English Partnerships, Groundwork UK, CABE, The Coalfields Regeneration Trust and The Arts Council of England.
2. Tonkin Liu was established in London by English architect Mike Tonkin, who set up his practice in Hong Kong in 1994, subsequently moving back to London in 1997 and joining forces with Anna Liu, a Taiwanese-American architect.
3. Fluid was set up in London in 1996 by English architects Steve McAdam, who previously worked with Bernard Tschumi, and Christina Norton who, prior to Fluid, worked with architect Nigel Coates as part of the NATO group; they both worked as architects for Ron Arad in London.
4. ZM Architects is a fusion of Zoo Architects and McGurn Architects launched in 2004 in Glasgow.
5. For an investigation of skateboarding as an urban practice, see Iain Borden's *Skateboarding, Space and the City: architecture and the body*, Berg, 2001.
6. In 1995.
7. Founded in London in 1979 and headed up by Jan Kaplicky and Amanda Levete.
8. Published by The Monacelli Press, New York, 1995.
9. André Loeckx, Chairman of Architecture, KU Leuven, Belgium, referred to this phrase which is taken from football at the second meeting of Young European Architects, 2004, a network organization established in 2003. The midfield connects the defence to the strikers; the architectural midfield mediates between clients and architects.
10. The UK's first independent architecture centre.
11. Creative Spaces: a toolkit for participatory urban design: www.creativespaces.org.uk.
12. Often describing the final, intense effort by architecture students to meet a project deadline, 'charrette' is derived from the French word 'cart'. Use of the term is said to originate from the Ecole des Beaux Arts in Paris during the 19th century, where teachers circulated a cart to collect final drawings from students.
13. Architect of Centaur Street in Lambeth, south London (2003).
14. Greenwich Millennium Village, completed in 1997, was the first in a programme advanced by English Partnerships.
15. And Ham Common near Richmond in 1953, one of the first private housing developments in the UK.
16. Founded in Rotterdam in 1995 by Rients Dijkstra and Rianne Makkink.
17. Essex County Council was the first public body to use design codes.
18. Jeremy Till and Sarah Wigglesworth, *9/10 Stock Orchard Street, A Guidebook*, The Bank of Ideas, 2001.
19. *The Future is Hairy*, Jeremy Till and Sarah Wigglesworth, essay published in *Architecture – the subject is matter*, edited by Jonathan Hill, Routledge, London and New York, 2001
20. *9/10 Stock Orchard Street, A Guidebook*, Ibid.
21. As Mies van der Rohe called it, 'Architecture and Technology', *Arts and Architecture*, vol. 67, no. 10, 1950.

Architect Biographies

David Adjaye – Adjaye Associates

David Adjaye was born in 1966 in Dar es Salaam, Tanzania, and raised in Egypt, Jeddah, Yemen and the Lebanon before moving to London when he was nine. He studied at South Bank University and at the Royal College of Art, graduating with a Masters degree in architecture in 1993. He is tutor of Diploma Unit 7 at the Architectural Association, and previously lectured at the Royal College of Art. After working for David Chipperfield Architects and Eduardo Souto de Moura, in 1994 he set up Adjaye & Russell with architect William Russell, designing the Social bar, Lunch café, Browns Focus boutique, studios for Chris Ofili (1999) and Jake Chapman, and private houses. In June 2000, Adjaye and Russell parted company and Adjaye established Adjaye Associates, with Karen Wong as Managing Director. His chief built projects, apart from a number of private apartments, include the live/work Elektra House (1998–2000) and Dirty House (2001–2); as well as a penthouse in Kensington Park Gardens (1999–2001); Fog House (2003); Idea Store, a new-build library in Poplar, east London (2001–4) with a five-storey flagship building on Whitechapel High Street due for completion at the end of 2005, the Shada pavilion with artist Henna Nadeem (1999–2000) at Limehouse, east London; Folkestone Library with Chris Ofili (1999–2002); the Asymmetric Chamber for CUBE, Manchester (2003); the exhibition spaces for the Frieze art fair, London, 2003 and 2004, and Chris Ofili's British pavilion at the Venice Biennale (2003). He was responsible for Selfridges' Beauty Hall & Accessories and Superbrands and jewellery halls at its Manchester and London stores (2001–2). In 2001 Adjaye was commissioned to design the Bernie Grant Centre in Tottenham, east London, a performing arts centre, including a 300-seat theatre, studios and café, and due for completion in 2006 and in 2003 Rivington Place, an arts centre in Shoreditch, east London, for inIVA and Autograph ABP. In progress are the Nobel Peace Center in Oslo (2002–), and the new Museum of Contemporary Art in Denver (2004), a prototype house in Nanjing, China, a new museum for the Thyssen-Bornemisza art organization in Croatia and Iceland, and the headquarters of Elpro in Berlin. Adjaye has co-presented two television series of *Dreamspaces* on modern architecture for the BBC. In 2005 Thames & Hudson published *David Adjaye: Houses*, ed. Peter Allison.

Alison Brooks Architects (ABA)

Alison Brooks set up her practice in London in 1996. Born in Welland, Ontario, Canada, in 1962, she trained at the University of Waterloo before coming to London in 1989. She joined architect and designer Ron Arad's One Off Studio, and in 1991 became a founding partner of Ron Arad Associates. There she completed the Tel Aviv Opera House foyer (1994), Arad's One Off Studio in Chalk Farm Road (1991) and the award-winning Belgo Centraal and Belgo Noord (1995) restaurants, both in London. Alison Brooks Architects' work spans urban design, housing, interiors and landscape. In 2002 she won an RIBA Award for VXO House in Hampstead, London (2001–4) and in 2000 a European Hotel Design Award for her Atoll hotel, Helgoland, Germany (1997–98). Private houses completed include Fold House, London (2001–4) and Salt House, St Lawrence Bay, Essex (2002–5). In 2003 ABA won an RIBA Housing Design Award for Brooklands Avenue, their three-part housing project in Cambridge, which won Best Housing Project of the Year in the National Homebuilder Design Awards in 2004, even before completion. Current work includes a hotel in Birmingham, artists' studios, landscape and housing projects throughout London, and an apartment building in Enfield. She has lectured extensively in the UK and internationally, and her work has been exhibited at numerous venues, ranging from the São Paulo Biennale to the RIBA, London.

Allford Hall Monaghan Morris (AHMM)

AHMM was co-founded in London in 1989 by its four partners, Simon Allford (born in London in 1961), Paul Monaghan (born in Liverpool in 1962), Jonathan Hall (born in Montreal, Canada, in 1960) and Peter Morris (born in Bramhall, Cheshire, in 1962). Each had previously completed his training in architecture at the Bartlett School of Architecture. Prior to that, Allford was educated at the University of Sheffield, and Hall and Morris at the University of Bristol. In keeping with this shared symmetry, all the partners worked for BDP; Allford also worked at Nicholas Grimshaw and Partners and Morris at Whicheloe Macfarlane before they founded the practice. Allford and Monaghan have run a Unit at the Bartlett since 1989, and have been visiting professors since 2004; they have taught at Nottingham University and are regular visiting critics and external examiners in the UK, as is Hall, while Morris has lectured at a number of architectural schools and for professional organizations. AHMM's main built projects include Cloth Hall Street, Leeds (2004), Raines Court housing, London (1998–2004), Jubilee School, London (1999–2002), Monsoon London (2000–1), Walsall Bus Station (1995–2000), Notley Green School, Essex (1997–99), Morelands Building, London (1999), CASPAR housing, Birmingham (1997–99), Dalston Lane housing, London (1998–99), North Croydon Medical Centre (1998) and St Mary's Nursery School, Kilburn (1996). Projects in progress include Rumford Place, Liverpool, Barking town centre masterplan (2002–), and, in London, the masterplan for the refurbishment of the Barbican Centre (2000–), Kentish Town Health Centre (2002–), the Johnson building, Westminster Academy, Tooley Street (mixed-use housing and offices) and Union Street (1999–). MoMo studied the feasibility of relocatable mass-produced housing (2001). Award-winning projects include Jubilee School (RIBA, AIA, Civic Trust), Notley Green School (RIBA, Royal Fine Arts Commission, CIBSE , Egan Demonstration Project, Construction Industry Award, Millennium Product Status), Raines Dairy (Housing Forum Demonstration Project, Housing Design Award, RIBA, British Construction Industry), CASPAR housing (Egan Demonstration Project, British Construction Industry Award), Dalston Lane (Civic Trust) and Walsall Bus Station (RIBA, Design Council, Civic Trust). AHMM exhibition venues include CUBE, Manchester and the Bartlett School of Architecture. *Manual*, by Iain Borden (Birkhäuser, Basel, 2003), provided a definitive critical account of the practice's first thirteen years of work.

Caruso St John

Adam Caruso (born in Montreal, Canada, 1962) graduated from McGill University in Montreal and worked for Arup Associates and Florian Beigel; Peter St John (born in Farnborough, Hampshire, 1959) graduated from the Bartlett School of Architecture, University College London and the Architectural Association prior to working for Richard Rogers Partnership, Arup Associates, Dixon Jones and Florian Beigel. They established Caruso St John in London in 1990. From 1990 to 2000 Caruso was Senior Lecturer at the University of North London (now London Metropolitan University) and, in 2002–4, Professor of Architecture at the University of Bath. St John was Senior Lecturer at the University of North London between 1991 and 1998, and in 2002–4 was Visiting Professor of Architecture, University of Bath. In 1999–2001 they were both Professors at Academy of Architecture, Mendrisio, Switzerland. Caruso St John's main realized projects include the New Walsall Art Gallery (1995–2000), the Barbican Concert Hall refurbishment (2000–1); galleries for Gagosian in Heddon Street (1999–2003) and Britannia Street, London (2003–4); the restoration of the Stortorget, Kalmar, Sweden (1999–2003), Brick House, London (2001–5) and refurbishment of the Bethnal Green Museum of Childhood (2002–, with phase 2 due for completion in 2006). Walsall Art Gallery won RIBA and Civic Trust Awards, Stortorget has won numerous awards, including an RIBA Worldwide Award. Under construction is the Nottingham Centre for Visual and Live Art (2004–). Publications by Caruso St John include *Knitting weaving wrapping pressing*, Edition Architekturgalerie Luzern/Birkhäuser, Basel, 2002, *L'architecture d'aujourd'hui* (St John, 344, 2003) *Quaderns* (Caruso, 228, 2001) and *OASE* (Caruso, 47, 1997). They have exhibited their work internationally.

dRMM (de Rijke Marsh Morgan)

dRMM was founded in London in 1994 by Alex de Rijke (born London, 1960), Sadie Morgan (born UK, 1969) and Philip Marsh (born UK, 1966). de Rijke studied at the Polytechnic of Central London and at the Royal College of Art, and worked in Amsterdam and London before setting up dRMM; Morgan and Marsh trained in interior design at Kingston Polytechnic, Morgan continuing her studies at the Royal College of Art, while Marsh trained as an architect at the Bartlett School of Architecture, going on to work with SOM before becoming a core member of dRMM. The trio ran a Unit at the Architectural Association for some years during the 1990s and de Rijke taught at the Royal College of Art, and has lectured in Europe, Asia and South America on the relationship between design concepts and new construction methods. Morgan has also taught at Kingston University and Chelsea College of Art. dRMM's principal realized projects to date include the extension of Kingsdale School, London (2001–4), One Centaur Street, London (2003), Moshi Moshi restaurant, Brighton (2000) and the Architects' Registration Board offices, London (2000). Projects in progress include Kingsdale School's new music block, sports hall and remodelled classrooms; Wansey Street, a housing project at Elephant & Castle for Southwark Council and Southern Housing; and Clapham Manor School consisting of a new wing and remodelling of the existing building. Their work on Kingsdale led to a contract from the DfES to design an exemplar secondary school as part of its Schools for the Future initiative. Awards include the RIBA London Building of the Year 2003, AJ First Building Award and CABE Building for Life Award for One Centaur Street. Exhibitions include 'Off the Shelf', an Architectural Association touring project and publication (2001, with essays by Alex de Rijke, Victoria de Rijke, Katherine Shonfield, Fred Scott). In 1999, *On the Road: the art of engineering in the car age*, a touring exhibition and book of de Rijke's photographs was launched by the Hayward Gallery and the Architecture Foundation, London. In 2005, dRMM won the new Next Generation Award launched by the Architecture Foundation and Pipers.

DSDHA (Deborah Saunt David Hills Architects)

DSDHA was established in 1998 in London by Deborah Saunt (born in Australia, 1965) and David Hills (born in the UK, 1968). Saunt graduated from Heriot-Watt University, Edinburgh in 1987, and from the University of Cambridge in 1991; Hills graduated from the University of Cambridge in 1993. Saunt worked for van Heyningen & Haward, Long & Kentish and Tony Fretton Architects, and Hills for Panter Hudspith Architects and Ronalds Farjadi Farjadi before setting up DSDHA; Hills worked concurrently with Erick van Egeraat Architects from 1999 to 2001. Both were Diploma Unit Masters at the University of Cambridge from 1998 to 2002, Diploma Unit 10 Masters at the Architectural Association, London, from 2002 to 2004 and are visiting critics at numerous schools of architecture as well as regularly contributing to journals and television broadcasts. In 2000, they won an RIBA Award for their first completed building, the Orangery in Norfolk. Their chief realized projects to date include the Hoyle Early Years Centre, Bury, Lancashire (2001–3), first prize winner in the CABE Neighbourhood Nurseries Competition; and which won the RIBA Award for Architecture in 2004; and the John Perry Nursery, Dagenham, Essex (2002–3). In 2004 they won a competition for £27 million of new school buildings in Guildford for Surrey County Council; in 2003 their designs won the CABE/IPPR Designs on Democracy competition for a new town hall in Letchworth, Hertfordshire; and in 2003 they won The Peabody Trust's competition for Artists and New Media Studios in Silvertown, east London.

Under construction or in progress are the Tittle Cott Bridge, their 2003 winning design for the Castleford Project for the town of Castleford, Yorkshire – a Joint Denominational School in Sheffield; Hurlingham Preparatory School; a mixed-use development, London; the Paradise Park Children's Centre, London; and affordable housing in Islington for developer Derwent Valley. Their most recent successes have been a commission at the end of 2004 for a luxury private house in Kensington Palace Gardens, and in collaboration with Foster and Partners as the winning team, a feasibility study for the development of Parliament Square, London.

FAT

FAT, an acronym for Fashion Architecture Taste, an art-architecture collective, was initially set up in London in 1991 by Sean Griffiths, Clive Sall and François Lefranc, all students at the Polytechnic of Central London (now University of Westminster), together with their tutor Kevin Rhowbotham. They designed competition entries and exhibitions and began making public art projects. Rhowbotham and Sall left FAT in 1994 and 1998 respectively, and architects Sam Jacob (1994–), Charles Holland (1996–) and Emma Davis (1995–99) joined. Griffiths (born in Liverpool, 1969) and Jacob (born in London, 1970) have taught extensively both in the UK (principally at the universities of Westminster and Greenwich) and as visiting critics and professors at institutions globally. Griffiths, Jacob and Holland (born in Chelmsford, 1969) have contributed to books, journals and magazines worldwide, and Jacob is currently architecture editor of *Contemporary* magazine. Projects include Kessels Kramer, the Dutch advertising agency (1998); the Brunel Rooms club and bar, Swindon (1995); their early private houses include one for comedian Steve Coogan, the conversion of a baptist chapel into a home. and Garner Street, Hackney, east London, (2002).Public art works include Adsite (1993), Home Ideas (1997, and exhibition), Utopia Revisited (1998), You Make Me Feel (Mighty Real), The New Civic (2000–1), all in London, a summer house for English Heritage, Northumberland (2000–1), and Highlife, Bristol (2002), where they became lead artist for Bristol Legible City. Key exhibitions have included 'Kill the Modernist Within', CUBE, Manchester (1999–2000) and 'Stealing Beauty', ICA (1999). In the Netherlands, at Boxtel they are designing the masterplan of a campus, with an extension and refurbishment of an art school; and at Hoogvliet Heerlijkheid, outside Rotterdam, a new community hall and park (2002–). In 2003, FAT won first prize in a competition for social housing at New Islington, Manchester, now under development; and first prize in 2004 in a London Borough of Newham competition to refurbish and extend Tanner Point, a 1960s' tower block.

Kathryn Findlay

Kathryn Findlay was born in Forfar, Scotland, and graduated from the Architectural Association, London,

in 1979. She moved to Japan with a scholarship from the Japanese Ministry of Education for postgraduate research at the University of Tokyo. She worked for Arata Isozaki and Associates (1980–82) before establishing Ushida Findlay Partnership in Tokyo with architect Eisaku Ushida in 1987. Findlay was an Associate Professor of Architecture at Tokyo University until 2001, a Visiting Professor at the Bartlett School of Architecture, UCL, at UCLA (1999), and at the Technical University in Vienna (2001). She is now Honorary Professor at the University of Dundee. Ushida Findlay's principal built projects include: Truss Wall House, Tokyo (1992–93); Soft and Hairy House, Baraki (1992–94); Kaizankyo Retreat, Wakayama (1993–94); Polyphony House, Osaka (1995–97); and Kasahara Amenity Hall (1999–2000, Kathryn Findlay Laboratory at the University of Tokyo); the Flagship building, Homes for the Future, Glasgow (1997–99), which won a Regional Award for Development in Scotland in 2000, and the Pool House, England (2000–1). Findlay relocated to London in 1997 and set up Ushida Findlay UK. Since 2004 she has practised under her name, Kathryn Findlay. Ushida Findlay won competitions to design Grafton New Hall, south Cheshire (2001); a Maggie's Cancer Centre, Wishaw, Lanarkshire (2004); Hastings Visitor Centre (2003). In Qatar, commissions include Villa Doha (2002–5), the Beach House (2002–), and the Al Koot Costume and Textiles Museum (2002–). The work of the practice has been exhibited extensively in the Far East and London, and in 2004 in 'Nine Positions', the British Pavilion exhibition curated by Peter Cook at the 9th Venice Architecture Biennale. Publications include a *2G* monograph (Gustavo Gili, 1998).

Foreign Office Architects (FOA)

Foreign Office Architects (FOA) was established in London in 1993 by Farshid Moussavi (born in Shiraz, Iran, 1965) and Alejandro Zaera Polo (born in Madrid, Spain, 1963). Zaera Polo graduated from Escuela Técnica Superior de Arquitectura (E.T.S.) en Madrid in 1988, and Moussavi from Dundee University (1987) and the Bartlett School of Architecture, University College London, in 1989. Both studied at the Graduate School of Design of Harvard University and in 1991 were awarded Masters in Architecture, Zaera Polo with distinction. Moussavi worked for the Renzo Piano Building Workshop in Genoa, Italy (1988), and Zaera Polo for Rafael Moneo (1989); both worked for OMA (Office for Metropolitan Architecture) in Rotterdam, the Netherlands, until 1993 when they moved to London. From 1993 to 2000 they were Masters of Diploma Unit 5 at the Architectural Association School of Architecture, London. Zaera Polo has been a critic for *El Croquis*, *Quaderns* and *AD*. He has been Dean of the Berlage Institute, Rotterdam, since autumn 2002, and has taught at UCLA and the universities of Columbia and Princeton in the USA, and at E.T.S. Madrid. Moussavi has been Professor of Architecture and Design at the Academy of Fine Arts, Vienna, Austria since autumn 2002, and has taught in the US at UCLA, Columbia, Princeton, as well as at the Hoger Architectuur Institute, Ghent, Belgium.

FOA's most important built projects to date are Yokohama International Port Terminal, Japan (1994–2002), which won the Enric Miralles Prize for Architecture and the Kanagawa Architecture Prize in 2003, and an RIBA Worldwide Award in 2004; the South Eastern Coastal Park and auditorium, Barcelona, Spain (2000–4); Municipal Police headquarters, La Vila Joiosa, Spain (2002-3); and Bluemoon, a hotel, Groningen, the Netherlands (1999–2000). Their earliest projects were restaurants and bars for Belgo,in London and New York. FOA were part of the multinational United Architects team shortlisted for the New York City Ground Zero competition in 2003, and were invited, with EDAW, Allies & Morrison, HOK

Sport and Fluid, to form the masterplanning team for the regeneration of London's Lower Lea Valley (2003–) and the park design for the London Olympic 2012 bid and were responsible for the main stadium design proposal (2004). Projects under construction or in preparation include the Zona Franca office park, Barcelona, Spain (2002–7) with Arata Isozaki; the Dul-Nyouk publishing headquarters, Paju Book City, Korea (2003–); the Technological Research Centre de la Rioja, Logroño, Spain (2003–6); the Cabo Llanos harbour masterplan, Santa Cruz de Tenerife (2003–6); the BBC Music Centre (2003–); T'Raboes Harbour facilities, Amersfoort, the Netherlands (2003–6); the Municipal Theatre Torrevieja, Spain (2000–5); the Spanish pavilion at the 2005 EXPO, Aichi, Japan; Mahler 4 offices, phase 3, Amsterdam (2000–7); housing in Spain; and a new building for Ravensbourne College of Design and Communications, London. Exhibitions staged include 'Breeding Architecture', ICA, London (2003-4), 'foa-phylogenesis', TNProbe Gallery, Tokyo, Japan (2003), the Museum für Angewandte Kunst, Vienna, Austria (2003); and at Harvard Graduate School of Design (2005). Publications about FOA include 'Foreign Office Architects: consistency and complexity, 1996–2002', *El Croquis*, 115/116, Madrid, 2003 (eds. Fernando Márquez and Richard Levine). FOA have published extensively, including an issue of *2G* (IV, Barcelona, 2000), with texts by Jeffrey Kipnis, Ciro Najle and FOA; *The Yokohama Project*, ed. Albert Ferré, Tomoko Sakamoto and Michael Kubo with FOA (Actar, Barcelona, 2002) and *Phylogenesis: foa's ark* (eds. Albert Ferré, Michael Kubo with FOA), ICA/Actar, 2003.

Gollifer Langston

Gollifer Langston was formed in 1994 in London by Andy Gollifer (born in Merseyside, 1960) and Mark Langston (born in Birmingham, 1960). Gollifer took his Masters degree in architecture at the Royal College of Art and Langston at Edinburgh College of Art in 1986. Between 1987 and 1989 Gollifer worked for Powell Tuck Connor Orefelt and Langston for Hamilton Associates, later Hawkins Brown (1990–93). The pair are visiting critics at Liverpool University. They first began collaborating on competitions in 1989, and in 1994, shortly after they established their practice, won the competition for the National Glass Centre in Sunderland, completed in 1998. Other realized projects include 601fx and Soho 601, film company offices in central London (1994 and 1996); Camden City Learning Centre (CLC), London (1999–2002); Brentford CLC (2003) and Platform1 CLC, King's Cross (2001–3), which won an RIBA Award in 2004. Projects under construction or in progress include the Music and Dance Building at Acland Burghley School, the Drama Building at Highbury Fields School, phase 1 nursery on the Broadwater Farm campus, a mobile classroom for Classrooms of the Future in Camden, all in London, and a multi-storey car park and residential project, part of a city centre redevelopment.

KDa (Klein Dytham architecture)

KDa was established in Tokyo in 1991 by Mark Dytham (born Northamptonshire, England, 1964) and Astrid Klein (born Varese, Italy, 1962). Dytham graduated with distinction in architecture from Newcastle University in 1985, and from the Royal College of Art, London, in 1988, where he took his Masters degree. He has worked for Skidmore Owings and Merrill, Chicago and London, and lectures at Tokyo Science University (1999–) and Hosei University, Japan (2001–). Klein graduated in interior design from the Ecole des Arts Décoratifs, Strasbourg, France (1986) and in architecture with a Masters degree from the Royal College of Art (1988), and has worked for Toyo Ito & Associates Architects, Tokyo. She lectures at Nihon University, College of Science and Technology (1997), Keio University and Tsukuba University (2002–). KDa's most noted works include the Idée Workstation, Shimouma, Tokyo, a furniture showroom (1996); Bartle Bogle Hegarty, Tokyo, an advertising agency interior (1999); Vroom! garage, Aichi Prefecture, (1999); Pika-Pika hoarding, Tokyo, (1999); i-fly virgin Wonderwall, an interactive hoarding for Virgin Atlantic (2000); Rin-Rin, Laforet, Tokyo (2000–1); Undercover Lab, a fashion company's headquarters (2001); Cat's Eyes at Foret, Tokyo (2002); Beacon, Tokyo, an advertising agency office interior (2002); Bloomberg ICE, Tokyo, an interactive installation (2002); Museum Café, Mori Arts Museum, Tokyo (2003); Green Green Screen, Omotesando, Tokyo (2003); the Leaf Chapel, Yamanashi, Japan (2004); and a ten-storey apartment building in Nagoya (2004). In 2003 KDa established SuperDeluxe, an events space, in Tokyo, an expanded version of Deluxe, run from their first office in Azabu-Juban. Their awards include the Kajima Space Design Award for the best young practice in Tokyo in 1993, and their design for Idée won both the Asahi Glass Design Award and the National Panasonic Award in 1996. In 2002 Dytham was given an MBE for services to British architecture in Japan. Publications include *Tokyo Calling*, Frame publishers, Amsterdam, 2001, and *Architect's Works File 2: Klein Dytham Architecture*, Xknowledge, Tokyo, 2002.

muf

muf is a practice that embraces art and architecture. It was established in 1996 by architects Juliet Bidgood, Liza Fior and artist Katherine Clarke, with the intention of working in the public realm. Bidgood left muf in 2002 to pursue her own research and to work with CABE, but remains an occasional contributor. The urban theorist Katherine Vaughan Williams (Shonfield), although never formally a partner, was also a key collaborator from the outset until her death in 2003. Clarke (born in Jersey, 1960) studied at Goldsmiths College, and has taught at Chelsea College of Art and the Architectural Association. Fior (born in London, 1962) trained at Polytechnic of Central London and Canterbury College of Art. She taught at the Royal College of Art and the Architectural Association, London. Chief muf projects include the Hypocaust building, St Albans (1999–2004); Open Spaces that are not parks, for the London Borough of Newham (2004); My Dream Today: Your Dream Tomorrow, community garden, Tilbury (2003-4); Security Mobility Pleasure, a New Deal for Communities (NDC) urban design framework (2001); SureStart on the Ocean, a playspace/meeting room (2000); Shared Ground, Southwark, London (1997); Pleasure Garden, Stoke on Trent (1998–2003); Bromford playstrip for the Scarman Trust, Birmingham (1998). muf's current projects include a mixed-use building in Hoxton, London, and stage one of Barking town centre, as part of the Mayor of London's 100 Public Spaces project for London. Their work has been exhibited at the Architecture Foundation, London, in 'Purity and Tolerance' (1995); at 'Arc en rêve', Bordeaux (2001) and Aedes Gallery, Berlin (2003). Publications include: *This is what we do, a muf manual*, ellipsis, London (2001), and *Architecture and Participation* (eds. Peter Blundell-Jones, Doina Petrescu and Jeremy Till), Spon (2004).

Sergison Bates

Sergison Bates was formed by Jonathan Sergison (born St Asaph, Wales, 1964) and Stephen Bates (born Essex, 1964) in London in 1996. Bates graduated from the Royal College of Art in 1989, and worked in Barcelona for Liebman Villavecchia and Lapeña Torres on housing and cultural projects, and in London for Bennetts Associates. Sergison graduated from the Architectural Association in 1989 and worked for David Chipperfield and for Tony Fretton on housing and cultural projects. Both partners have taught at various UK (Bates was Unit Master at the Architectural Association from 1995–98) and European schools of architecture and are currently visiting professors at the Swiss Federal Institute of Technology (ETH), Zurich. Principal built projects include the award-winning public house, Walsall (1997-8), in collaboration with Caruso St John; prototype social housing, Stevenage (1998–2000); assisted self-build housing, Tilbury, Essex (2001); as part of the Classrooms of the Future pilot project, Bedfordshire (2001–3); and a mixed-use scheme, Wandsworth, London (1999–2003). Current projects include a masterplan for 2,500 homes at the Royal Arsenal, Woolwich, the new Department of Dramatic Arts and Audio Visual Technology, Erasmushogeschool, Brussels and a new library in Blankenberge, Belgium. In 2001 the practice published *Papers*, a collection of illustrated texts by the partners.

S333

S333 architecture + urbanism was officially founded in 1997 in Amsterdam in the Netherlands by Burton Hamfelt (born in Montreal, Canada, 1964), Christopher Moller (born in Wellington, New Zealand, 1961), Dominic Papa (born in London, 1965) and Jonathan Woodroffe (born in London, 1964). Prior to that the practice was formed more loosely in London in 1990, staging workshops, producing publications and entering competitions. Papa and Woodroffe trained at University of Portsmouth, with Papa completing his education at the Architectural Association, London. Moller trained at the University of Auckland, and Hamfelt at University of Toronto. All four partners gained experience with established practices before founding S333, Papa with Terry Farrell and Wiel Arets, Woodroffe with the Architects Collaborative (Boston), Gensler (New York), Wilkinson Eyre (London), and Neutelings Riedijk (Rotterdam), for whom Hamfelt also worked, along with Xaveer de Geyter (Antwerp) and Bruce Mau Design (Toronto). Moller worked with practices in New Zealand, Terry Farrell and as senior urbanist, Groningen City Council; Papa and Hamfelt currently teach the First Year Studio at the Berlage Institute, Rotterdam, and Papa is design tutor in Housing and Urbanism, Architectural Association, London, where for four years he was Unit Master with Woodroffe, and Moller was for six years design tutor. Hamfelt also teaches at the Academie van Bouwkunst, Amsterdam and previously taught at the Architectural Association, University of Toronto, Hoger Instituut St Lucas (Ghent), and, like Woodroffe, at the TU Delft, and Academie Van Bouwkunst (Tilburg).

S333's principal built projects in the Netherlands include Schots 1 & 2, the award-winning CiBoGa Terrain, Groningen (1997–2003) and Bloembollenhof, Vijfhuizen (1999–2003); Beaumont Quarter in Auckland, New Zealand (2001–5) is a scheme of row houses and cliff dwellings. Their urban plan for the new town centre of Nieuw-Vennep was completed in 2003. In progress are a commercial centre at Eschmarke (2001–5) and Block 7 + 9, a mixed-use scheme, Almere (2002–5); Coast Wise, Bergen, Norway, an urban framework plan for the city (2004); Oldham Beyond, Manchester, a comprehensive urban strategy (2003–4); and Tarling Estate, London, housing/mixed-use scheme (2000–), in collaboration with Stock Woolstencroft. Urban studies include Waste Space (2000–1); Eikenlaan, Groningen (a new tram route, 2003–); the Intense City on housing and urban expansion (2004–5). In 1994 (Groningen) and 1996 (Manchester), S333 won the Europan housing competitions, and in 2000 were given an Anglo-Dutch Award for Enterprise. Exhibitions include 'Remaking Holland' (Hanover 2000 Expo, and at at arc en rêve, Bordeaux, and 'Lille, Metropolis in Europe', Euralille, Lille, 2004.

Project credits

Adjaye Associates

Elektra House, London >Architect: David Adjaye. Kensington Park Gardens, London >Design team: David Adjaye, Lucy Tilley. Folkestone Library, Kent >Client: Kent County Council. Design team: David Adjaye, Josh Carver. Artist: Chris Ofili. Nobel Peace Centre Oslo, Norway >Client: The Norwegian Nobel Institute. Design team: David Adjaye, Nikolai Delvendahl, Mansour El-Khawad, John Moran, Jennifer Bohiem, Sebastian Spengler, James Carrigan, Fiona Scott, Fawzia Ghafoor, Hannah Booth. Shada Pavilion, London. Architect: David Adjaye. Artist: Henna Nadeem. Idea Store, Chrisp Street, London >Client: London Borough of Tower Hamlets. Design team: David Adjaye, Yohannes Bereket, Nikolai Delvendahl, Josh Carver, Cornelia Fischer, Soyingbe Gandonu, Jessica Grainger, Andrew Heid, Haremi Kudo, Yuko Minamide, Josh Carver, Ana Rita, RP Silva, Go Tashiro. Engineers: Arup. Bernie Grant Centre, London >Client: Bernie Grant Trust. Design team: David Adjaye, Josh Carver, Joseph Franchina, Ixone Altube, Dieter DeVos, Craig Tan, Bertil Donker, Mansour El-Khawad, Achille Corradin, Juanita Cheung, Davide Marelli. Rivington Street, London >Client: inIVA/Autograph. Design team: David Adjaye, Joseph Franchina, Mansour El-Khawad, Nikolai Delvendahl, Rashid Ali, Fawzia Ghafoor, Sebastian Spengler, Yuko Minamide.

Alison Brooks Architects

Atoll hotel, Helgoland, Germany >Client: KG Weber Helgoland GmbH. Design team: Alison Brooks, Sara Yabsley (project architect), Thorsten Overberg, Antonia Infanger, Wolfgang Frese VXO House, London >Design team: Alison Brooks, Steven Cox (project architect), Bethune D'Souza. Structural consultant: Price & Myers. Artist: Simon Patterson. Brooklands Avenue, Cambridge >Client: Countryside Properties PLC/Kajima Construction Europe. Design team: Alison Brooks, Dominic Mckenzie (project architect), Juan Francisco Rodriguez, Juana Canet Rossello, Scott Barker, Angel Martin Cojo, Irene Konschill, James Taylor. Structural consultants: Richard Jackson Partnership/Atkins. M&E consultants: Kajima Design Engineering PLC. Fold House, London >Client: Alistair & Rachel Kelly. Design team: Alison Brooks, Matthew Potter (project architect). Structural consultant: Price & Myers. Salt House, St Lawrence Bay, Essex >Client: John & Margaret Skerritt. Design team: Alison Brooks, Angel Martin Cojo (project architect), Juan Francisco Rodriguez. Structural consultant: Price & Myers

Allford Hall Monaghan Morris

Notley Green School, Essex >Client: Essex County Council. Design team: Simon Allford, Jonathan Hall, Paul Monaghan, Peter Morris, David Archer, Scott Batty, Ceri Davies, George Dawes, Demetra Ryder Runton, John Thornberry. Structural engineer: Atelier One. Services engineer: Atelier Ten. Landscape architects: Jonathan Watkins Landscape. Public art: Hartley & Kovats. Barking Town Centre, Essex >Client: Barking & Dagenham Council/Urban Catalyst. Design team: Simon Allford, Paul Monaghan, Jonathan Hall, Peter Morris, Ross Hutchinson, Susie Le Good, Jonathan Picardo, Paulo Costa, Matt Thornley, Heidrun Schuhmann, Kerstin Bedau, Gabriel Musat, Georgia Tzika, Fiona Selmes, Charlotte Harrison, Steve Ritchie, Dan Marshall, Sarah Hunneyball, Maya Koljonen. Structural engineer: Buro Happold. Services engineer: Faber Maunsell. Landscape architect: Grant Associates. CASPAR, Birmingham >Client: Joseph Rowntree Foundation. Design team: Simon Allford, Jonathan Hall, Paul Monaghan, Peter Morris, Harriet Brown, Victor Kite, Demetra Ryder Runton. Structural engineer: Adams Kara Taylor. Landscape architect: Jenny Coe. Planning & development: Alsop Zogolovitch Urban Studio. Dalston Lane, London

>Client: Peabody Trust. Design team: Simon Allford, Jonathan Hall, Paul Monaghan, Peter Morris, David Archer, Victor Kite, Jenny Lovell, Demetra Ryder Runton. Structural engineer: Campbell Reith Hill. Landscape architects: Jonathan Watkins. Raines Court, London >Client: Peabody Trust. Design team: Simon Allford, Jonathan Hall, Paul Monaghan, Peter Morris, Karen Scurlock,Will Lee. Structural engineer: Whitby Bird. Services engineer: Engineering Design Partnership. Module manufacturer: Yorkon. MoMo >Design team: Simon Allford, Jonathan Hall, Paul Monaghan, Peter Morris, Morag Tait, Will Lee Consortium team WH Davis (manufacturer). Structural, services & façade engineers: Buro Happold. Jubilee School, London >Client: London Borough of Lambeth. Design team: Simon Allford, Paul Monaghan, Jonathan Hall, Peter Morris, Susie Le Good, Anthony Martin, Ben Gibson, Tara de Linde, Fiona Selmes. Structural engineer: Elliott Wood. Environmental engineer: Atelier Ten. Graphic design: Studio Myerscough. Furniture design: Andrew Stafford. Artist: Martin Richman. Landscape architect: Robert Rummey Associates. Acoustics: Paul Gillieron Acoustic. Rumford Place, Liverpool >Client: Rumford Investments. Design team: Simon Allford, Paul Monaghan, Jonathan Hall, Peter Morris, Steven Ritchie, Jeremy Young, Gabriel Musat, Peter Mayhew, Leonardo Lattavo, Susie Le Good, Heidrun Schuhmann, Jonathan Crossley, Dan Marcel. Structural engineer: Faber Maunsell. Environmental engineer: Hoare Lea. M&E engineer: Hoare Lea. Barbican Arts Centre >Client: Barbican Arts Centre/Corporation of London. Design team: Simon Allford, Jonathan Hall, Paul Monaghan, Peter Morris, Frank Strathern, Peter Sargent, Robert Burton, Charlotte Harrison, Sonia Grant, Hazel Joseph. Structural engineer: Faber Maunsell. Environmental engineer: Sir Frederick Snow & Partners. Graphic designers: Studio Myerscough, Cartlidge Levene. Lighting design: Minds Eye. Acoustic consultant: Sandy Brown Associates. Furniture design: Andrew Stafford

Caruso St John
New Art Gallery, Walsall >Client: Walsall Metropolitan Borough Council. Design team: Adam Caruso, Peter St John with Laurie Hallows, Alun Jones, Martin Bradley, Andrés Martinez, Silvia Ullmayer. Structural engineer: Arup. Services engineer: Arup. Gagosian Gallery, London >Client: Gagosian Gallery. Design team: Adam Caruso, Peter St John with Stephanie Webs. Structural engineer: Price & Myers. Services engineer: Max Fordham & Partners. Stortorget, Kalmar, Sweden >Client: Municipality of Kalmar & Statens Konstråd (Swedish National Council for Public Art). Design team: Adam Caruso, Peter St John with Adam Khan, Lorenzo De Chiffre. Artist: Eva Löfdahl. Brick House, London >Client: private. Design team: Adam Caruso, Peter St John with Rod Heyes, Lorenzo De Chiffre, James Payne. Structural engineer: Price & Myers. Services engineer: Mendick Waring. Bethnal Green Museum of Childhood, London >Client: Victoria & Albert Museum. Design team: (phase 1) Adam Caruso, Peter St John with Tim Collett, Rod Heyes, Adam Khan; (phase 2) Adam Caruso, Peter St John, David Kohn, Kerstin Treiber. Structural engineer: Alan Baxter & Assoc. Services engineer: Max Fordham & Partners. Artist (phase 1): Simon Moretti

dRMM (de Rijke Marsh Morgan)
Module Grass House >Client: dRMM research project. Design team: Alex de Rijke, Sadie Morgan, Philip Marsh, Janek Schaefer. Structural engineer: dRMM. Capsule Hotel >Client: dRMM/ Architectural Association research project. Design team: Intermediate Unit 4/Architectural Association, Alex de Rijke, Philip Marsh, Sadie Morgan. HH House, Cornwall >Design team: Alex de Rijke, Michael

Spooner. Structural engineer: Michael Hadi Associates. ARB headquarters, London >Client: Architects Registration Board. Design team: Alex de Rijke, Sadie Morgan, Rosie Berry. Structural engineer: Michael Hadi Associates. Environmental engineer: Ibsec. Moshi Moshi, Brighton >Client: Moshi Moshi. Design team: Alex de Rijke, Michael Spooner, Satoshi Isono. Structural engineer: Michael Hadi Associates. Environmental engineer: dRMM. Centaur Street, London >Client: Solid Space. Design team: Alex de Rijke, Sadie Morgan, Michael Spooner, Roger Zogolovitch. Structural engineer: Michael Hadi Associates. Environmental engineer: Monalco. Kingsdale School, London >Client: London Borough of Southwark. Design team: Philip Marsh, Alex de Rijke, Michael Spooner, Satoshi Isono, Sadie Morgan. Structural engineer: Michael Hadi Associates. Environmental engineer: Fulcrum Engineering. Quantity surveyor: Appleyard & Trew. Artist: Atelier Van Lieshout

DSDHA (Deborah Saunt David Hills Architects)
Hoyle Early Years Centre, Bury >Client: Bury Metropolitan Borough Council. Design team: David Hills, Deborah Saunt, Claire McDonald, Brent Crittenden, Fred Collin. Structural engineer: Price + Myers. Services: Atelier Ten. John Perry Primary School, Dagenham >Client: London Borough of Barking & Dagenham. Design team: David Hills, Deborah Saunt, Sam Potter, Maisie Rowe. Structural engineer: Price & Myers. Services: Atelier Ten. The Bermondsey Twist >Client: Urban Catalyst. Design team: David Hills, Deborah Saunt, Wolfram Schneider, Martin Pearson. Structural engineer: Adams Kara Taylor. Letchworth Town Hall >Client: North Hertfordshire District Council. Competition Sponsor: IPPR / CABE. Design team: David Hills, Deborah Saunt, Brent Crittenden, Claire McDonald, Sam Potter, Jean Dumas. Services: Max Fordham. Structural engineer: Jane Wernick. Tittle Cott Bridge, Castleford >Client: Wakefield Metropolitan District Council. Sponsor: Channel 4/Talkback Productions. Design team: David Hills, Deborah Saunt, Sam Potter, Wai Piu Wong. Structural engineer: Jane Wernick

FAT
Brunel Rooms, Swindon >Client: Norman Fraser Ltd. Design team: FAT (all projects). Structural engineer: Techniker. M&E engineer: Phil Reynolds. Specialist lighting: Tony Gottelier. Scala cinema, London >Client: Primartarium Ltd. Structural engineer: Vic Shore. M&E engineer: Eddie Mayhew. Kessels Kramer, Amsterdam >Client: Kessels Kramer. Garner Street, London. Structural engineer: Elliot Wood Partnership. Hoogvliet Heerlijkheid, Hoogvliet, the Netherlands >Client: Wimby. St Lucas, Boxtel, the Netherlands >Client: St Lucas. Tanner Point, London >Client: London Borough of Newham. Structural engineer: Adams Kara Taylor. M&E engineer: BDSP partnership. New Islington social housing, Manchester >Client: Manchester Methodist Housing Group/Urban Splash., Structural engineer: Whitby & Bird. Bristol road designs >Client: Bristol City Coucil. Graphic designer: Graphic Thought Facility

Kathryn Findlay
Truss Wall House, Tokyo, Japan >Client and contractor: Truss Wall Co. Design team: all projects Ushida Findlay unless otherwise stated
Kasahara Amenity Hall, Gifu Prefecture, Japan. Architect: Kathryn Findlay Laboratory, The University of Tokyo. Assistants: Tomoko Taguchi, Takanori Yukawa. Grafton New Hall, south Cheshire >Client: Ferrario Burns Hood. Structural engineer: Atelier One. Mechanical/electrical engineer: Atelier Ten. Landscape design: Jonny Bell. Hastings Visitor Centre >Client: Hastings Borough Council. Structural engineer: Arup.

Artist: David Ward. Al Koot Costume and Textiles Museum, Qatar >Client: Government of Qatar. Structural engineer: Fluid. Mechanical/electrical engineer: XCO2. Villa Doha, Qatar >Client: Minister of Culture, Qatar. Structural engineer: Buro Happold. Mechanical/electrical engineer: Atelier Ten. Landscape design: B&B/Jonny Bell. Beach House, Qatar >Client: HRH Sheikha Mosa, wife of the Emir of Qatar. Structural engineer: Buro Happold. Mechanical/electrical engineer: Atelier Ten

Foreign Office Architects (FOA)
International Port Terminal, Yokohama, Japan >Client: City of Yokohama Port and Harbor Bureau Construction Department Osanbashi Passenger Vehicle Terminal Maintenance Subdivision. Design team: (competition) Farshid Moussavi, Alejandro Zaera Polo with Iván Ascanio, Yoon King Chong, Michael Cosmas, Jung-Hwang, Guy Westbrook, Hernando Arrazola (basic design stage 1) Farshid Moussavi, Alejandro Zaera Polo with Kenichi Matsuzawa, Jordi Mansilla, Santiago Triginer, Félix Bendito; (basic design stage 2) Farshid Moussavi and Alejandro Zaera Polo with Lluís Viu Rebés, Kenichi Matsuzawa, Xavier Ortiz, Dafne Gil, Victoria Castillejos, Oriol Montfort, José Saenz, Julian Varas, Thomasine Wolfensberger; (detail design) Farshid Moussavi and Alejandro Zaera Polo with Lluís Viu Rebés, Xavier Ortiz, Yasuhisa Kikuchi, Kensuke Kishikawa, Izumi Kobayashi, Keisuke Tamura, Kazutoshi Imanaga,Tomofumi Nagayama, Eisue Kurosawa, Masami Suzuki, Masanori Sodekawa, Kenichi Matsuzawa: (supervision) Farshid Moussavi, Alejandro Zaera Polo with Kenichi Matsuzawa, Lluís Viu Rebés, Yasumasa Kikuchi, Kensuke Kishikawa, Izumi Kobayashi and Keisuke Tamura. Local architect: GKK (Shuichi Iida, Masaya Koizumi). Structural engineer: Structure Design Group (SDG)/Kunio Watanabe (1998–2002), Arup (1995–96). Services engineer: PT Morimura & Associates. Lighting: Kado Lighting Design Laboratory. Acoustics: Nagata Acoustics Inc. Disaster prevention consultant: Akena Fire Research Institute. Traffic consultant: Urban Traffic Engineering. General contractor: Shimizu Corporation (first division), Kajima Corporation (second division), Toda Corporation (third division). South Eastern Coastal Park and Auditoriums, Barcelona, Spain >Client: City of Barcelona. Design team: Farshid Moussavi, Alejandro Zaera Polo with Lluís Viu Rebés, Niccoló Cadeo, Danielle Domeniconi, Marco Guarnieri, Sergio López-Piñeiro, Terence Seah, Daniel Valle, Lluís Viu Rebés, with (basic design phase), Marco Guarnieri, Sergio López-Piñeiro, Pablo Ros, Lluís Viu Rebés, Juanjo Gonzállez (detailed design phase). Landscape architect: Teresa Galí, Barcelona. Structural engineers: Obiol, Moya y Asociadoes SLMechanical/electrical engineers: Proisotec. Bluemoon Hotel, Groningen, the Netherlands >Client: City of Groningen. Design team: Farshid Moussavi, Alejandro Zaera Polo, with Xavier Ortiz, Lluís Viu Rebés, Marco Guarnieri. Local architect: Artes, Groningen. Structural engineer: Adams Kara Taylor, London. The Bundle Tower (first proposal for the World Trade Center). Design team: Farshid Moussavi and Alejandro Zaera Polo with Daniel López-Pére, Erhard Kinzelbach, Edouard Cabay, Chu Ka Wing Kelvin. 'United We Stand' (Ground Zero competition entry). Design team: Foreign Office Architects, Greg Lynn Form, Los Angeles; Imaginary Forces, Los Angeles/New York; Kevin Kennon Architect, New York; Reiser + Umemoto, New York; UN Studio, Amsterdam. D38 Parque Empresarial en la Zona Franca, Barcelona, Spain >Client: Habitat ES. Design team: Farshid Moussavi, Alejandro Zaera Polo with Pablo Ros, Nerea Calvillo, Jordi Pagès I Ramon, Marco Guarnieri, Izumi Kobayashi, Pablo Ros. Structural engineer: Brufau, Obiols, Moya. Mechanical engineer: Idom. BBC Music Centre and Offices, London >Client: BBC. Design team: Farshid Moussavi, Alejandro Zaera

Polo with Nerea Calvillo, Kelvin Chu Ka Wing, Kazuhide Doi, Eduardo Fernández-Moscovo, Laura Fernández, Kensuke Kishikawa, Friedrich Ludewig, Kenichi Matsuzawa, Jordi Pagès i Ramon. Structural engineers: Adams Kara Taylor, London. Acoustics: Sandy Brown Associates, London. Lighting: Speirs and Major Associates. Theatre consultant: Ducks Sceno, Vaulx-en-Velin. Service engineer: Cameron Taylor Brady, London. La Rioja Technology Transfer Centre, Logroño, Spain >Client: Regional Government of La Rioja. Design team: Farshid Moussavi, Alejandro Zaera Polo with Kensuke Kishikawa, Jordi Pagès i Ramon, Pablo Ros. Structural engineer: Brufau, Obiols, Moya. Landscape architect: Teresa Galí, Barcelona Municipal Theatre and Auditorium, Torrevieja, Spain >Client: Torrevieja city council. Design team: Farshid Moussavi and Alejandro Zaera Polo with Jorge Arribas, Marco Guarnieri, Clara Jorger, Sergio López Piñeiro, Natalia Rodriguez, Daniel Valle, Nuria Vallespin, Lluís Viu Rebés. Associate architect: Antonio Marquerie, Torrevieja. Acoustics: UPV, Audiotec. Structure: NB35

Gollifer Langston
National Glass Centre, Sunderland >Client: Tyne & Wear Development Corporation and the National Glass Centre Ltd. Project Manager: Turner and Townsend. Design team: Sundeep Bhamra, Louise Clayton, Andy Gollifer, Mark Langston (project architect), David Rhodes, Gordon Shrigley, Naoki Shimura, Tom Whitehead. Associate executive architects: Ryder Company, Newcastle. Structural engineer: Techniker. Mechanical and electrical engineer: Battle McCarthy. Façade engineer: Ove Arup and Partners. Landscape architect: Liversedge Landscape, Wardell Armstrong. Platform 1, King's Cross, London >Client: CEA@Islington for London Borough of Islington. Design team: Tim Bell, Andy Gollifer, Anand Sagoo (project architect). Structural, M &E engineer: Buro Happold. South Camden CLC (phase 3), London >Client: Camden Local Education Authority (Camden LEA). Design team: Mary Duggan, Mark Langston (project architect). Structural engineer: Michael Hadi Associates. Mechanical and electrical engineer: SEA. 601fx, London >Client: Soho 601 Productions Ltd. Design team: Andy Gollifer (project architect), Julian Vaughan-Williams

KDa (Klein Dytham architecture)
Bloomberg ICE, Tokyo, Japan >Client: Bloomberg LP; LED technology: Starlet; media artist: Toshio Iwai. Design team: KDa (all projects): Idée Workstation, Tokyo, Japan >Client: Idée Co. Ltd. Pika-Pika Pretzel, Tokyo, Japan >Client: Veloqz. Balloon manufacturer: Cameron Balloons. Museum Café, Mori Art Museum, Tokyo >Client: Mori Building Co.Ltd. Green Green Screen, Tokyo, Japan >Client: Mori Building Co. Ltd. Graphic design: Super Future, Namaiki. Rin-Rin, Tokyo, Japan >Client: Mori Building Ryutsu System Co. Ltd. Cat Eyes (Foret Harajuku), Tokyo, Japan >Client: Mori Building Ryutsu System Co.Ltd. Manufactured reflector: Kashima Co.Ltd. Lighting consultant: Raffine, Tsuneo Iwahashi. Beacon Communications, Tokyo, Japan >Client: Beacon Communications k.k Vrooom!, Aichi Prefecture, Japan >Client: confidential. Undercover Lab, Tokyo, Japan >Client: UNDER COVER Co,.Ltd. Leaf Chapel, Kobuchizawa, Japan >Client: Risonare (Hoshino Resort). Lighting engineer: ICE (Masanobu Takeishi, Michiru Tanaka). Landscape design: Studio On Site(Hiroki Hasegawa, Chisa Toda, Kazutaka Tanbe)

muf
Shared Ground, Southwark, London >Client: London Borough of Southwark. Design team: muf (all projects). Consulting engineer: Arup. Landscape architect: Carolyn Roy. 100 Desires video, Katherine Clarke/muf > Client: Architecture

Foundation. SureStart on the Ocean, Stepney, London >Client: SureStart on the Ocean/Tower Hamlets Health Authority. Consulting engineer: Stockdales At Home. Video: Sue Ayrton. Security, Mobility and Pleasure urban design framework/The Mounding over the Greenway, London >Client: Westham and Plaistow NDC. Structural engineer: Arup. My Dream Today, your Dream Tomorrow, community garden, Tilbury, Essex >Client: Thurrock Borough Council and B.R.A.T.S. Consultant: Stockdales. A Horse's Tail, Tilbury >Client: Countryside Agency Local Heritage Initiative. Gardèn, Camden Arts Centre, London >Client: Camden Arts Centre. Hypocaust Museum, St Albans, Hertfordshire >Client: St Albans City & District Council/ Verulamium Museum. Structural engineer: Atelier One

Sergison Bates
Urban mixed use development, Wandsworth, London >Client: Baylight Properties PLC. Design team: Stephen Bates, Nicolaj Bechtel, Andrew Davy, Guy Derwent, Aidan Hodgkinson, Tim Rettler (project architect for medical centre), Juliette Scalbert, Jonathan Sergison, Joanna Sutherland, Mark Tuff (project architect for main project), Jessica Zagres. Structural engineers: Price & Myers. Environmental engineers: Max Fordham & Partners. Graphic designer: JANE. Prototype social housing, Stevenage >Client: William Sutton Trust. Design team: Stephen Bates, Sally Richards, Cornelia Schwaller, Jonathan Sergison, Mark Tuff (project architect). Structural engineers: Baldock Quick Partnership. Assisted Self-Build Housing, Tilbury, Essex >Client: New Islington & Hackney Housing Association, for New Essex Housing Association/ Community Self-Build Agency. Design team: Matthias Amann, Stephen Bates, Andrew Davy, Sophie Marée, Tim Rettler (project architect), Jonathan Sergison, Mark Tuff. Structural engineers: Price & Myers. Classrooms of the Future, Bedfordshire >Client: Bedfordshire County Council, for Maple Tree Lower School, Burgoyne Middle School and Sandy Upper School. Design team: Stephen Bates, Rebecca Behbahani, Guy Derwent, Sophie Marée, Jonathan Sergison, Joanna Sutherland (project architect). Collaborator: The Science Museum/NSMI Trading Ltd. Structural engineers: Greig-Ling Consulting Engineers. Service engineers: Arup. Graphic designer: JANE. Public House, Walsall, West Midlands >Client: Walsall Metropolitan Borough Council. Developer: Chartwell Land. Design team: Stephen Bates, Martin Bradley, Marie Brunborg, Becky Chipchase, Jonathan Sergison, Mark Tuff. Collaborating architects: Caruso St John. Structural engineers: Waterman Partnership. Environmental engineers: Waterman Gore. Graphic designer: JANE. Bibliotheek, Blankenberge >Client: Stadbestuur Blankenberge. Design team: Stephen Bates, Sigalit Berry, Aidan Hodgkinson, Angela Hopcroft, Tim Rettler, Jonathan Sergison, Mark Tuff, Jan Vermeulen (project architect). Structural engineers: Technum NV. Services engineers: Bureau Bouwtechniek. RITS, Brussels >Client: Erasmushogeschool Brussels. Design team: Stephen Bates, Angela Hopcroft, Tim Rettler, Jonathan Sergison, Val Tse, Mark Tuff, Jan Vermeulen (project architect). Structural engineers: Technum NV. Services engineers: Technum NV. Acoustic engineers: DBA Consult

S333
Dutch Mountain, Zaanstad, the Netherlands >Client: Municipality of Zaanstad, NL. Design team: Burton Hamfelt, Chris Moller, Dominic Papa, Jonathan Woodroffe with Stig Gothelf, Frank Lang, Rachel Pigg, Jacob Sand, Rasmus Hansen. Schots 1 & 2, the CiBoGa Terrain, Groningen, the Netherlands >Client: IMA development consortium (ING Vastgoed, Amstelland Ontwikkelling, Bouwbedrijf Moes BV, Amvest Vastgoed and Nijestee Vastgoed). Design

team: Burton Hamfelt, Chris Moller, Dominic Papa, Jonathan Woodroffe with Hotao Chow, Stig Gothelf, Zvonimir Prlic, Jacob Sand, Line Thorup Schultz, Melanda Slemint, Fabien van Tomme, Francesca Wunderle. Supervising urbanist: Alsop Architects. Structural engineers: Ingenieursbureau Wassenaar BV. Landscape: Van Ginkel Veenendaal BV. La Ville Forêt, Grenoble, France >Client: City of Grenoble and Europan. Design team: Burton Hamfelt, Chris Moller, Dominic Papa, Jonathan Woodroffe with Thomas van Arman, Lucas Chirnside, Rasmus Hansen. Landscape: Studio Engleback. Engineers: Battle McCarthy. Model: Made by Mistake. Bloembollenhof, Vijfhuizen, the Netherlands >Client: City Council of Haarlemmermeer and Durabouw Amsterdam BV. Design team: Burton Hamfelt, Chris Moller, Dominic Papa, Jonathan Woodroffe with Elsa Caetano, Stig Gothelf, Gimill Mual, Zvonimir Prlic, Jacob Sand, Fabien van Tomme, Francesca Wunderle, Kees Draisma. Urban plan: Atelier Zeinstra van der Pol. Structural engineers: Constructie-adviesbureau Steens BV. Landscape: Bureau Alle Hosper. Installations: Haarmans installatietechniek. Building physics: Breman Noord-Holland BV. New Town Centre Nieuw Vennep, the Netherlands >Client: de Woonmaatschappij & City Council of Haarlemmermeer. Design team: Burton Hamfelt, Chris Moller, Dominic Papa, Jonathan Woodroffe with Thomas van Arman, Dagobert Bergmans, Frank Lang. Beaumont Quarter, Auckland, New Zealand >Client: Melview Developments Ltd, Auckland. Design team: Burton Hamfelt, Chris Moller, Dominic Papa, Jonathan Woodroffe, Dagobert Bergmans, Elsa Cataneo, Kees Draisma, Stefan Kurath, Omar Al-Omari, Thom McKenzie. Associate architects: Studio of Pacific Architecture, Wellington. Engineer: Holmes Consulting Group. Landscape: Steven Tupu. ROCvA Zuidas (Regional Opleidings Centrum Zuidas), Amsterdam, the Netherlands >Client: Regional Opleidings Centrum of Amsterdam (ROCvA) in collaboration with PRC Bouwcentrum and Amstelland MDC. Design team: Burton Hamfelt, Chris Moller, Dominic Papa, Jonathan Woodroffe with Gimill Mual, Omar Al-Omari, Mikkel Ryberg. Block 3, Tarling Development, London >Client: Toynbee Housing Association and Galliford Try. Design team: Burton Hamfelt, Chris Moller, Dominic Papa, Jonathan Woodroffe with Thomas van Arman, Gimill Mual, Nicolas Thioulouse, Omar Al-Omari, Helena Serrano. Associate architects: Stock Woolstencroft. Landscape: Farrer Huxley. Oldham Beyond, Manchester >Client: Oldham Local Strategic Partnership. Design team: Burton Hamfelt, Chris Moller, Dominic Papa, Jonathan Woodroffe with Thomas van Arman, Claudia Frankenreiter, Gimill Mual. Consultant team: Urbed, Manchester, S333, Co-Media, London, King Sturge, Manchester and WSP Consultant Engineers, Manchester